The Czech Black Book

THE
CZECH
BLACK
BOOK

Prepared by the Institute of History
of the Czechoslovak Academy of Sciences

EDITED BY
ROBERT LITTELL

FREDERICK A. PRAEGER, *Publishers*
New York · Washington · London

FREDERICK A. PRAEGER, PUBLISHERS
111 Fourth Avenue, New York, N.Y. 10003, U.S.A.
5, Cromwell Place, London S.W.7, England

Published in the United States of America in 1969
by Frederick A. Praeger, Inc., Publishers

The Czech Black Book was prepared by the Institute of History of the
Czechoslovak Academy of Sciences and published by the Academy under
the title *Sedm Pražských Dnů: 21.–27. srpen 1968,* late in the fall of 1968.

Translation © 1969 by Frederick A. Praeger, Inc.

Library of Congress Catalog Card Number: 75–76955

Printed in the United States of America

EDITOR'S INTRODUCTION

Dates are handy pegs on which to hang history. So, for the record, the period that became known as the Czechoslovak spring can be said to have begun on Friday, January 5, 1968. Of course, the enormous economic and political dislocations that set the stage for the events of that spring had been accumulating for years before then. But on that day, the 110-member Central Committee of the Czechoslovak Communist Party assembled in the ornate Spanish Hall of Hradcany Castle, which stands sentinel-like on a pinnacle overlooking Prague, and formally ended the fourteen-year reign of Antonin Novotny as boss of the Czechoslovak Communist Party. In the process, the Central Committee sent the fate of Czechoslovakia spinning off like a top the players could channel but not control.

The man chosen to replace Novotny as First Secretary of the Communist Party, a forty-six-year-old Slovak named Alexander Dubcek, was scarcely known outside of Czechoslovakia, and the few biographical details that were available were not auspicious. Dubcek was, from all appearances, the archetypal *apparatchik*: a man who had been raised and educated in the Soviet Union and had devoted his life to the Party, working his way, rung by rung, up its ranks to become head of the Slovak Communist organization and a member of the ruling Presidium of the Czechoslovak Communist Party. Just how much of a Party man Dubcek was thought to be by his superiors can be gleaned from the fact that in 1955 he was sent to the Soviet Communist Party's prestigious college in Moscow—run, presumably, for conventional Communists who are not expected to do much in the way of counterrevolution.

Whether Dubcek was a reformer who had been quietly boring from within or a conventional Communist who bent with the wind is still not clear. Once in power, Dubcek, pulled along by the almost insatiable appetites of a people who had once tasted democracy and material comfort and craved both again, proceeded to humanize Communism in Czechoslovakia.

The substantive changes were immediate and spectacular. The press, freed of censorship, poured forth a torrent of criticism; no person or subject was sacrosanct. Government and Party decisions—indeed, the very process of decision-making, which had long been shrouded in secrecy—were opened to public scrutiny. On a personal level, the reformers pressed ahead with the formal rehabilitation of victims of Stalinist purges and, more crucial, began weeding out members of the old guard from their entrenched positions in the Party and Government bureaucracies. On March 5, 1968, for instance, the Presidium transferred responsibility for ideology from Novotny's closest associate, Jiri Hendrych, to reformer Josef Spacek. On March 22, the liberals forced Novotny to step down as President of the Republic, a position he had held since 1957.

At times, the reformers plunged ahead of the people; at others, they raced after them. Either way, the pace was dizzying. Reformation filled the atmosphere. It was evident in the tone of the times and in the rhetoric of the reformers. At the twentieth anniversary of the coup that put the Communists in power in Prague, Dubcek, speaking from a platform shared by none other than Soviet Communist Party leader Leonid Brezhnev, declared that "everything must be really and thoroughly changed." The formal scenario of change, the Action Program published by the Communist Party in April, spoke of the "unique experiment in democratic Communism." "The Communist Party," the Action Program said, "does not fulfill its leading role by ruling over society [but] relies on the voluntary support of the people." The Program went on to recognize that a "clash of opinions is necessary in the search for the best solution."

The clash of opinions—in the newspapers, on the radio, in the

lowest and highest precincts of the Party, on every street corner
—unnerved the Soviet leaders. And with good reason. The Czechoslovak spring represented a profound challenge to the men who
ruled in the Kremlin—more profound, in many respects, than the
Hungarian Revolution. Previous challenges, such as the one that
occurred in Hungary in 1956 or even in Yugoslavia in 1948, had
been rebellions against Stalinism and the tyrannical excesses that
the word implies. The Czechoslovaks, however, were posing the
first serious challenge to Leninism in the history of the Communist movement. They were questioning the desirability of
three things Lenin superimposed on classical Marxism: democratic centralism (whereby ideas tend to originate at the top),
the monopoly of power by the Communist Party, and the ideological dogmatism with which power is exercised. Viewed from
Moscow, the center of power of the Communist Party, such
questioning was heretical. It would have been odd indeed if
some Soviet leaders had not seen in the Czechoslovak spring the
dreaded Thermidor—the first stage of counterrevolution.

At a number of summit sessions and at a meeting of the Czechoslovak Presidium and the Soviet Politburo in the Slovak frontier
town of Cierna nad Tisou, the Russians tried to talk Dubcek into
toning down the reformation. Dubcek argued forcefully that the
reforms did not endanger the leading role of the Communist
Party but, in fact, strengthened it by building public support.
The Soviet leaders never accepted this argument. By the summer of 1968, the Soviets and Czechoslovaks were squared off
for a confrontation that left little room for compromise. The
Czechoslovaks were seeking nothing less than national salva-
tion; the Soviet leaders were struggling to preserve The System.

The actual decision to intervene militarily in Czechoslovakia
was most likely made on the weekend before the invasion. The
final vote in the sharply divided Soviet Politburo, according to
excellent sources in Moscow, was 7 to 4 for the use of force,
with Aleksei Kosygin, Mikhail Suslov, Nikolai Podgorny, and
Gennadi Voronov lining up on the dove side. The decision was
probably conveyed to the leaders of East Germany, Poland, Hungary, and Bulgaria on Sunday, August 18; the top Bulgarian
Communists are known to have flown to Moscow and back to

Sofia on that day. At 8 P.M. on Tuesday, August 20, officers of Warsaw Pact units in East Germany, Poland, Hungary, and the Ukraine assembled their troops and read them a letter from some conservative factory workers in Prague requesting assistance. Two hours later, the units moved out toward the Czechoslovak border. What happened after that is the subject matter of this book.

The Soviet leaders followed the big stick with the big lie. As the Warsaw Pact columns crossed the frontier into Bohemia, Moravia, and Slovakia, the Soviet propaganda machine began churning out material claiming that the troops had been invited by Czechoslovak Party and Government leaders—though the Soviet press conspicuously omitted giving the names of these leaders. Obviously, the Russians expected to form a collaborationist government at any moment; one of the revelations in THE CZECH BLACK BOOK is that they apparently came within a hair's breadth of doing just that. Eventually, when it became evident that the few collaborators available were too timid, the Soviet leaders quietly dropped the story about having been invited to Czechoslovakia and rested their case for intervention on what became known as the Brezhnev doctrine. Briefly stated, this ex post facto line of reasoning held that Moscow had the moral right to intervene anywhere in the "socialist commonwealth" to prevent counterrevolution.

The Brezhnev doctrine depended on the Soviets' demonstrating that there was, in fact, a counterrevolutionary condition in Czechoslovakia that required intervention. Proving this was not easy; there had been no open hostilities, as in the Hungarian case. On September 11, the official Soviet Communist Party newspaper *Pravda* displayed its ideological elasticity by formulating a theory that eliminated the dilemma. It discovered "a new phenomenon of history" called "peaceful counterrevolution."

Soon after, the Soviets set out to prove the charge of "peaceful counterrevolution." Though the controlled press hammered away at this theme, the main documentation was contained in a publication entitled "On Events in Czechoslovakia," but promptly nicknamed "The White Book" because of its white cover and because it attempted to whitewash Soviet intervention in Czecho-

slovakia. "The White Book"—a collection of articles and statements by Czechoslovak leaders, quotations from speakers at
club meetings in Prague, analyses and reports from Western
publications, excerpts from leaflets and underground newspapers
printed in Czechoslovakia—purported to prove that the Warsaw
Pact intervention had been the only alternative to the "peaceful"
counterrevolution raging in Czechoslovakia. "The aim of the
counterrevolution," wrote the Soviet journalists (also unnamed)
who prepared "The White Book," "was to deprive the Czechoslovak Communist Party of its leading role, to wrest power from
the workers and the peasants, to destroy state and public organizations founded by the people . . . to divert Czechoslovakia
onto the path of restoring capitalism."

In Czechoslovakia, where occupation troops distributed hundreds of thousands of copies of "The White Book," the prestigious
Czechoslovak Academy of Sciences put together a page-by-page
refutation of the Soviet version, pointing out everything from
quotations taken out of context to outright fabrications. But the
definitive refutation of the Soviet case—that is to say, the Czechoslovak version of what happened when the Warsaw Pact armies
invaded the country—was contained in a "study document" prepared by the Institute of History of the Czechoslovak Academy
of Sciences and entitled *Seven Days in Prague*. The book, which
quickly became known as "The Black Book" because of the color
of its cover and because of its obvious contrast to the Soviet
"White Book," was printed late in the fall in an extremely limited
edition and was distributed to intellectuals and key Party people
throughout the country within hours of coming off the presses, in
order to forestall the possibility that it would be confiscated by
the occupation troops.

By any standard, THE CZECH BLACK BOOK is stunningly unique.
It is the victim's description of the crime, recorded while the
crime was being committed. Slowly, agonizingly, in passionate,
mimeographed leaflets, in disjointed underground-newspaper
articles, in coldly correct official records, in crisp clandestine
radio reports, in emotional eyewitness accounts, the crime un-
folds. Certain threads run through the story: the outrage and
impotency of the victims; contempt for collaborators (who are

often accused by name); pride that the Soviets had been unable to set up a collaborationist government; uncertainty over what was happening at the negotiations taking place in Moscow; above all, the growing realization by the people of Czechoslovakia that this tragic hour was also their finest hour.

In the original Czech, "The Black Book" is 494 pages long; a complete English translation would be somewhat longer. In editing the material, I have tried to preserve the spontaneity of the document and to retain every item that might be of value to scholars piecing together the events of those days. Most of the deleted material was repetitious (resolutions of support from countless organizations, for example) or available elsewhere (the Soviet press, the texts of speeches in the United Nations, and so on). What remains is the heart of the matter—the hour-by-hour, day-by-day account of the Warsaw Pact invasion of Czechoslovakia.

Robert Littell

New York City
January, 1969

CONTENTS

The Czech Black Book

INTRODUCTION

Quite often, the historian is plagued by inadequate source materials. This usually happens whenever the normal pace of developments accelerates to a point where historical time must be figured not in years or months but in days, hours, or even minutes. Attempts to catch up years later with what contemporaries failed to document are rarely successful. Even the most meticulous effort can then accomplish little more than assemble a fraction of the required documentary evidence, and personal testimony taken ten or twenty years after the event usually lacks authenticity.

The bitter experience of generations of historians leads us to the experiment of this volume. We have been guided by a sense of duty that derives from the function of the Institute of History as a research center. Equally important, we wanted to stimulate efforts at documentation in the various regions and districts of the country and in the industrial enterprises.

The materials in the following pages represent a partial documentation of the first stage of the entry of foreign armies onto the territory of Czechoslovakia. We have focused on the period beginning with the night of August 20 and ending on the evening of August 27, when the people of Czechoslovakia learned the content of the Moscow communiqué and heard the addresses of President Ludvik Svoboda and the First Secretary of the Central Committee of the Communist Party of Czechoslovakia, Alexander Dubcek. We made only two concessions to this narrow time span. We included data that pertains to some of the impor-

3

tant events that took place before 11 P.M. on August 20 and that
are closely related to everything that followed. We also included
official speeches and documents given or published on August 28
and 29 that are closely related to the Moscow communiqué.
Finally, we included [in the Epilogue] some of the immediate,
grass-roots reactions to the Moscow communiqué from Party and
trade union organizations, factories, public offices, schools, and
other institutions.

Limitations on the content of the book were determined, in
part, by time and the technical resources available to us. However, there are involuntary omissions—a deficiency we hope to
overcome by collecting additional personal accounts. We turn,
therefore, to the Prague factories, whose materials we perhaps
missed the most, to newspapermen, to radio and television reporters, to colleagues in other historical institutions, to museum
curators, archivists, and librarians, to officials of all the parties
and organizations of the National Front, and to all those who
will read this study, with a plea for help and advice. We turn
not only to the citizens of Prague but to all citizens of the Republic. For the benefit of those who would like to contribute
new materials, we give our address: Institute of History, Czechoslovak Academy of Sciences, Prague 1, Jirska 3; telephone 53 92 44.

Last but not least, we want to thank all those who helped us
bring this study into existence and so fulfill our professional duty
to our people as historians.

INSTITUTE OF HISTORY
CZECHOSLOVAK ACADEMY OF SCIENCES

Prague
September, 1968

1

TUESDAY, AUGUST 20:
PROLOGUE

2 P.M.

A session of the Presidium of the Central Committee of the
Communist Party of Czechoslovakia, originally scheduled to start
at 10 A.M., was called to order.

4 P.M.

An extraordinary conference of selected members of the
Czechoslovak State Security forces headed by Deputy Minister of
Interior Viliam Salgovic was held, and the plan for the occupation of Czechoslovakia was divulged. Members were assigned
tasks for the night of August 20–21.

Around 6 P.M.

Miroslav Sulek, then Director General of the Czechoslovak
News Agency, returned unexpectedly from a vacation in the
Soviet Union and ordered that no news about Czechoslovakia
was to be sent abroad without his permission.

In the Evening

Several Soviet civilian aircraft, which later in the night directed
the landings of Soviet air-borne forces, landed on the Prague
airfield at Ruzyne.

Ruzyne, Tuesday Night

The first surprise at Ruzyne Airport came just before 8:30 P.M., when an unscheduled aircraft from Moscow landed on the field. One hour later, another special Soviet plane, this one arriving from Lvov, landed. About 30 minutes later it is said to have returned to Lvov. This was shortly after 10 P.M. From this time on, until a little after midnight, the field was quiet. Just after midnight, the airport dispatcher learned from arrogant voices on the telephone that the airport could neither receive nor dispatch any additional air traffic, despite the fact that planes from Yugoslavia and Bulgaria were expected. At the same time, suspicious-looking men in civilian clothes began arriving in the airport building. Soon a Soviet colonel, accompanied by a representative of the Soviet [state airline] Aeroflot, made his appearance.

None of the employees or foreign tourists paid any attention to him, and everyone went about his regular business. But not for long. Shortly after midnight, two gigantic airplanes with Soviet markings touched down on the airfield, and several dozen armed Soviet soldiers jumped out. They immediately surrounded and entered the main airport building and began chasing out into the area in front of the building all airport personnel as well as the tourists. Most of these people were not even allowed to put on their coats and gather up their belongings.

Outside the building, the Russians separated the men from the women, leaving the men outside and allowing the women to sit in the airport waiting room. After half an hour, during which time Soviet aircraft were landing one after the other at about one-minute intervals, the men were allowed to return to the waiting room. Here, in the din of the landing and departing airplanes and the rumbling of tanks and armored cars, they made us wait, despite many protests, until about 5:30 in the morning, when a Soviet major arrived and announced to the airport personnel and the tourists and visitors such as myself that everyone could go home. In answer to questions about transportation, he said: "On foot. Our armies also must march a great many miles on foot." Protests were to no avail, and everybody, including the foreign tourists, departed on foot.

Everyone was ordered to leave, and administration of the airport was taken over by Soviet and [East] German troops, who took up positions on the airfield and the surrounding roads. As we were leaving the airport area, heavy military aircraft continued to land and disgorge tanks, other military equipment, and soldiers. As soon as the planes were unloaded, they would take to the air again.

While we waited in the airport, we tried numerous times to speak with the young Soviet soldiers who were guarding us. Even though they were reluctant to talk, or had been ordered not to, we learned that they had been stationed in Poland and the German Democratic Republic and had come to Czechslovakia on military orders. When asked whether they knew that they had not been invited here, they answered: "We have faith in our leadership which gave us the orders, and that is what matters to us." All of them agreed that they firmly believed what the Soviet press, and specially *Pravda*, said.

On our way from the airport to the center of Prague, we passed columns of Soviet troops traveling in Soviet as well as Czechoslovak cars, in tanks, and in armored vehicles.

From Zemedelske Noviny, *August 21, 1968*

An Unusual Night

I was awakened before daybreak by an unusual noise, just as were the majority of Prague inhabitants. Outside my windows, one tank after another rolled toward the center of the city. I could not understand this, but the unusually heavy traffic at Ruzyne Airport persuaded me to leave quickly for my office. I arrived there shortly before 6 A.M. and automatically turned on the teletype connection with the airport operation control. It came on and relayed a report that in the next hours became a document of tremendous value. Interspersed in the teletype reports about the occupation of our country by allied armies were accurate reports about the operation at Ruzyne Airport, where it had all begun. Despite the fact that some readers are already familiar with some of the details, I think I should repeat them.

The arrival of a special aircraft from Moscow had been announced for 10 P.M.[1] There was nothing unusual about this, for many Aeroflot airplanes were scheduled as special flights. The airplane, a civilian An-24, did indeed arrive, but it remained parked on the edge of the runway. At 11 P.M., another special An-24 arrived, this one from Lvov; from it emerged a number of civilians, who were cordially welcomed at customs. They then left for the city, and after about half an hour the airplane departed. Thereafter the airfield was quiet. Only at the customs office, where usually just a few people can be found, was there heightened activity. In fact, an unusually large number of employees was there at this late hour. The reason for this became apparent soon enough. Just before 2 A.M., cars belonging to Soviet Aeroflot arrived at the airport carrying not only civilians but also army officers. They entered the foreign departures area where they were cordially welcomed by Colonel Elias, Commander of the Security Air Squadron of the Ministry of Interior, and Lieutenant Colonel Rudolf Stachovsky, chief of passport control at Ruzyne. And then it all began. An unannounced An-12 landed on the airfield. It contained an air-borne unit of the Soviet Army, whose members immediately entered the airport buildings and chased all employees and tourists outside. After a long wait in front of the main building, the Soviet soldiers separated the men from the women and children and allowed the women and children to re-enter the waiting room. By this time, in precise one-minute intervals, one military An-12 after another was landing on the field. People at the airport were slow to grasp what was happening. The military air traffic was being directed from the special An-24 from Moscow, which remained parked on the edge of the runway; even the later take-offs by military planes were directed from this aircraft. We also had difficulty understanding that those who had welcomed the Soviet intruders were really traitors.

In the early morning hours, the interned airport workers were released and sent home. Even the tourists had to return to Prague on foot. But those who manned the teletype were forgotten, and it was thanks to them that I learned the terrible truth. The tele-

---

[1] This account places the time of arrival of the planes at about an hour and a half later than the previous account. The discrepancy is not explained in the study.

type at Ruzyne was in operation until almost noon. It broadcast to the whole world the shocking truth that the Czechoslovak Socialist Republic had been assaulted by the allied armies of the Warsaw Pact. Shame to the traitors and collaborators, among them Colonel Elias, Commander of the Security Air Squadron of the Ministry of Interior, and Lieutenant Colonel Stachovsky, chief of passport control at Prague Airport.

From Letectvi a Kosmonautika, *August 27, 1968*

Before 11 P.M.

The Prague military garrison was put on alert.

Around 11 P.M.

Military units of the five countries (the Soviet Union, Poland, Hungary, East Germany, and Bulgaria), estimated during the first phase of the operation at two hundred thousand men and later at half a million,[2] crossed the state borders of Czechoslovakia.

After 11 P.M.

Soviet Ambassador Stepan Chervonenko called on the President of the Republic, Ludvik Svoboda, and notified him that the armies of the five countries had crossed the Czechoslovak borders.

11:40 P.M.

Premier Oldrich Cernik announced to the Presidium of the Party Central Committee that he had just received the report of the military action of the five countries against Czechoslovakia.

Around Midnight

The President of the Republic arrived in the building of the Central Committee and then returned to the presidential palace.

Minister of Interior Josef Pavel arrived in the Central Committee building and after an hour returned to the Ministry.

[2] The Czechoslovak Ministry of Defense later estimated that six hundred thousand Warsaw Pact troops were in the country, but Western intelligence sources put the figure at somewhere between two hundred fifty thousand and three hundred fifty thousand.

2
WEDNESDAY, AUGUST 21

Around 1 A.M.

Czechoslovak Radio in Prague alerted listeners to stand by for an important announcement by the Central Committee of the Communist Party.

Shortly After 1 A.M.

The Presidium of the Central Committee approved, with four opposing votes (Vasil Bilak, Drahomir Kolder, Emil Rigo, Oldrich Svestka), the text of a proclamation to the people of Czechoslovakia.

To All the People of the Czechoslovak Socialist Republic:

Yesterday, August 20, 1968, at about 11 P.M., the armies of the Soviet Union, the Polish People's Republic, the German Democratic Republic, the Hungarian People's Republic, and the Bulgarian People's Republic crossed the state borders of the Czechoslovak Socialist Republic. This took place without the knowledge of the President of the Republic, the Presidium of the National Assembly, the Presidium of the Government, and the First Secretary of the Communist Party Central Committee. The Presidium of the Central Committee was then in session, preoccupied with the preparations for the Extraordinary Fourteenth Party Congress. The Presidium calls upon all citizens of the Republic to keep the peace and not resist the advancing armies, because the defense of our state borders is now impossible.

For this reason, our army, the Security Forces, and the People's Militia were not given the order to defend the country. The Presidium considers this action [the invasion] to be contrary to the fundamental principles of relations between socialist states and a denial of the basic norms of international law.

All leading officials of the Party and the National Front remain at their posts, to which they were elected as representatives of the people and members of their organizations according to the laws and regulations of the Czechoslovak Socialist Republic. The appropriate constitutional organs have called into session the National Assembly and the Government of the Republic, and the Presidium of the Central Committee is convening the Party Central Committee in order to deal with the situation that has arisen.

> Presidium of the Central Committee of the
> Communist Party

From Prace, *August 21, 1968*

After 1:30 A.M.

In the studios of Prague Radio, the text of the proclamation of the Presidium of the Central Committee was broadcast several times before 2 A.M. However, on order from the Director of the Central Communications Administration, Karel Hoffman, the medium-wave transmitter had been turned off, so that the majority of listeners heard only a part of the first sentence of the proclamation. The broadcast was probably heard only on the wire transmissions of Prague Radio.

After 2 A.M.

The Leading Secretary of the City Committee of the Party in Prague, Bohumil Simon, departed to advise Alexander Dubcek of the proposals of the leadership of the City Committee for certain urgent measures: (1) to convene a conference of delegates elected to the Extraordinary Fourteenth Party Congress, (2) to organize a general strike, and (3) to prepare an appeal to the Communist parties of the world.

Around 3 A.M.

Czechoslovak Premier Oldrich Cernik was arrested in the building of the Government Presidium by Soviet air-borne troops.

The Arrest of Oldrich Cernik

According to information from officials of the Government Presidium, at 3 A.M. on August 21, Soviet parachutists broke into the office of the Premier, lined up all the officials present against the wall, and led Oldrich Cernik away at bayonet point. Twenty minutes later, Alexander Dubcek called Cernik on the telephone, but the official who answered could only tell the First Secretary that Cernik could not speak to him because he had been taken away. The official himself was then under military surveillance. Dubcek responded that his situation was not quite so bad and asked everyone to hold out. The entire building of the Government Presidium was occupied by troops, and its occupants were interned until 5 o'clock in the afternoon. The soldiers destroyed the main telephone switchboard. During the course of this action, some of the employees of the Ministry had their watches taken.

After 3 A.M.

Bohumil Simon was again sent to confer with Dubcek. However, when it became apparent that it was no longer possible to establish contact with Dubcek, the leadership of the City Committee in Prague proceeded on the basis of its original proposals.

After 4 A.M.

The first Soviet armored cars reached the building of the Secretariat of the Central Committee of the Party. About an hour later, the occupation of the building began. First Secretary of the Party Dubcek and a number of other leading officials were interned in the building until the afternoon hours.

Information About the Fateful Night

What took place at the last session of the Presidium of the Party Central Committee?

Czechoslovak Radio broadcast a taped recording of the testimony of one of the responsible Party officials who had been present at the last session of the Central Committee Presidium during that fateful night. Here is a substantial extract of this eyewitness account:

The Presidium was discussing two issues. The first, which was introduced by Comrade Dubcek, was the draft report of the Central Committee to the Extraordinary Fourteenth Party Congress [scheduled for September] and a draft resolution for the Congress. The second issue on the agenda was a question carried over from the preceding meeting of the Presidium.

When Comrade Dubcek concluded his remarks concerning the Central Committee report to the Congress, Comrade Kolder took the floor to suggest that this item be passed over in favor of a discussion of the second issue on the agenda. This proposal was rejected, and the Presidium proceeded to deal with the draft report and the draft resolution for the Extraordinary Fourteenth Party Congress.

In the late evening hours, the meeting turned to discussion of the second agenda item. I happened, by chance, to be present at this discussion. Forgive me for not giving my name here, but I can assure you that my information about this discussion is absolutely authentic. I should first describe the substance of the issue under discussion. It concerned material submitted by Comrade Jan Kaspar. The material represented an imprecise, pseudo-scientific attempt to analyze the internal political situation since Cierna and Bratislava.[1] The material contained an array of correct conclusions and impressions, but it was also tendentious in its thrust. It tried to prove that the forces that supported the progressive development were superficial and unstable, while the

[1] Late in July, the entire Czechoslovak Presidium met with all but two members of the Soviet Politburo in the Slovakian border town of Cierna nad Tisou to discuss Soviet objections to the Czechoslovak liberalization program. Under intense pressure from Moscow, Dubcek and his reform-minded colleagues reportedly agreed to rein in the aspects of the "reformation" that were most offensive to Moscow. The meeting ended in an apparent compromise that was then immediately confirmed at a six-nation conference (attended by the Soviet Union, Czechoslovakia, Poland, Hungary, Bulgaria, and East Germany) in Bratislava. With that, the threat of Soviet armed intervention seemed to recede.

forces that supported the conservatives were steadfast and stable and would grow in strength as time went on.

This analysis, which was couched in scientific terms, was not prepared by the Party secretaries responsible for the different sectors; as a result, it stressed some aspects of the situation and neglected other important ones. By itself, however, this report would not have sparked a crisis. However, the material submitted by Kaspar interested some notorious Presidium members such as Comrade Kolder, Secretary Alois Indra, and others, who kept pointing out that this was important material that the Presidium had not had in its possession before.

In addition, another subject came up for discussion. It had previously been decided that a commission headed by Comrade Indra should prepare proposals for certain measures. But Comrade Indra never convened this commission; instead, together with Comrade Kolder, he prepared a position paper about fifteen pages long. This paper proposed no concrete measures, but the two comrades presented it to the Presidium for adoption.

When I arrived at the Presidium session, Comrade Cernik had the floor. He described the attitude of the comrades [Indra and Kolder] as treason. Comrade Frantisek Kriegel analyzed the position paper very critically and charged that it adopted the attitude of the letter of the Warsaw Pact signatories [2] and liquidated the results of the Cierna and Bratislava conferences. He concluded by saying that adoption of the position paper would mean acceptance of the Warsaw letter theses. Comrade Kriegel then not only demanded that the Presidium refuse to adopt this document, but that it categorically and formally reject it and also reject what Comrade Kolder planned—namely, that if the Presidium failed to adopt the statement, he, Kolder, would come out with it in public. Other members of the Presidium and Central Committee secretaries then joined the discussion and, for the most part,

[2] In July, leaders of the Soviet Union, East Germany, Poland, Hungary, and Bulgaria met in Warsaw and fired off a sternly worded diplomatic note to Prague accusing the new Czechoslovak leaders of endangering Communist Party control. The note added the ominous warning that "the situation in Czechoslovakia jeopardizes the common vital interests of other socialist countries" and that "a decisive rebuff to the forces of anti-Communism" was "not only your task but ours, too."

rejected the document. At about 10:30, Comrade Bilak took the floor and expressed his approval of the attitude of the two comrades [Kolder and Indra]. He was then joined by others, including Comrade Rigo. The discussion was interrupted while Comrade Antonin Kapek [a Presidium candidate member] spoke, by and large approvingly, about the statement presented by comrades Kolder and Indra. Before Kapek took the floor, Comrade Jan Piller had also spoken about the material presented by Comrade Kaspar, declaring that it was a valuable piece of work, despite its imperfections, and that we could support its approach. He added, however, that neither the Kaspar report nor the Kolder-Indra position paper should be published but that future policy should be carried out in the spirit of the two documents.

I should like to backtrack for a moment. Two sessions before, some comrades had criticized Comrade Dubcek on the grounds that he enjoys too much personal popularity and that he is not making use of this popularity to increase the authority of the body over which he presides: So far, only his personal popularity is high and not the authority of the Presidium. Signs of such criticism had become increasingly evident, especially on the part of Comrade Bilak and several others. This criticism had been rejected, especially by Comrade Stefan Sadovsky [a Party Secretary], who had argued that the authority of the Party Presidium grows with the authority of its members. Discussion of this question had finally been brought to a conclusion with the statement of Comrade Zdenek Mlynar [also a Party Secretary] that everyone ought to remember that personal authority depends on the results of personal accomplishment. I had gathered from all this that, even then, preparations were already under way to undermine Comrade Dubcek. And it was evidently the intention of the Kolder-Indra position paper to create a split in the Presidium in order to force Comrade Dubcek to side with Kolder and Indra, thus preparing the ground for the following events.

While the discussion about the Kaspar report and the Kolder-Indra position paper proceeded, Comrade Cernik occasionally stepped into the antechamber to speak on the telephone. From what I could overhear, it was evident that he was seeking information about the situation on our borders, because certain reports

had come in earlier. At 11:40 P.M. Comrade Cernik returned
from the telephone for the last time and, after Comrade Dubcek
interrupted the debate, announced the following: "The armies of
the five parties have crossed the borders of our Republic and have
begun occupying our country."

The Presidium was in a state of shock—at least, some of its
members were, particularly Comrade Dubcek, who declared:
"This is a tragedy, I didn't expect this to happen." Several others
reacted in the same way. As far as I was able to observe, Bilak,
Kolder, and Indra did not seem to be surprised, and I think that
I could say the same of Svestka. Comrade Dubcek then read a
letter he had received the previous Monday night from the Central Committee of the Communist Party of the Soviet Union, that
is, from Comrade Leonid Brezhnev. No one else had seen this
letter. The Soviet Central Committee reproached our Party for
not respecting what had been agreed upon in Cierna and in Bratislava and charged that counterrevolutionary tendencies continued to make themselves felt in our country. In short, the criticisms
of the Warsaw letter were being repeated, only in sharper form.
As he read the letter, Comrade Dubcek commented on some of
the passages. He declared, for example: "This is what they keep
on saying, but they do not take into consideration what the real
situation is. After all, we are taking measures." He continued
reading the letter, in which there was not a single remark or
indication that the Soviet Central Committee wanted to resolve
the situation as they were resolving it—through military occupation of Czechoslovakia. Comrade Dubcek said: "I declare on my
honor as a Communist that I had no suspicion, no indication, that
anyone would want to undertake such measures against us." This
was stated despite the fact that the previous Saturday Comrade
Janos Kadar [Hungarian Communist Party leader] had conferred
with Comrade Dubcek—I know this second-hand—in Slovakia.
Thus, up to the last minute, the leading comrades of the so-called
fraternal parties gave Comrade Dubcek no indication of the steps
they were about to take. Thereafter, I was charged with certain
tasks, and I was no longer continually present at the Presidium
session.

After the reading of the letter, the comrades evaluated the

situation. They saw it as a great tragedy for the entire workers' and Communist movement and foresaw tragic historical consequences. In short, they were extraordinarily disturbed. I remember Comrade Dubcek saying: "That they should have done this to me, after I have dedicated my whole life to cooperation with the Soviet Union, is the great tragedy of my life." I saw tears in his eyes. He called the Presidium to order and announced that he would prepare a draft proclamation.

I was present again at the proceedings that followed, and I know that, when the discussion opened, some comrades, in particular Comrade Indra, were missing. Comrade Dubcek, with great emphasis, demanded to know where he was and asked that he be called. This was done, and the discussion then turned to the proposed proclamation for the press.

When I returned at about 1:30 A.M. to the Central Committee building, the proclamation was not yet ready. The comrade journalists were pointing out that broadcasting stops at 2 A.M., and so on. The proclamation was issued at about 1:45 A.M., and then the Presidium dispersed. Some comrades left, and others remained in the Central Committee building. When I myself departed, sometime between 4 and 5 A.M., comrades Dubcek and [National Assembly Chairman Josef] Smrkovsky were still there. I also saw comrades Vaclav Slavik, Josef Spacek, and Frantisek Kriegel. Many other people were also there, including some department heads. Comrade Cernik left sometime after 2 A.M. for a session of the Government, but then the report came that the Government had been interned and that tanks were heading for the Central Committee building. As I emerged from the building, three (I think) armored cars, led by a black Volga from the Soviet Embassy, pulled up in front of the Central Committee building. The Volga stopped in front of the entrance, and I managed to move off to the right, where my car was waiting, and watch for a while from there. I saw more Soviet armored cars arrive, and soldiers prevented anyone from entering or leaving the building.

Comrades, dear friends, citizens, I should like to add one more thing, which I was unable to verify exactly but which I did notice during the course of the events. You know that almost imme-

diately after the radio began, at about 1:55 A.M., to broadcast
the Presidium's proclamation, transmission was interrupted. We
ascertained at the radio that the Director of the Central Communications Administration, Karel Hoffman, had ordered the
dispatchers not to broadcast. He had also forbidden long-distance
telephone calls, and I was told that if I wanted to place such a
call I could do so only with Hoffman's consent. I also found out
that Czechoslovak News Agency Director General Sulek arrived
at about 6 o'clock at his office and gave the order, even though he
was then officially on leave, that all information was to be chan-
neled through him. Some comrades know that several days earlier
Karel Hoffman had frequently been seen on the premises of the
Central Committee where he conferred with Alois Indra. I don't
think that we would be far from the truth if we evaluated the Kolder-Indra position paper as a preparation for what eventually
happened—as an attempt to replace Dubcek as leader of the
Party. This conclusion is consistent with the fact that the four
votes cast against adoption of the published proclamation of
the Presidium were those of Svestka, Bilak, Rigo, and Kolder.
Indra, as a Secretary, does not vote, but his solidarity with the
four is well known, and he was joined in his attitude by another
Secretary, Comrade Sadovsky, who expressed his full solidarity
with him.

I should like to call attention to the fact, which is not generally
known, that Comrade Frantisek Barbirek did not give the impression of supporting the memorandum submitted by comrades
Indra and Kolder. As far as I know, Comrade Barbirek does not
support the statement, issued by some members of the Central
Committee who met in the Praha Hotel, which aimed at accepting
the occupation regime.[3]

From Rude Pravo, *August 23, 1968*

Report on the Situation in Prague

Heavy aircraft with foreign markings cruised over Prague
through the night. Prague Radio went off the air. The sentence

---

[3] On August 21, a number of Central Committee members and candidate
members met in the Praha Hotel, and conservatives—including Kolder, Bilak,
and Indra—appealed to those present to cooperate with the Soviets.

"Yesterday, August 20, 1968, around 11 P.M. troops crossed . . ." was interrupted by silence. Gradually, all Czechoslovak stations went silent, and on the 210-meter wave-length the radio station *Vltava*[4] came on, broadcasting communiqués of the Soviet news agency *Tass* in Czech and Slovak. "Personalities of the Czechoslovak Communist Party," it said, "requested military aid from the Soviet Union, because our Republic was threatened by counterrevolution and anti-socialist elements which in combination with outside forces . . . ." The grammatical errors, the poor pronunciation, the entire style are reminiscent of times one does not forget.

I am standing in front of the Central Committee building. There are reporters and young people present. They discuss their disapproval of the occupation. A few girls weep. We want to speak with Alexander Dubcek or with other representatives of the Communist Party. It is not possible. And what about the Government? Why hasn't it come out yet with a statement about the situation? Why isn't anybody saying anything? The office of the Premier is said to be occupied.

Then comes the report: Soviet troops are on their way from Ruzyne. And instantly comes another: They are already on the bridge!

It is already 4:30 A.M. Soviet tanks and armored cars arrive in front of the Central Committee building. Soviet soldiers emerge in gloomy darkness and occupy the building. Others take up positions outside. They stand with their machine guns about 20 yards apart. I approach one of them: "We are your brothers. I am a Czech." Their commander appears and chases me away. "Do not speak with anyone," he shouts at the soldier. A while later, I walk up to another soldier: "In 1945, we welcomed Soviet soldiers in Prague." "Do not speak with anyone," the order comes again. The soldier opposite me releases the safety catch on his gun and chases me away. "We will shoot," he shouts in Russian. More tanks emerge from the darkness.

The strange radio station *Vltava* again tries, in broken Czech, to explain the occupation. The armies, it says, will be withdrawn

[4] The occupation radio, believed to have been transmitting from East Germany.

as soon as the dangers threatening socialism are removed. The occupation is not directed against any state; "it serves the cause of peace and the interests of European security."

We are used to great hypocrisy; our history is filled with truths and lies. But this lie and this violence we shall never forget. We cannot. We must not.

I learn that foreign airplanes are dropping leaflets—where did they print them?—stating that [former President] Antonin Novotny is the legal President of the Republic.

We all lived through this tragic night as honorable Czech people. At this time, when our country bleeds, the only ones who enjoy satisfaction are perfidious traitors, dogmatists, and enemies of their own people.

I have lived in the streets of Prague, the streets of my native city, through the humiliation of Munich. On Prikopy Street on March 15, 1939, we defied the Nazis. On October 28, 1939, we demonstrated for freedom. In May, 1945, we welcomed the new freedom in the first issues of *Mlada Fronta*. After January, 1968, we opened the road to a new life.

Our history is filled with tragedies. We were often oppressed. But we always lived to regain liberty. This time, too, freedom will arise again in our land.

From Mlada Fronta, *August 21, 1968*

4:30 A.M.

Czechoslovak Radio in Prague began its regular morning transmission. It broadcast the proclamation of the Presidium and other reports and commentary about the entry of foreign armies onto sovereign Czechoslovak territory. The two-week-long heroic epic of Czechoslovak Radio had begun.

The Command of the occupation armies distributed a proclamation to Czechoslovak citizens:

Our brothers, Czechs and Slovaks!

The governments of the Bulgarian People's Republic, the Hungarian People's Republic, the German Democratic Republic, the Polish People's Republic, and the Union of Soviet Socialist Republics appeal to you.

Responding to the request for help received from leading Party and state leaders of Czechoslovakia who have remained faithful to socialism, we instructed our armed forces to go to the support of the working class and all the people of Czechoslovakia to defend their socialist gains, which are increasingly threatened by plots of domestic and foreign reactionary forces.

This action is based on the collective commitment that the Communist and workers' parties of the fraternal countries adopted at Bratislava and on the commitment to support, strengthen, and defend the socialist gains of every nation and to stand up to imperialist plots.

Counterrevolutionaries incited and supported by imperialists are grasping for power. Anti-socialist forces that seized positions in the press, radio, and television have attacked and smeared everything created by the hands of industrious Czechs and Slovaks in the twenty-year-long struggle for socialism.

Enemies have incited people against the cadres dedicated to socialism; they have undermined the foundations of legality and the legal order, wantonly removed class-conscious workers and peasants from the political life of the country, and persecuted honest members of the intelligentsia who refused to take part in their actions. Trampling under foot socialist laws, counterrevolutionary forces preparing to seize power have created their own organizations.[5] And all this was being masked by demagogic phrases about democratization! We believe that the Czechoslovak people, dedicated to the ideals of socialist democracy, will not be deceived. True freedom and democracy can be guaranteed only through strengthening the leading role of the working class and of its vanguard—the glorious Communist Party of Czechoslovakia.

The January session of the Central Committee of the Czechoslovak Communist Party, which marked the beginning of the effort to rectify the mistakes of the past, had called for the attainment of this very goal. Our parties and nations supported the

[5] A reference to the clubs established after January, such as Club 231 (an organization of former political prisoners) and the Club of Involved Nonpartisans. Moscow feared that these clubs would evolve into political movements and would eventually challenge the Communist Party's monopoly of political power.

justified aims to strengthen and further perfect socialist democracy.

In recent months, the anti-socialist forces, which worked in clever disguise, have concentrated their efforts on undermining the foundations of socialism. A number of people who had penetrated the state and Party leadership of Czechoslovakia offered cover for these subversive actions and thus helped the counterrevolution to rally its forces for the final struggle to seize power.

Czechoslovak leaders kept declaring at the Soviet-Czechoslovak meeting at Cierna nad Tisou and at Bratislava that they intended to guard the interests of the workers and defeat the reactionary forces that were attempting to undermine socialism. They promised that they would strengthen the unity of Czechoslovakia and the fraternal socialist countries.

These assurances and commitments, however, were not fulfilled, which further encouraged the anti-socialist forces and their foreign protectors to strengthen their hostile activities. The enemy was preparing to throw the country into chaos.

The counterrevolutionaries expected that, in the complicated and strained international situation brought about by the aggressive actions of American imperialism and especially by the revanchist forces in West Germany, they could succeed in detaching Czechoslovakia from the community of socialist states. But these are vain hopes. The socialist states have sufficient strength to support a fraternal country and defend the cause of socialism.

Dear friends!

Your class brothers have come to your aid today.

They did not come to meddle in your internal affairs, but to help you fight the counterrevolution, defend the cause of socialism, and remove the danger threatening the sovereignty, the independence, and the security of your homeland.

The armies of the fraternal allied countries came so that no one could take away your freedom gained in our common struggle against fascism, so that no one could bar you from advancing on the shining road to socialism. These troops will leave your territory after the danger to the freedom and independence of Czechoslovakia has been removed.

We believe that the close unity of the fraternal nations of the

socialist commonwealth will prevail over the plots of the enemy.
Long live socialist Czechoslovakia!

Long live the friendship and brotherhood of the nations of the
socialist countries!

Council of Ministers of the Bulgarian People's
Republic
Council of Ministers of the Hungarian Peo-
ple's Republic
Council of Ministers of the German Demo-
cratic Republic
Council of Ministers of the Polish People's
Republic
Council of Ministers of the Union of Soviet
Socialist Republics

From leaflets dropped by helicopters and airplanes

Around 5:25 A.M.

The illegal station *Vltava* broadcast in Czech and in Slovak a
statement by *Tass* on the occupation of Czechoslovakia:

Tass is authorized to state that Party and Government leaders
of the Czechoslovak Socialist Republic have asked the Soviet
Union and other allied states to render the fraternal Czechoslovak
people urgent assistance, including assistance with armed forces.
This request was brought about by the threat that has arisen to
the socialist system existing in Czechoslovakia, emanating from
the counterrevolutionary forces that have entered into collusion
with foreign forces hostile to socialism. Further aggravation of
the situation in Czechoslovakia affects the vital interests of the
Soviet Union and other socialist states.

The decision [to intervene] is fully in accord with the right of
states to individual and collective self-defense provided for in
treaties of alliance concluded between the fraternal socialist
countries. The decision is also in line with vital interests of our
countries in safeguarding European peace against forces of militarism, aggression, and revanchism, which have more than once
plunged the peoples of Europe into wars.

Soviet Army units together with units of other allied countries
entered the territory of Czechoslovakia on August 21. They will
be promptly withdrawn from the Czechoslovak Socialist Republic

as soon as the threat to the security of the countries of the socialist community is eliminated and the legal authorities find that the further presence of these armed units is no longer necessary.

The actions that are being taken are not directed against any state. They serve the purpose of peace and have been prompted by concern for its preservation.

The fraternal countries firmly and resolutely counterpose their unbreakable solidarity to any threat from outside. No one will ever be allowed to wrest a single link from the community of socialist states.

From Pravda, *August 21, 1968*

Proclamation to Save Socialism in Czechoslovakia

According to reliable testimony, this proclamation was issued by a group of Czechoslovak state and Party officials who allegedly asked the Soviet Union and other socialist countries to save socialism in Czechoslovakia. The proclamation was supposed to have been published in Czechoslovakia shortly before the entry of the occupation forces on Czechoslovak territory. It was, in fact, delivered to the Czechoslovak News Agency at 8 A.M., August 21, by the former Director General of the Agency, Miroslav Sulek. The News Agency, however, did not release the proclamation.

Citizens of Czechoslovakia, workers, peasants, working intellectuals, men and women, young people!

We appeal to you at a time when the achievements of our socialist order are threatened by forces that abuse the progressive steps launched by the Party itself at the January plenum of the Central Committee. Unfortunately, this post-January period of transformation has been abused by right-wing forces that, for many years, waited for a favorable moment to discredit the Party and challenge its political and moral right to guide society. Certain forces inside the Party actually met these right-wing forces half way. They organized an inflammatory campaign designed to discredit individual Party functionaries, including some members of the new leadership of the Communist Party who found the courage to publicly draw attention to the impending danger. They violated public order and aroused nationalist passions. They demanded changes in our foreign policy. Their campaign of slander culminated with attacks on the alliance with the Soviet Union, especially in connection with the staff exercises of the armed forces of the Warsaw Pact, as well as attacks on the friendship with the other socialist countries. In this way, they created an atmosphere absolutely unacceptable for a socialist country.

The Communist Party, the Government of the Republic, the National Assembly, and the National Front maintained exceptional patience and understanding. However, it was emphasized more than once, especially at the May plenum of the Central Committee, that the paramount task was to frustrate the plans of the right-wing anti-socialist forces and not to let any mistake jeopardize implementation of the Action Program; to make sure that the question of the future Party line not be settled by exponents of extremist views but by the sound, progressive nucleus of the Party; and to render publicly full support to the Party and state apparatus, the army, the Security Forces, the Prosecutor's office, the courts, the People's Militia—in a word, to consolidate the internal political situation.

The extremist right-wing forces stepped up their activity still further. During daily spontaneous meetings in Prague, attended by thousands of people, different elements attacked the Party and insulted its representatives, whom they themselves made attend such meetings. A public campaign was launched in the center of the city to collect signatures in favor of liquidating the People's Militia. Communists who expressed their views at these unsanctioned street meetings were rudely silenced, and force was used against them more than once. Many who signed the letter at the Auto Praha factory in Prague [6] were shamelessly persecuted to the point of dismissal, and the press, although indirectly, continued to abuse leading functionaries by other, more sophisticated methods. This organized subversion came to a head in recent days when the Central Committee building in Prague was openly

[6] In July, ninety-nine Czechoslovak factory workers wrote to the Soviets voicing agreement with Moscow's alarm over trends in Czechoslovakia and advocating the presence of Warsaw Pact forces there as a "guarantee of our safety."

attacked. Thus there arose a situation in which commitments made at Bratislava were being systematically and publicly violated.

Comrades and fellow citizens, everything that our working people have built up in the last twenty years and all the gains of socialism are now at stake. Conscious of our supreme responsibility to our people, filled with feelings of true patriotism and international socialist solidarity, and conscious of our international commitments, we have assumed the initiative of rallying all patriotic forces in the name of the socialist future of our homeland. The danger of fratricidal struggle has forced us to make a historic decision and appeal to the Soviet Union and other fraternal socialist countries for help. Our allies came to our help as they did in 1945, when our very existence was in question.

We appeal to the whole population to support the military units of our allies. After the danger of a reactionary coup is removed, the allied troops will leave Czechoslovakia.

Guided by a profound sense of responsibility to our people, we appeal at this crucial moment to you, citizens of the Republic, to rally around the realistic core of the Party, which holds dear the cause of socialism, progress, and the new post-January path, as well as the friendship with the Soviet Union and the other fraternal countries.

We reject pre-January policies. We shall not permit any return to discredited pre-January methods, which were strongly rebuffed by an overwhelming majority of our people and which jeopardized the leading role of the Party and the socialist gains of our working people. On the contrary, we want to defend and implement fully the progressive January ideas that will lead us to the creation of a truly modern, rejuvenated, and humane socialist society—a society that the founders of Marxism-Leninism envisaged and that their followers, after the victorious 1917 October Revolution, began translating into reality. We shall bring to full conclusion the constitutional reorganization of our Republic on a federative basis. We shall guard as the apple of our eye the ties of our fraternal alliance and friendship with the Soviet Union and its people, with the people of all countries of the world socialist community, and with all forces of peace, democracy, progress, and socialism—the values that give us a guarantee of our independence and national and state sovereignty, without which we would again face the threat of a new Munich and those who planned it in 1938. Czechoslovakia can develop only as a socialist country and as an inseparable part of the socialist community.

Citizens, we urge all of you—from the Sumava border mountains to Cierna nad Tisou, from the Krkonose to the banks of the Danube—to maintain the unity and mutual trust that we need in the days to come. Our guiding principles must be foresight, order, truth, progress, and the prospect of socialism, state sovereignty, and united solidarity.

Long live and flourish democratic socialist Czechoslovakia!

Around 6 A.M.

Czechoslovak Radio in Prague broadcast a personal message from Alexander Dubcek. Comrade Dubcek requests that the Czechoslovak people go to their regular places of work, for that, at this moment, is the only possible thing to do.

Two officials of the State Security took Cestmir Cisar, a Secretary of the Central Committee and Chairman of the Czech National Council, from his home to the Security headquarters in Bartolomejska Street and questioned him.

6:35 A.M.

Czechoslovak Radio broadcast an appeal to the people to remain calm and meet the occupation with passive resistance.

6:45 A.M.

Czechoslovak Radio repeated its appeal for calm and asked that armed conflict be avoided.

Before 7 A.M.

Czechoslovak television in Prague went on the air. Since the transmitter on Petrin in Prague was occupied by Soviet troops, the transmitter at Cukrak near Zbraslav broadcast directly. After the occupation of the Strahov station transmitting the signal to

Cukrak (at 11 A.M.), the technicians improvised a direct connection.

From Lidova Demokracie, *August 21, 1968*

The Presidium of the Czechoslovak Academy of Sciences in Prague convened in extraordinary session. At 7 A.M., a statement was adopted and at 8:12 A.M. was broadcast by Czechoslovak television. The Presidium of the Czechoslovak Academy of Sciences thereafter remained in session and dealt every day with urgent questions of work at its institutions. It adopted an array of documents, proclamations, and appeals addressed to the Embassy of the Soviet Union (protest against the illegal occupation), to the Soviet troops, to the scientists of the world, and so on.

From materials of the Czechoslovak Academy of Sciences

Document 1: The Presidium of the Czechoslovak Academy of Sciences on the Occupation of Czechoslovakia

The Presidium of the Czechoslovak Academy of Sciences met in the early morning hours of August 21, 1968, the first day of the illegal occupation of the Czechoslovak Socialist Republic—an act accomplished against the will of the constitutional leaders of Czechoslovakia and of all its people. This appeal was sent to UNESCO in Paris:

The Czechoslovak Academy of Sciences stands unanimously behind the Dubcek leadership of the Party, behind the legally elected President of the Republic, Ludvik Svoboda, and the Cernik Government.

We condemn the occupation of Czechoslovakia by the armies of the Warsaw Pact. The occupation is an action contrary to alliance commitments and represents a flagrant transgression of the principles of international law and state sovereignty and which, in its consequences, damages the cause of socialism in the eyes of all the nations of the world.

The Presidium of the Czechoslovak Academy of Sciences has succeeded in establishing contact with a large portion of the members of the Academy and with a majority of Academy institutions. They all express their agreement with this declaration, as well as their support for further actions by the Academy Presidium.

The Academy Presidium has also sent the following telegram to the Embassy of the Soviet Union in Prague:

Dear Comrades: Since we are unable to establish contact with Soviet scientists, we ask you to transmit to the leadership of the Academy of Sciences of the Soviet Union our protest against the forcible and illegal occupation of Czechoslovakia.

Signed: Academician Ivan Malek, Academician J. Macek, Corresponding Member J. Pluhar, Ladislav Nemec, Corresponding Member F. Vodicka, Academician J. Filip, Corresponding Member B. Rosicky, Dr. J. Mach, Dr. M. Smidak.

The Presidium of the Academy has also issued the following appeal, drafted in several languages, to all the scientists of the world:

At this time when our country is being illegally occupied by occupation armies, we turn to you with an urgent appeal to help our just cause with all means at your disposal.

In the name of Czech and Slovak scientists,
Czechoslovak Academy of Sciences

7 A.M.

Czechoslovak Radio received a resolution from the military unit Mlada asking for the immediate convocation of the Extraordinary Fourteenth Congress of the Czechoslovak Communist Party.[7]

[7] The Extraordinary Fourteenth Party Congress had been originally scheduled to convene on September 9. The delegates, most of whom were liberals, had planned to create a new Central Committee and Presidium more overwhelmingly reform-minded than the existing bodies. On August 22, 1,192 Congress delegates—many disguised in work clothes—met secretly in the suburban Prague CKD plant and selected a new Central Committee and Presidium, removing many conservatives in the process. At Soviet insistence, the work of this Extraordinary Fourteenth Party Congress has since been nullified.

After 7 A.M.

Czechoslovak Radio broadcast an appeal of the District Committee Prague 2 demanding the immediate reconvening of a city Party conference and the convocation of the Extraordinary Fourteenth Party Congress.

7:10 A.M.

Czechoslovak Radio announced that queues were forming in front of Prague food stores.

There Will Be Bread

Since the early morning hours citizens have been forming long queues in front of food and dairy stores. This is understandable, since the occupation troops have barricaded with tanks the streets and bridges of Prague. Enough food is available, however, and there is no need for concern. We telephoned this morning the Prague Bakeries in Holesovice and were told that bread is in full production; the delivery trucks are encountering difficulties in passing through the streets. The Prague Dairies in Radlice, Vysocany, Hostivice, and in other locations promise that milk will be brought into the stores as usual even if the milk trucks have to make detours around the main centers of Prague. From Prague Foods we learn that, in order to prevent a panic, rationing is going into effect. Everyone can purchase four pounds of flour, two pounds of sugar, one pound of butter, half a pound of fat, five eggs, one piece of soap, three cans and ten pounds of potatoes. But citizens should have no fears; there is enough food, and it is only a question of how to get it into stores. So far, this is a problem in Prague only.

From Mlada Fronta, *2nd special edition, August 21, 1968*

7:15 A.M.

Czechoslovak Radio requested the people who were congregating in the Old Town Square to disperse and maintain calm. Self-control is our best weapon.

Czechoslovak Radio announced that an extraordinary session

of the Czechoslovak Socialist Party was called to meet in the morning.

Czechoslovak Radio again requested citizens not to build barricades. We need the streets free. It also announced that the first clashes with the occupation troops had taken place.

The Reporting of the Radio

Shortly before putting this special edition to bed, we received a report that the first clashes had taken place:

We appeal for calm and self-control. Do not allow yourselves to be provoked! Armed defense is out of the question. Reports arrive that the first shots are being fired in front of the Prague building of Czechoslovak Radio, where six tanks are stationed in position; the troops fire tracer bullets (perhaps even live ammunition). We do not know how much longer the radio will be able to continue broadcasting.

We are in a hurry. One more report: Czech National Council Chairman Cestmir Cisar was taken by two men in civilian clothes from the Central Committee building, which is occupied, to an unknown destination. People on Wenceslas Square are trying to stop vehicles of the occupation troops with their bodies.

From Mlada Fronta, *August 21, 1968*

7:18 A.M.

A message from Alexander Dubcek: "I beg you to maintain calm and to bear with dignity the present situation. I appeal to you for calm."

So do we!

7:20 A.M.

Czechoslovak Radio broadcast an appeal to all members of the Association of Anti-Fascist Fighters to attend a meeting called for 8 A.M.

7:25 A.M.

A column of Soviet tanks reached the immediate vicinity of the building of the Czechoslovak Radio.

7:30 A.M.

Czechoslovak Radio reported that six tanks are in front of the radio building and no one knows how much longer it will be possible to go on broadcasting.

7:35 A.M.

Czechoslovak Radio reported that occupation troops approaching the radio are firing tracer bullets and live ammunition. They are a few dozen yards from the building. A barricade facing Wenceslas Square has been erected. Several hundred people are trying to stop the advancing tanks with their bodies. The radio building has been hit by dozens of shots and is being buzzed by aircraft of the Antonov type and by large fighter planes. Czechoslovak Radio asks the people to try and engage the troops in conversations—it is our only weapon.

The broadcasting of Czechoslovak Radio is coming to an end. The national anthem is being played. This means that the radio has been occupied.

A moment after the playing of the anthem, however, a familiar voice announces over the air that the staff is remaining in the studio and will continue broadcasting the news as long as possible.

When you hear voices on the radio you are not familiar with, do not believe them!

From Mlada Fronta, *August 21, 1968*

Statement by the Editors of Rude Pravo.[8]

In this serious hour, the editorial board of *Rude Pravo* stands unequivocally behind the Central Committee Presidium and fully supports its proclamation.

We stand firmly behind the Dubcek leadership, behind the

---

[8] This statement is particularly interesting, since *Rude Pravo* (the official Czechoslovak Communist Party newspaper) was in the midst of a power struggle between the conservative editor, Presidium member Oldrich Svestka, and his liberal colleagues on the staff. In the end, Svestka's pro-Soviet views resulted in his ouster.

President of the Czechoslovak Socialist Republic, Ludvik Svoboda, and behind the Cernik Government.

We call on all Czechoslovak Communists, all citizens of the Czechoslovak Socialist Republic. Comrades, citizens! At this serious moment in our history, it is essential that we maintain a dignified calm and self-control. It is the only possible way of creating the conditions that will lead to rapid liquidation of the present situation. Let us demonstrate that the Czechoslovak people can solve their serious problems independently, with calm and with the dignity and courage they have displayed more than once in their history.

This country and its people do not want to have their internal problems solved by violent means. Their socialist traditions and ideals do not allow for an occupation, by enemies or by friends. We are deeply convinced that the ideological struggle, which in these days has reached its peak, cannot and must not become the grounds for any kind of repression.

We are convinced that the action of the allied armies is the result of insufficient information about our true internal condition. We assume, therefore, that we are facing an action that will change in complexion within several days. We firmly believe that our Government and Party organs, the President of the Republic, and the National Assembly will, after establishing direct contact with the governments of the socialist states, achieve a radical change in the political attitude of these states. We are convinced that the causes of the serious misunderstanding will be eliminated and supplanted by a consciousness of the injustice committed.

The ideals of socialism are strong enough to prevail under our democratic conditions without the intercession of force.

Maintain calm and follow the work of our Government and Party organs. Trust them.

The unity of our [Czech and Slovak] nations is a powerful force.

The socialist unity of our people is invincible.

From Rude Pravo, *special edition, August 21, 1968*

Similar statements from editorial boards were printed by several other dailies, including, for example, *Mlada Fronta, Zeme-*

delske Noviny, Vecerni Praha, Lidova Demokracie, and others.

7:45 A.M.

Czechoslovak Radio reported that the Ministry of Foreign Affairs requests Czechoslovak Radio to repeat several times that this occupation is unjustified. The Ministry of Foreign Affairs is surrounded by troops.

Old Town Square After the Hour Had Struck

Prague, August 21, 1968, 8 A.M. The Jan Hus monument is surrounded by hundreds of Prague citizens. A Czechoslovak soldier and a civilian have placed a Czechoslovak flag on top of the statue. Directly under the tower of the Old Town City Hall, honored artist Vlasta Chramostova has engaged a Soviet captain in the following dialogue: "Why did you come? After all, you are our friends. And friends do not come visiting armed. We want peace, freedom, sovereignty, and friendship." An official of the Union of Czechoslovak-Soviet Friendship joins in: "I have been a Communist and a friend of the Soviet Union for twenty-five years. Ninety per cent of the people stand behind Dubcek. Dubcek wants socialism. Why, then, did you come?"

A group of Soviet soldiers in an amphibious vehicle discusses with several Prague citizens a special edition of *Rude Pravo.* From the other side of the Square, one can hear the constant calls, "Dubcek, Dubcek, Dubcek." The approach to the Old Town Square from Celetna Street is closed by Soviet troops. Flags still flutter over the head of the majestic Hus. In one corner of the Square, citizens sing the national anthem. The discussion with the Soviet captain continues. He says: "Everything will be all right." The people object: "But when? Not until you go home. After all, you do want to remain our friends."

There are tears in many eyes. The Soviet soldiers and commanders knew what they meant. No, we are not traitors.

From Prace, *2nd special edition, August 21, 1968*

8:15 A.M.

Czechoslovak Radio broadcast an address by the President of
the Republic.

Dear fellow citizens:

During the last few hours a complicated situation has arisen
in our country. At the present moment I cannot tell you any
more. As President of the Czechoslovak Socialist Republic, I address you with the full responsibility I accepted when I assumed
office, and I urgently ask you to maintain reason and complete
calm.

Aware of your civic responsibility and in the interest of the
Republic, do not allow any unpremeditated actions to occur. With
the dignity and discipline you have shown during the past few
days, await further measures by the constitutional authorities of
the Republic.

From Prace, *2nd special edition, August 21, 1968*

Shortly Before 9 A.M.

The announcers of Czechoslovak Radio are temporarily silent.
The radio building is occupied by Soviet troops. Machine-gun
and automatic-weapons fire—along with the Czechoslovak national anthem—can be heard on the radio.

Report on the Situation in Prague

Young people who arrived from Ruzyne Airport, where they
had witnessed the arrival of the occupation troops, began assembling early in the morning in the middle of Wenceslas Square.
The blocking of the Square and of the entire center of the city
forced people who were on their way to work to leave the streetcars and continue on foot.

We learned from people on Wenceslas Square that there had
been shooting in front of the Central Committee building on the
bank of the river. Young people carried a blood-stained Czechoslovak flag as their corpus delicti.

We left immediately for the hospital at Frantisek. There, in an ambulance, lay an unconscious young man (his identity had not yet been ascertained) with a wound in his head. His condition, according to the doctor, was almost hopeless.

Another of the persons who had been shot, according to the medical record, was wounded by a Soviet soldier at 5:10 A.M. His injury (he had been shot through the shoulder) is not serious.

The third case is the saddest. This victim of the shooting in front of the Central Committee building died.

A woman who was said to have been run over by an occupation personnel carrier was in the hospital on Charles Square. Her condition is not serious.

The last scene: There are crowds of people with flags in front of the radio building. Military carriers try to reach the site. They are followed by the crowd, and immediately barricades of automobiles spring up on other approach streets.

False information is rife. On our way to the radio, we stopped the driver of an ambulance. He told us that the occupation troops are unwilling to let ambulances pass on their missions. He said that our doctors have been shot at, particularly near the hospital at Frantisek. We were there, and no shooting at our doctors had taken place.

After our return to the editorial office, we heard another alarming report: In Karlin, our people are marching with flags against armed occupation soldiers.

The situation in Prague remains tense. Please, maintain calm! Do not allow provocations to cause further bloodshed!

❖   ❖   ❖

In one of the cross streets near the radio building, I saw a Soviet captain open fire from a troop carrier. This was a signal to soldiers in other vehicles to start shooting like barbarians at the already badly chipped building fronts of Vinohrady. I stood five yards from the firing soldiers. I stood there, horrified at the defenselessness of the people around me, and I asked myself what could have made the Russian soldiers fire their automatic rifles in a friendly country. What caused this shooting? On Vinohradska Street, Soviet troops fired through the windows of a streetcar and demolished a civilian automobile. I believe that the young occupation soldiers were very nervous. We must not forget that many Prague citizens, especially the young ones, know Russian, and one can assume that what they had been saying to the armed soldiers was not very agreeable.

Why this nervousness? Why the violence? Why the resort to arms? Where is the famous Soviet diplomatic calm and decisiveness? I used to like the Soviet people, especially young people. But looking at the Soviet troops, I was ashamed for my former friendship. Not just for myself, but for them as well.

What I have just written was written with a heated pen, which apparently will not cool off today. It might seem that the present situation would be a godsend for a newspaperman. Do not believe it. The shooting and the sight of the old people running for shelter made me terribly sad.

The occupation troops wander around. Their commanders hold consultations. Do the occupation soldiers have any idea what this is all about? What do they want, why did they come? All that aimless movement, the shooting, the gaze of the young Soviet boys in occupation uniforms who helplessly cluster around their officers only reinforce my belief that they do not know what they want.

Where is that Soviet "This is your affair" we heard in past days?

8:45 A.M.

At this moment, Prague asked Ostrava to take over broadcasting. Ostrava immediately came on the air and began broadcasting telegrams and letters from factories all over the country expressing determination to continue supporting the legal authorities of our Republic.

While we are listening to television and the radio, crowds of Prague citizens carrying Czechoslovak flags and cheering for Dubcek pass under the windows of our editorial office. From the opposite direction come Soviet tanks, and they are greeted with hisses and clenched fists. People weep in the streets. The scenes look as if they had been cut out of periodicals dated March 15, 1939.

❖   ❖   ❖

From the office into the street, coming and going, that is the nature of the reporting activity of most Prague newspaper editors today. It is 8:30 A.M. Czechoslovak Radio is broadcasting. Aren't you reminded of those memorable words coming from radio receivers in 1945? Oh, yes. But today the meaning is reversed.

At 8:35 A.M., several trucks filled with people left the radio building. They held flags in their hands, and on the hood of the leading vehicle sat a boy of about nineteen with a fractured forehead. We asked him how he was wounded. "A Soviet officer struck me with his rifle butt." Another boy on the sidewalk showed us Soviet bullet shells. A column of vehicles carrying singing people ("There is lightning over the Tatras, and terrible thunder" [9]) passed through Wenceslas Square heading toward Old Town Square. They were followed from the radio building by Soviet troop carriers and tanks.

What do the simple soldiers with their startled faces think about us and all these events?

A record of a conversation: A Russian corporal from a personnel carrier with the identification mark 3–10 in a white triangle says, "We are here to maintain order." But what kind of order, since we had not suffered from any disorder? There is an old Czech proverb that says, "Put your own house in order."

Here is another bit of information revealed in discussion between citizens of Prague and the Soviet occupation army. A Russian corporal: "We won't do you any harm, we have no interest in hurting you. We'll only take a few people."

One of the citizens of Prague asks: "And what about Dubcek, is he a capitalist?" Soviet soldier: "Dubcek is a capitalist, yes, but also a nationalist."

8:50 A.M.

In front of the radio building, Soviet occupation troops demolished automobiles. Plaster flies off building façades. Glass litters the streets. Occupation troops use force to move the people away from the building but do not succeed without violence.

---

[9] Lines from the Slovak anthem.

Jaroslav Zeleny, a student born in 1945, is bayoneted by a Soviet soldier.

9 A.M.

The vehicles that went to Old Town Square return to Wenceslas Square. Shouts ring out from them: "Russians go home!" In front of the radio building, an occupation tank rammed a truck barricading the street. The impact started a fire, which engulfed the truck as well as the tank. The Soviet troops were thrown into confusion. In their effort to escape the flames, the tanks smashed into the buses and trucks that formed the barricade. More than fifteen tanks appeared at the museum from Vinohradska Street and without any apparent cause began firing not only at the nearby buildings but also at the National Museum itself.

On the steps in front of the museum lay people who had been struck down by the falling plaster and shells.

A procession of Prague citizens with a bloodstained flag marched down Wenceslas Square.

We were among the people under fire at the radio. We can give a realistic picture of this situation. We can only add that this action of the Soviet troops is incomprehensible.

From Svobodne Slovo, *August 22, 1968*

9:30 A.M.

On August 21, 1968, at 9:30 A.M., I [National Assembly Deputy Alois Polednak] called the office of the President of the Republic. After a short pause, Ludvik Svoboda came to the telephone. He told me that he had just requested permission to drive through Prague in order to observe the situation and visit the Presidium of the Party's Central Committee. He said that a decision would be made regarding his request, but he did not say by whom. He asked if I knew the whereabouts of Comrade Smrkovsky, and I told him that we have had no contact with him and that we do not know where he is.

10 A.M.

Soviet troops began clearing the editorial offices and the printing plant of *Rude Pravo* in Prague.

Citizens, Comrades, Friends!

The editorial offices of *Rude Pravo* were occupied by a military unit. As far as possible, we remained in our places and continued to work. At 1 P.M., following an ultimatum, all editors, typesetters, and printers are to leave the publishing house.

We must therefore temporarily interrupt the publication of our paper, but, we hope, not for long. *Rude Pravo* will unconditionally support the Dubcek leadership, fight for the sovereignty of our state and for the right of our Communist Party to seek its own road for building socialism in its own country. The principal slogan of the renewal process of socialism was "Return to Social-ism Its Human Face!" To this goal we shall dedicate all our efforts. We know, as all of you know, that a humane socialism cannot be built in the shadow of gun barrels. We resolutely re-quest the leaders of the intervening states to recall their armies from our territory!

Rude Pravo will again be published, even, if necessary, at the risk of its editors' lives.

Editorial board of Rude Pravo

10:07 A.M.

The extraordinary eighty-fifth session of the Presidium of the National Assembly was convened (the session was interrupted at 10:20 A.M.). The Presidium of the National Assembly adopted a declaration addressed to the prime ministers and the chairmen of the parliaments of the five states taking part in the occupation of Czechoslovakia and signed by sixteen members of the Presidium of the National Assembly. It also approved a letter from the Pres-idium of the National Assembly addressed to the Soviet Embassy and selected a delegation charged with the task of acquainting the Soviet Ambassador with the attitude of the National Assembly on the situation. The composition of the delegation: deputies Zdenek Fierlinger (head of the delegation), Alois Polednak, Dusan Spalovsky, Josef Zednik, Andrej Ziak, and Secretary Gen-eral of the National Assembly Vladimir Kaigl. The delegation left at 10:20 A.M. for the Soviet Embassy.

The Presidium of the National Assembly, duly convened on August 21, 1968, adopted at its session the following declaration:

To the chairmen of the governments and the chairmen of the parliaments of the Soviet Union, the Polish People's Republic, the Hungarian People's Republic, the German Democratic Republic, the Bulgarian People's Republic:

The Presidium of the National Assembly expresses its deep and fundamental disagreement with the action of the allied armies, which today, without cause, began occupying our country. A violation of our state sovereignty has just taken place, an act absolutely inadmissible in our mutual relations.

At this moment, while shots ring out in the streets of Prague, we demand most urgently that you order an immediate withdrawal of all armies from the territory of the Czechoslovak Socialist Republic.

From materials of the National Assembly

10:15 A.M.

An appeal from representatives of the creative artists' unions was broadcast on television and repeated on the radio: At 12 noon a two-minute demonstration will take place during which all traffic in the streets will halt. In this way we shall honor the memory of those who have already fallen.

After 10:15 A.M.

Throughout the entire day and night, until 6 A.M., August 22, officials in the building of the Prague City Committee maintained telephone contact with the regional secretariats of the Communist Party and with the Bratislava City Committee. In the process, they ascertained the whereabouts of delegates elected to the Extraordinary Fourteenth Party Congress.

The Prague City Committee held a session first in Celetna Street and later in Snemovni Street. Before noon, it dispatched representatives to the various regions in order to assure the arrival in Prague of the delegates to the Extraordinary Fourteenth Party Congress.

To the Communist and Workers' Parties of the Entire World!

Comrades, the Czechoslovak Socialist Republic was occupied today by the armies of five states of the Warsaw Pact, against the will of the Government, the National Assembly, the leadership of the Communist Party, and all the people.

In view of the fact that the Central Committee building, where the Presidium is now in session, is occupied by troops, the Prague City Committee appeals to all Communist and workers' parties.

Comrades, protest against this unprecedented violation of socialist internationalism!

Demand the immediate withdrawal of the occupation armies!

We ask you to consider the need for immediate convocation of a conference of Communist and workers' parties, which would adopt an appropriate attitude toward the act of lawlessness suffered by the people of Czechoslovakia and its Communist Party.[10]

The Presidium has decided to inform the Rumanian and Yugoslav embassies about the present situation and to ask them to forward messages to the Central Committees of their Communist parties.[11] The Presidium requests these organs to give urgent consideration to the present situation in the Czechoslovak Socialist Republic.

> City Committee of the Czechoslovak Communist Party in Prague

From Vecerni Praha, *August 21, 1968*

In the Course of the Day

A number of organizations published statements of their attitudes toward the occupation.

Statement of the Association of Anti-Fascist Fighters

The Presidium of the Central Committee of the Association of Anti-Fascist Fighters and all resistance branches express their unconditional support for the constitutional leadership of the Czechoslovak Socialist Republic headed by the President of the

---

[10] The Czechoslovak Communists were confident of strong backing at any international Communist meeting, especially from the French, Italian, Rumanian, and Yugoslav Communist parties. This analysis proved to be correct. Although no international meeting was called at the time, a great many Communist parties condemned the Warsaw Pact invasion of Czechoslovakia.

[11] Rumanian Communist Party leader Nicolae Ceausescu and Yugoslav President Josip Broz Tito had both visited Czechoslovakia earlier in the month as a sign of their support for developments in that country.

Republic, Ludvik Svoboda. They express their full faith in and support for the Central Committee, led by Comrade Alexander Dubcek, and the entire Dubcek leadership.

From Prace, *2nd special edition, August 21, 1968*

Statement of the Defense and Security Committee of the National Assembly

The Defense and Security Committee of the National Assembly appeals to all members of the Czechoslovak People's Army and the National Security Corps to remain faithful to Alexander Dubcek, the Central Committee, and the President of the Republic, Ludvik Svoboda.

From Prace, *2nd special edition, August 21, 1968*

Statement of the Presidium of the Union of Czechoslovak Journalists

The Presidium of the Union of Czechoslovak Journalists has met at this difficult time to express its firm faith in the road upon which our Communist Party, our Government, and our entire nation embarked after January. We want to declare once again before the whole nation that we shall firmly support President Svoboda, the duly elected Presidium of the Communist Party, Comrade Dubcek, the legal Government led by Oldrich Cernik, and the leadership of the National Assembly headed by Comrade Smrkovsky. We will not and cannot serve anyone else. We appeal to all journalists to persevere in support of the progressive and democratic traditions of our people and to do nothing of which they could be ashamed in the future.

From Vecerni Praha, *August 21, 1968*

To All Trade Union Organizations of the World!

During the night of August 20–21, 1968, the Czechoslovak Socialist Republic was occupied by the armies of the Soviet Union, the German Democratic Republic, the Polish People's Republic, the Bulgarian People's Republic, and the Hungarian People's Republic.

This action was taken without the knowledge of the President of the Czechoslovak Socialist Republic, the Government, the National Assembly, and the Central Committee of the Communist Party. This groundless, treacherous occupation of our peace-loving socialist homeland is contrary to international law and to the Charter of the United Nations. Our country was occupied because we have been striving for a humane and profoundly just socialism in a manner that best corresponds to our conditions and potential.

In the name of five and one-half million Czechoslovak trade unionists and of all working people, we appeal to you to protest against this violent act.

> Secretariat of the Central Trade Union
> Council and Chairmen of the Central
> Committees of Trade Unions

10:45 A.M.

The Presidium of the National Assembly issued a report on its session.

Report of the Presidium of the National Assembly

The Presidium of the National Assembly has been sitting in extraordinary session since the early morning hours of August 21, 1968, and has been discussing the serious situation that has occurred as a result of the occupation of the Czechoslovak Socialist Republic by the armies of the Soviet Union, the German Democratic Republic, the Polish People's Republic, the Hungarian People's Republic, and the Bulgarian People's Republic.

The Presidium of the National Assembly has been trying to make contact with the Ambassador of the Soviet Union in Prague and with the commander of the armies on the territory of the Republic in order to initiate negotiations.

The Presidium of the National Assembly appeals to the population to avoid all actions that could be considered provocative, so as to avoid unnecessary bloodshed.

The Presidium of the National Assembly again calls on all of the assembled deputies to appear without delay for the meeting of the Assembly plenum. It asks the deputies to make use of all available means of transportation. It also asks the Regional and

District National Committees to help provide the assembled deputies with transportation facilities.

> Josef Valo,
> First Deputy Chairman of the National Assembly

From materials of the National Assembly

11:30 A.M.

The Central Committee of the Socialist Party [12] met during the morning hours of August 21 and issued a statement on the situation.

The Only Possible Solution—Departure of the Troops

As a political party, we fully support the President of the Czechoslovak Socialist Republic, Ludvik Svoboda, as the only legal President of our country; we fully support our National Assembly, headed by its Chairman, Josef Smrkovsky, and our Government, headed by Premier Oldrich Cernik; and we fully support the present leadership of the Communist Party of Czechoslovakia headed by Alexander Dubcek.

If the occupation of Czechoslovakia by the five armies of the Warsaw Pact is not brought to an end in the shortest possible time, all responsibility for the consequences must be borne by the countries who are occupying us. We believe that no collaborationist government can persuade the Czechoslovak people that socialism can be built under the shadow of bayonets, even if those bayonets belong to allied and fraternal armies. Such a government (if it should be formed) will be hated and isolated by the Czechoslovak people. Under the leadership of such a government, Czechoslovakia would really become the weakling in the Warsaw Pact.

From Svobodne Slovo, *August 22, 1968*

12 Noon

Exactly at 12 o'clock, all movement in the streets of Prague came to a halt. Citizens obeyed the appeal of the representatives

[12] A member of the Communist-dominated National Front.

of the creative artists' unions for a two-minute protest strike against the occupation of our country.

From Lidova Demokracie, *August 21, 1968*

Around Noon

Soviet troops surrounded the radio transmitter at Cukrak, near Zbraslav.

12:25 P.M.

Czechoslovak Radio broadcast a request of the Prague City Committee asking that all Communist Party Regional Committees express their views on an immediate convocation of the Fourteenth Congress of the Communist Party.

Czechoslovak Radio broadcast in several languages an appeal to writers, intellectuals, and artists of the entire world, in which, among other things, the following was stated:

Stalinism precluded any prospects for a humane socialism. The Czechoslovak Socialist Republic stood in the vanguard of a new approach opposed to this evil. The occupation of the Republic dealt a blow to all the progressive forces of mankind. We request progressive figures the world over to come to the defense of our country.

> Union of Writers,
> Union of Plastic Artists,
> Union of Architects,
> Union of Film and Television Workers,
> Union of Journalists

12:30 P.M.

The Czechoslovak News Agency was informed by the Prague Rescue Service that twenty-five people suffering from gunshot wounds have been reported in hospitals. Deaths have also been reported.

Czechoslovak News Agency received an unofficial report that comrades Dubcek, Smrkovsky, Cernik, and Kriegel are still being held in the Central Committee building and that Comrade Cisar is in the Bartolomejska Street police headquarters.

12:55 P.M.

Czechoslovak Radio broadcast a statement issued by some members of the Czechoslovak Government:

1. We stand firmly behind all the legally elected constitutional and political authorities, and we firmly support today's proclamation of the Presidium addressed to all the people.

2. We consider the occupation of the Czechoslovak Socialist Republic, which took place without the agreement and knowledge of the Czechoslovak Government, an illegal act, contrary to international law and the principles of socialist internationalism.

> Julius Hanus, Vladimir Kadlec, Josef Krejci, Bozena Machacova, Frantisek Penc, Stanislav Razl, Bohumil Sucharda, Vaclav Vales, Michal Stancel, Vladislav Vlcek, Vaclav Hromadka

According to a Czechoslovak News Agency report from the office of Minister Vales, ministers Miroslav Galuska, Bohuslav Kucera, and Josef Pavel have associated themselves with the declaration of the ministers by adding their signatures.

From Lidova Demokracie, *2nd special edition, August 21, 1968*

Report on the Situation in Prague

The Director of the Northwest Railroad, L. Kaspar, informed the Czechoslovak News Agency today that the Main and Center Railroad stations in Prague have been occupied and shut down. The movement of trains across the Smichov railroad bridge has been interrupted. Trains bound for Prague let passengers off at stations on the outskirts.

Passenger transportation has also been interrupted in Brno and Plzen. Freight traffic is functioning normally and is almost entirely devoted to moving civilian supplies. At the occupied railroad stations, foreign troops interfere with the movement of the railroad personnel and even interrupt telephone communications.

The public is requested to curtail their railroad travel.

According to a report from the Deputy Director of the Prague Transport Enterprise, J. Kucera, bus and streetcar traffic in Prague has come to a complete halt. No fuel is available, as the national enterprise Benzina has been occupied by foreign troops. According to incomplete reports, some twenty buses and ten streetcars have been damaged or destroyed during the occupation of Prague.

From Lidova Demokracie, *August 21, 1968*

Shortly After 2 P.M.

Dubcek, Smrkovsky, Kriegel, and Spacek were taken by a Soviet armored personnel carrier from the Central Committee building to an unknown destination.

2:35 P.M.

A previously interrupted meeting of deputies of the National Assembly, which, as the extraordinary twenty-sixth session of the National Assembly plenum, had approved recent measures of the National Assembly Presidium, discussed the current situation and issued the following proclamation:

1. We fully endorse the Central Committee proclamation and that of the Presidium of the National Assembly, which calls the occupation of Czechoslovakia by the armies of five countries of the Warsaw Pact a violation of international law, a violation of the provisions of the Warsaw Pact, and a violation of the principles of equal relations between nations.

2. We demand that our constitutional leaders, primarily the President of the Republic, Ludvik Svoboda, the Premier, Oldrich Cernik, the Chairman of the National Assembly, Josef Smrkovsky, the First Secretary of the Communist Party, Alexander Dubcek, the Chairman of the National Front, Frantisek Kriegel, the Chairman of the Czech National Council, Cestmir Cisar, and others be released from internment. Moreover, the delegation from the National Assembly, which we sent this morning to the Soviet Embassy, has not yet returned.

3. We protest against the measures that have prevented the National Assembly, the Government, members of the National Front, and the leaders of these bodies from exercising their legal rights. We demand their freedom of movement and assembly.

4. We categorically demand the immediate withdrawal of the armies of the five states of the Warsaw Pact, the honoring of the provisions of the Warsaw Pact, and full respect for the state sovereignty of the Czechoslovak Socialist Republic. We appeal to the parliaments of all countries and to world public opinion to support our lawful demands.

5. We entrust a delegation of the National Assembly, consisting of Marie Mikova, Josef Macek, Frantisek Vodslon, Pavol Rapos, Josef Pospisil, and Vaclav Kucera, with contacting Chairman of the National Assembly Comrade Josef Smrkovsky, President of the Republic, Ludvik Svoboda, and Premier Cernik, in order to inform them about this resolution and consult with them about further steps. The delegation will immediately report to the Czechoslovak people on the results of its negotiations.

6. We call on all the people of our country not to use violence against the occupation troops and not to allow themselves to be provoked by elements that seek justification for the intervention.

Working people, citizens!

Stay at your places of work and defend your enterprises! Use all democratic means for the further development of socialism in Czechoslovakia!

If necessary, you will surely be able to defend yourselves by a general strike. Normal life can be guaranteed in this country only by the people who live and work in it.

We are living through difficult hours. We believe that we shall prevail with heads held high.

This proclamation was adopted by all the deputies present.

> Josef Valo,
> First Deputy Chairman of the National Assembly

From materials of the National Assembly

Report on the Situation in Prague

Wenceslas Square, Wednesday afternoon: Over Vinohradska Street the smoke from burning houses still rises into the sky. We pass a smoke-smudged youth carrying a sad souvenir—the shell of an 85-mm gun. The fountain below the museum splashes quietly, just as it did yesterday, as if nothing had happened, but when you raise your eyes to the façade of the museum, you freeze in your steps. Against the dark background shine hundreds of white spots, as if evil birds had pecked at the façade. The antenna of a tank had touched a trolley wire—and that was enough to provoke gunfire, which will mark for many years the historical edifice at the head of Wenceslas Square.

"Soldiers, go home! Quickly!" implores an inscription in Russian fastened to the pedestal of Saint Wenceslas' statue. And below, around the statue, silently sit the young and the old. Saint Wenceslas is decorated with Czechoslovak flags. There are also a few leaflets demanding that the occupation armies leave. The inscription on the statue, which normally is unnoticed, is endowed today with new and vital meaning: "Do not let us perish, nor our heirs!" The inscription is supplemented by a sign expressing the opinion of us all: "Dubcek hurrah!" People sit dejectedly on the pedestal. On the street corner, small groups of people listen to transistor radios.

From Rude Pravo, *August 22, 1968*

Charles University in Prague

Charles University, loyal to the traditions of humanism, science, progress, and the truth, protests categorically against the action of the five friendly governments of the Warsaw Pact, which violated the principles governing the relations between socialist countries, as well as the fundamental norms of international law.

Science and humanity can flourish only where freedom, independence, state sovereignty, and peace reign. Charles University supports with all its strength the representatives of our state power and of the Communist Party who in the post-January period began creating the conditions for the peaceful and successful development of our socialist state. Therefore, it demands the immediate withdrawal of occupation forces from the territory of our state.

Moreover, Charles University believes that the scientific world will loyally support its position.

From a leaflet

Leaflet from the University in Prague [13]

We, the former students who on November 17, 1939, were dragged off to Nazi concentration camps, solemnly declare that we firmly and loyally support our President, Army General Ludvik Svoboda, the Chairman of the National Assembly, Josef Smrkovsky, the legal Government of the Czechoslovak Socialist Republic headed by Oldrich Cernik, and the Action Program of the Communist Party of Czechoslovakia and of its Central Committee headed by First Secretary Alexander Dubcek.

We therefore ask the people of the whole world for support, and we turn particularly to former inmates of Nazi concentration camps and to students of the world with the following appeal: Prevent the second occupation of Czechoslovakia!

Association "17th of November,"
Association of Anti-Fascist Fighters

Appeal to the Warsaw Pact Soldiers!

Comrades!

You came to us convinced that you were defending the cause of socialism in our country. You yourselves have seen that there is peace here and that no counterrevolutionary elements are active. The Communist Party of Czechoslovakia continues to lead the people on the basis of socialism and Marxist-Leninist teaching. That is why we see no reason for the occupation of our territory by allied armies of the Warsaw Pact. After our own sad experiences with German militarism, we are capable of defending our western frontier in the knowledge that we are defending it not only for our sake but for the entire socialist peace camp, of which we are a part. We therefore do not view your arrival here as we did in 1945, when you came to liberate us from Hitlerite oppression; we view it as an unwanted occupation. This armed strike against the sovereignty of our state will disturb our mutual friendly relations for a long time to come.

We ask therefore: Leave our territory as friends and do not interfere with our internal development. A further step-up in

[13] Originally in German.

your activity here will create a tragic misunderstanding in our mutual relations.

In the name of all the workers of the national enterprise Polygrafia, Prague 2

5:10 P.M.

Czechoslovak Radio broadcast a proclamation of the Czech National Council adopted at an afternoon meeting:

Members of the Czech National Council from Bohemia, Moravia, and Silesia who were able to meet in Prague protest categorically, in the name of the entire Czech National Council, the arrest of Cestmir Cisar.

They declare that all persons who kidnapped the Chairman of the Czech National Council bear full responsibility for this crime. We ask that they immediately set Comrade Cisar free.

From Svoboda, *August 22, 1968*

Around 5 P.M.

During his transfer from the Bartolomejska Street police station to the Soviet Embassy, Cestmir Cisar succeeded in escaping and left Prague.

Around 6 P.M.

Prague City Committee Secretary Bohumil Simon was taken from the Central Committee building in a Soviet military vehicle to an unknown destination.

In the Afternoon

During the absence of the Premier and the deputy premiers, the Government met in extraordinary session under the chairmanship of Minister Bozena Machacova and adopted the following resolution:

The Government has been prevented from executing its duties. Throughout the day, individual members of the Government were not allowed to enter the building of the Presidium of the Government or to contact the Premier or the deputy premiers. The Government has also been prevented from contacting the Chairman of the National Assembly, Comrade Smrkovsky.

The Government has resolved to request the President of the Soviet Union for an immediate audience in order to discuss the consequences of the military occupation of the Czechoslovak Socialist Republic.

The Government has approved the action of the Ministry of Foreign Affairs, which has transmitted through the Czechoslovak embassies in Moscow, Warsaw, Budapest, Berlin, and Sofia a diplomatic note requesting the withdrawal of the troops of the Warsaw Pact countries from the territory of Czechoslovakia.

In the Course of the Day

The Czechoslovak Ministry of Foreign Affairs has dispatched to the ambassadors of the Czechoslovak Socialist Republic in Moscow, Berlin, Warsaw, Budapest, and Sofia two notes to be transmitted to the governments to which they are accredited.

Statement of the Ministry of Foreign Affairs of the Czechoslovak Socialist Republic

The Ministry of Foreign Affairs, on behalf of the Government of the Czechoslovak Socialist Republic and with the agreement of the President of the Republic, today instructed the Czechoslovak ambassadors in the Soviet Union, the Polish People's Republic, the German Democratic Republic, the Hungarian People's Republic, and the Bulgarian People's Republic to deliver immediately an energetic protest with the request that the illegal occupation of Czechoslovakia be immediately ended and all troops withdrawn from Czechoslovak territory.

From documents of the Ministry of Foreign Affairs

Note of the Ministry of Foreign Affairs to the Ambassadors of the Czechoslovak Socialist Republic in the Capitals of the Warsaw Pact Nations

The Embassy of the Czechoslovak Socialist Republic, on behalf of the Ministry of Foreign Affairs of the Czechoslovak Socialist Republic, in the name of the Government and with the agreement of the President of the Czechoslovak Socialist Republic, informs the Ministry of Foreign Affairs of —— of the following.

In the night of August 20–21, 1968, the air and ground forces of the Soviet Union, the Polish People's Republic, the German Democratic Republic, the Hungarian People's Republic, and the Bulgarian People's Republic launched a joint massive invasion of the territory of Czechoslovakia. The troops penetrated Czechoslovak territory simultaneously at various points and occupied the entire country.

In order to prevent irrevocable, catastrophic consequences for Czechoslovakia's relations with ——, as well as a threat to international peace and security, the constitutional representatives of the Czechoslovak Socialist Republic and the Presidium of the Central Committee of the Czechoslovak Communist Party have called upon citizens of the Republic to keep calm and offer no resistance to the advancing armies. For the same reason, the Czechoslovak Army, the Security Forces, and the People's Militia have received no order to defend the country.

This stand of the Czechoslovak Government in the face of armed occupation of the country will be appreciated in history as the contribution of a small country to the maintenance of international peace.

The Government of the Czechoslovak Socialist Republic declares that neither it nor any other constitutional authority of this country has agreed to the invasion and occupation of Czechoslovakia.

The armed occupation of Czechoslovakia is contrary to the Charter of the United Nations, the Warsaw Pact, and the fundamental principles of international law. By their joint action, the five countries have assaulted the independence of Czechoslovakia and violated in an unprecedented manner its territorial integrity.

The Government of the Czechoslovak Socialist Republic protests this act most resolutely. In the name of the entire Czechoslovak people and in the name of international peace and cooperation, it demands that the illegal occupation of Czechoslovakia be ended and all troops withdrawn from Czechoslovak territory.

The Czechoslovak Government reserves the right to undertake

all necessary measures if its demand for the immediate end of the occupation of Czechoslovakia is not complied with.

From documents of the Ministry of Foreign Affairs

Second Note of the Ministry of Foreign Affairs

The Embassy of the Czechoslovak Socialist Republic makes reference to its note bearing today's date in which, in the name of the Government and with the approval of the President of the Republic, it most resolutely protested the invasion and armed occupation of Czechoslovak territory.

The Embassy calls to the attention of the Government of —— the fact that the work of the constitutional authorities of the state, such as the President, the Government, the National Assembly, and other national and local bodies of state power, is being seriously impeded in the territory of Czechoslovakia. The grave nature of the situation is further aggravated by the absolutely illegal detention of political and public officials, such as the Chairman of the Czech National Council and the Secretary of the Central Committee of the Czechoslovak Communist Party. Neither the Czechoslovak state authorities nor any other organs have been informed about the fate of Mr. Cisar. The delegation from the National Assembly that was sent to the Embassy of the Soviet Union in Prague has not returned. The immediate release of Mr. Cisar and of the delegation of the National Assembly is a demand that corresponds to elementary principles of law. The Czechoslovak authorities expect that similar occurrences will under no circumstances be repeated.

In various places, there has been bloodshed among the civilian population, public and residential buildings have been damaged, and incalculable losses have been inflicted upon the entire national economy. The distribution of supplies to the population and medical care for the wounded are being threatened, and transport and communications are paralyzed. Numerous public buildings and installations have been seized by the occupation troops.

In the name of the Government, the Embassy, apart from the

fundamental demands contained in the preceding note, urgently requests the Government of —— to take all measures that will make possible a return to normal life in the country and demands that all violent actions against the population of Czechoslovakia be ceased without delay.

From documents of the Ministry of Foreign Affairs

Around 7 P.M.

Czechoslovak Radio broadcast the proclamation of the Government of the Czechoslovak Socialist Republic:

To All the People of Czechoslovakia!

Against the will of its Government, the National Assembly, the leadership of the Communist Party, and its people, Czechoslovakia was occupied today by troops of five Warsaw Pact states. Thus, for the first time in the history of the international Communist movement, an act of aggression directed against a state led by a Communist Party and carried out by allied armies of socialist countries has taken place.

A state of crisis has existed since early morning. The constitutional authorities of the Republic are deeply disturbed. Individual members of the Government, the National Assembly, the leadership of the Communist Party, the National Front, and other organizations are prevented from having contact with each other and with the citizens of this country, who in recent months have spontaneously demonstrated their confidence in them.

A number of Government and Party leaders have been interned. The last remaining link to the people is the semi-illegal Czechoslovak Radio, which is functioning only because of the utmost efforts of its workers. But the radio is gradually being silenced.

Yet even under such circumstances, the Czechoslovak Government and other constitutional organs, as well as the leadership of the Party, wish to discharge their constitutional functions and ensure normal life in the country.

We turn to you, Czechs, Slovaks, members of national minorities, all citizens of the Czechoslovak Republic with the following appeal:

1. We demand the immediate withdrawal of the troops of the five Warsaw Pact states; we demand adherence to the Warsaw Treaty and full respect for the sovereignty of Czechoslovakia.

2. We urgently demand that the governments of the Soviet Union, the German Democratic Republic, the Polish People's Republic, the Hungarian People's Republic, and the Bulgarian People's Republic issue orders for the cessation of armed action, which is leading to bloodshed and the material destruction in our country.

3. We demand that Government and Party leaders be released from internment so that they can resume their work.

4. We demand the immediate convocation of the plenum of the National Assembly so that the entire Czechoslovak Government can present to it its views on the resolution of the present situation.

To all our citizens!

We ask you to support these demands of the Government in the following manner:

1. By showing, as you have often done in recent months, statesmanlike self-control and by rallying around the duly elected Czechoslovak Government, which exists and in which, in April, you expressed your confidence.

2. By not allowing the establishment of any government other than one elected under free and democratic conditions.

3. By encouraging the work forces of our plants, cooperative farms, and other enterprises to express their support for the Czechoslovak Government to the commands of the occupation troops and to the governments of the five Warsaw Pact countries.

4. By insuring the maintenance of order, avoiding all spontaneous actions against members of the occupation armies, providing the population with the necessary food, water, gas, power, and so forth. Provide everywhere for the defense of factories and other important installations and prevent further economic losses.

Dear fellow citizens!

We are living through difficult times. Only the people who live and work here can guarantee the happy life of this country.

We believe that at this time you will give your Government your full support and that you will place all your forces at the service of our Socialist Republic.

Citizens!

With your help, it is still in our power to complete the great task of renewal we began in January. The Government believes that with your help we shall achieve this, and without unnecessary sacrifice and bloodshed.

Government of the Czechoslovak Socialist
Republic

From Prace, *August 22, 1968*

In the Evening

Czechoslovak Radio reported that deputies of the National Assembly heard from the delegation that visited the Soviet Embassy to deliver a statement from the National Assembly. [Soviet] Counsellor S. I. Prasolov assured the delegation that he would transmit the demands to the proper authorities and that he would report by telephone when and with which military commander the National Assembly could negotiate. (He did not keep his promise.)

Deputy Marie Mikova tried to enter the Central Committee building but did not succeed; the Soviet Embassy also refused to admit her.

[Soviet news agency] *Tass* issued a statement on the situation in Czechoslovakia:

As reported earlier, the Soviet Union and other allied countries have satisfied the request of Party and state leaders of the Czechoslovak Socialist Republic to render urgent aid, including aid with armed forces, to the fraternal Czechoslovak people.

In fulfillment of this decision, troops of allied socialist countries entered Czechoslovakia on August 21 and reached all regions and towns, including Prague and Bratislava. The advance of the troops of the fraternal countries took place unobstructed. Military units of the Czechoslovak People's Army remain in the areas of their deployment. The population is calm. Many Czechoslovak citizens express their gratitude to soldiers of the allied armies for their timely arrival in Czechoslovakia, for their help in the struggle against counterrevolutionary forces.

In Prague, however, and in some other places, right-wing and anti-socialist elements are organizing hostile attacks against the healthy forces in the Czechoslovak Socialist Republic and against the allied troops that have come to their assistance. These hostile moods have found their expression in the organization of provocations on the streets, in circulation of hateful rumors and fabrications, and in distribution of slanderous leaflets. There have also been incendiary statements on the radio, on television, and in the press.

Subversive activities are conducted by the very same anti-socialist elements that, in recent months, daily attacked the foundations of socialism in the Czechoslovak Socialist Republic, the Communist Party of Czechoslovakia, and friendship with the Soviet Union and other socialist countries. Behind all this counterrevolutionary activity, one senses the guiding hand of imperialist circles.

By resorting to methods of provocation and blackmail, anti-socialist elements are trying to cast doubt on the aims of the fraternal countries, which are now fulfilling their international duty of protecting socialist gains in Czechoslovakia.

Thus, despite the clear statement by the allied countries that their military units would not interfere in the internal affairs of Czechoslovakia, rumors are being circulated to the effect that the goal of the allied countries is to install in the leadership of the country the former President of the Republic, Antonin Novotny. However, the fraternal parties and governments of the allied countries have more than once expressed their support for the decisions of the January plenum of the Czechoslovak Communist Party.

The progressive forces in Czechoslovakia, as is clear from the appeal published by some members of the Central Committee, are firmly determined to continue in the course mapped out by the Party at the January plenum and supported by the Bratislava conference. This appeal is an important political document, and it is supported by all those people who treasure the freedom, independence, and sovereignty of socialist Czechoslovakia.

Throughout the day of August 21, a statement by the President of the Republic, Ludvik Svoboda, was widely publicized all over Czechoslovakia. In it he called on the people to display reason and calm in order to prevent, in the interest of the Republic, rash actions.

From Svoboda, *August 22, 1968*

10 P.M.

After firing colored rockets, Soviet troops opened fire in several parts of Prague. This maneuver was repeated several days in a row and always lasted intermittently until 10:30 P.M.

10:30 P.M.

Czechoslovak Radio broadcast a second address on the situation by the President of the Republic, Ludvik Svoboda.

Dear Fellow Citizens,

I am addressing you for the second time on this fateful day. We are going through exceptionally grave moments in the history of our nation. Military units of the Soviet Union, together with units of the Polish People's Republic, the Bulgarian People's Republic, the German Democratic Republic, and the Hungarian People's Republic entered the territory of our Republic. This took place without the agreement of the constitutional authorities of the state, which, however, because of their responsibility to the nations of our homeland, must urgently deal with the situation that has arisen in order to bring about an early departure of the foreign troops.

As far as current conditions allow, I have sought during this day to work toward that end. Today I convoked a plenary session of the National Assembly. This evening I spoke with members of the government about some of the urgent problems related to the task of restoring normal conditions to the country. Tomorrow I shall continue these discussions—hopefully, also with Premier Oldrich Cernik. I am aware of all the problems and difficulties called forth by the present situation. I turn to you again, dear fellow citizens, with the urgent request that you maintain the greatest prudence and avoid everything that could provoke regrettable actions with irreparable consequences. I sincerely address this appeal especially to our youth.

I appeal to all of you—workers, peasants, members of the intelligentsia—to demonstrate again by your attitude your relationship to socialism, freedom, and democracy.

For us there is no way back. The Action Program of the Communist Party expresses the vital interests and the needs of all the people of our homeland. We must therefore continue in the task we have begun. We shall not lose faith. We will all join together, and together with the Communist Party and the National Front we will remain united for the sake of a better life for our nations.

From documents of the Ministry of Foreign Affairs

In the Evening and During the Night

Meeting of Some of the Members of the Communist Party in the Praha Hotel

According to reliable information, about fifty members of the Central Committee of the Communist Party of Czechoslovakia met during the night of August 21–22, 1968, in the Praha Hotel, in order to adopt a statement on the situation resulting from the occupation of our Republic by foreign troops. Soviet officers who arrived with some of the Central Committee leaders—among them Vasil Bilak, Frantisek Barbirek, Drahomir Kolder, and Alois Indra —never left the meeting hall. On the initiative of some of the Central Committee leaders, a resolution was passed that aimed at a codification of the existing situation. There is no demand in the resolution for the departure of the occupation troops or for the release from internment of the leaders of the Party and the state.

From Zemedelske Noviny, *August 22, 1968*

After 11 P.M.

Czechoslovak Radio broadcast [14] a statement by the Institute of History of the Czechoslovak Academy of Sciences in Prague:

Dear Fellow Citizens!

The first long day of aggression and undeclared war by five states of the Warsaw Pact against our country is coming to an end. The occupiers failed to bring us to our knees; they failed to install a collaborationist regime; they failed to cause panic, disintegration, or fratricidal war; they failed to push us into thoughtless actions resulting in massacres.

In the present crisis created by the military invasion, we perceive the most valuable feature of our internal development to be the fact that no collaborationist group or clique of traitors has come forward to offer the aggressors the opportunity to camouflage in the international forum the treacherous breach of allied bonds and commitments and thus enable them to make the desired political arrangements. To prevent political collaboration with the occupiers remains in our view the most important task of the day. This is within our power! Everyone who would want to disrupt our present unity and plunge a knife in the back of our constitutional leaders must know that he will be cast aside by the hatred of our entire people and that history would never forgive such a deed. The eight months of 1968, even though they were only the beginning of our renewal process, are a living reminder that we have something to lose! Our entire effort for a humane socialism is at stake. Also at stake are freedom of speech and creative scientific work, which has enabled those of us who are historians to come to you freely during the past months with the results of our efforts.

The history of our state and our nation already knows one Munich. We paid for that capitulation dearly—not only with the loss of sovereignty and immeasurable suffering of hundreds of thousands and millions of people, but also with the terrible shock, from which it took our nation a long time to recover.

[14] For technical reasons, this statement was broadcast in part only.

We cannot live on our knees. We want to live and work standing up. It is in our power!

From a document in the archives of the Institute of History of the Czechoslovak Academy of Sciences

The Evening of the First Day in the Streets of Prague

The sound of machine-gun fire brought me late Wednesday night to the Savings Bank on Wenceslas Square. Until about 11, when an ambulance arrived, I walked about on the broken glass with a Soviet captain, exchanging views. The captain was asked to accompany the ambulance to a wounded man on Jirasek Square; it was possible to reach him only through Resslova Street, which was then under fire. I went along, and all of us—the Soviet captain, our officer, the two ambulance attendants, and myself— finally reached our destination safely. The wounded man had died in the meantime. It was a Soviet soldier, shot, it was said, by a sniper, perhaps from the window of one of the buildings across the street. There was more shooting. We stood, sheltered by the armor of the tanks, near Jirasek Bridge, and again there was a lively discussion. A Soviet lieutenant colonel commanding the sector between Resslova Street and Jirasek Square and down the river bank to Manes explained what they were doing in Czechoslovakia. They had come to protect us from the counterrevolution. They were four against our four: the two ambulance attendants, who had already gathered up five dead (the Soviet soldier was their sixth) and had taken thirty wounded to hospitals; a captain from our army who had just returned from fighting an accidental fire in a house on Naplavni Street; and a citizen who had daringly traveled from Ruska Street to several Prague hospitals, where he had offered his blood (he had earlier donated blood seven times for North Vietnam).

We presented our arguments, and when we parted we all said: We shall not say *au revoir*, we shall not wish you luck, and we shall not even shake your hands. This was perhaps the ultimate argument. I actually saw tears in the eyes of the Soviet captain. There was even a small spasm in the lieutenant colonel's face. The soldiers who had earlier just listened stood about hanging their heads. As we were leaving, the captain followed us a few steps and said: "We shall reflect about what we discussed here. I am afraid that you are right about a number of things. It is a terrible tragedy. And you can print this if you want to." "If that is really so," I said, "perhaps we shall shake hands after all some day."

From Rude Pravo, *August 23, 1968*

Developments in the State Security Apparatus on August 20–21, 1968

During the night of August 20–21, 1968, the main administration of the State Security Forces was put on alert. Around midnight, the employees were told that Soviet troops and troops of other member states of the Warsaw Pact had crossed our borders. Many were astounded and outraged by this news and began expressing their opposition. Some chiefs, such as Lieutenant Colonel Vanek, were labeling people by loyalty to "their countries." As early as the preceding day it was possible to notice that Lieutenant Colonel Vanek's self-esteem had risen considerably. He did not fail to boast before the assembled employees that he had been informed about the impending arrival of the troops in Czechoslovakia as early as 4 P.M., August 20, 1968, during an extraordinary conference with the Deputy Minister of the Interior, Viliam Salgovic. According to Vanek, all chiefs of section of the second department of the Ministry of Interior had taken part in that conference. On that occasion, the various section chiefs received their special assignments; the second section was given the task of guarding all capitalist foreign missions, including the embassies of Yugoslavia and Rumania. Specifically, their assignment was to prevent Czechoslovak citizens from seeking asylum in these missions.

The seventh section, on direct orders from Lieutenant Colonel Josef Rypl, was asked to prevent the Czechoslovak Radio from broadcasting the declaration of the Presidium on the occupation of Czechoslovakia. Lieutenant Colonel Vanek later stated that the broadcast had been interrupted through the action of State Security authorities. When the Presidium declaration was broadcast in full at 4:30 A.M., on August 21, 1968, Vanek declared that it was a forgery. His activity on the whole had considerably influenced the thinking of others. In the night of August 21–22, employees of the seventh section (about forty people) searched for the sites from which our legal radio stations were broadcasting.

A story circulated at the Ministry of Interior—and it was not considered a secret—that a special airplane carrying officials of the Soviet KGB had landed as early as August 17, 1968, at Ruzyne Airport. These Soviet secret police officials, together with chiefs of the State Security, then prepared the measures that were to be taken at the time of the occupation. While issuing orders, Salgovic maintained as late as August 21 that all the measures taken were being carried out in agreement with the Central Committee of the Czechoslovak Communist Party and that he had a direct telephone line to Comrade Dubcek. He later took back this statement. Salgovic and Rypl are known to have held meetings at which Soviet security agents were present.

In the tenth section, during the voting on the Central Committee resolution condemning the occupation, ten employees, headed by their chief, Coufal, refrained from voting.

While issuing orders, Lieutenant Colonel Vanek could not refrain from making deprecatory remarks about the Minister of Interior, Comrade Josef Pavel, such as, for example, "That clown must now be hiding in some cellar" or "They won't let that boy in anymore." Almost all State Security chiefs interfered with the work of Party organs, which were doing their best to allow the truth to come out and to give every Communist the opportunity to express himself about the events. One had the impression that the chiefs were waiting for something, some decisive step that would bring about a sudden reversal of the situation. This expectation, however, was not fulfilled. Apparently, they had been informed about the strategic as well as the tactical plans of the occupiers. When, by August 22, most people had clearly expressed themselves against the occupation, they began complaining about what would happen to the families of State Security members in the event of the withdrawal of Soviet troops.

From the Party organ of the State Security in Prague came word that Prague region State Security chief Lieutenant Colonel Bohumil Molnar from Bartolomejska Street had sent State Security agents to arrest Comrade Smrkovsky. He even ordered the arrest of the young members of State Security who had supported Comrade Pavel.

One of the first to arrive in the building of the main administration of the State Security after the state of alert was announced was the former Deputy Minister and chief of staff of State Security Klima. The former chief of the sixth department, Bokr, who had been dismissed a few weeks earlier, was also present in the building that day. According to some comrades, he was called in for consultations on how to locate the sites of the legal broadcasting stations. The direction of intelligence was again taken over by the previously discharged Colonel Houska [former chief of the Ministry of Interior, first department], the former deputy chief of the second department, Spelina, the former chief of inspection, Kral, and others. Rypl, together with five officers of the occupation Security Forces, personally arrested Comrade Pesek [a State Security officer], who was then imprisoned with other comrades. On the twenty-second, Vanek ordered the arrest of British journalists who were reported to be delivering to their Embassy films and tapes recording the misdeeds of the occupiers in Prague. As late as the afternoon of the twenty-second, Vanek defended the occupiers' viewpoint against the majority of the comrades. On the twenty-third, he argued against issuing an openly anti-occupation statement, saying: "Wait until the discussions are over in Moscow; a reasonable compromise will surely be reached there!"

When the state of alert was being announced in the night of August 20 at the regional State Security administration in Prague, some of the comrades were not notified. When they arrived in the building, some of the young members (including comrades Beran, Kravciak, Lapacek, and others who in June, 1968, had formed the so-called Aktiv of Young Members for Minister Pavel) were interned.

It was the talk of the State Security in Prague that Comrade

Cisar had been there since the morning. No one knew, however, whether he was interned or whether his personal security was involved. On Friday, it was said at the Aktiv that Molnar had released Comrade Cisar. Earlier, however, it was said that on Wednesday Comrade Cisar had been taken somewhere and that he had declared that if the troops had arrived two days later he and Comrade Smrkovsky would have strengthened the regime in Czechoslovakia. On Thursday, some people spread the slander that Cisar and Smrkovsky wanted to invite the [West German Army] to Czechoslovakia.

On Wednesday the twenty-first, sometime after 9 A.M., several people gathered in the office of Lieutenant Colonel Molnar. Among them were Hoffman, Sr., Peroutka, Dubsky, Simonicek, Stambersky, Balaban, Lukas, Klika, Zimmerhanzel, Cisar, and perhaps others. Molnar pointed to three members of the Soviet KGB and told the comrades that they would accompany them to the Central Committee building, where they would take into custody comrades Dubcek, Smrkovsky, Kriegel, and Pavel and would bring them to the regional command of National Security in Prague. Someone asked whether they should take guns along. Molnar said they should. Five automobiles then departed: two Soviet Volgas and three cars of ours with the drivers Skobla, Janik, and one other. They sped to the Soviet Embassy, where an elderly man who turned out to be in charge of the whole action, a Soviet colonel, and another officer climbed into the Soviet cars. The vehicles then left for the Central Committee building. There, a Soviet major in battle dress and armed with an automatic rifle reported to the group. He was probably the commander of the special detachment assigned to seize the Central Committee building. On the second floor, in room 70, a man wearing glasses inquired where the offices of comrades Dubcek, Smrkovsky, Kriegel, and Pavel were and asked who knew the comrades personally. According to reports, he then said to the State Security men: "Who among you is a hero? Who will go to Dubcek and say: 'In the name of the Revolutionary Government, led by Comrade Indra, you are hereby taken into custody?'" All are said to have refused. Later, Hoffman, Sr., volunteered and with great zeal memorized the formula. Six selected men were then taken to the office of Comrade Cisar, where later comrades Dubcek, Smrkovsky, and Kriegel were also brought. In the front office, other comrades of the Central Committee were gathered. The Soviet officers were very anxious to find Interior Minister Pavel. When the Soviets brought comrades Smrkovsky and Kriegel into the office, the two were forced to raise their arms, and they were searched. Comrade Dubcek, too, was supposed to have been searched. In the afternoon, the comrades were led out of the office by the Soviet authorities. Of our people, Hoffman, Peroutka, and Dubsky took an active part in making the arrests.

Lieutenant Colonel Zdenek Machacek was very actively engaged on another mission. On about Thursday, Molnar said that he had seen a list of prospective members of a new government that was said to be acceptable to the Soviets as well as to the public. He said that the new government would present itself on Friday and announce its support of the decisions of the January plenum of the Central Committee and condemn the counter-revolutionaries.

❊ ❊ ❊

At State Security headquarters, a member of the Soviet State Security, Vinokurov, asserted that the allies had occupied Czechoslovakia because the conditions set at the conferences in Cierna and Bratislava were not being fulfilled; instead of suppressing counterrevolution, the authorities had facilitated its growth. This was shown primarily in the anti-Soviet demonstrations of the youth and in the additional actions aimed against the People's Militia. Because of the real danger that the counterrevolution might come out into the open any day, the allies decided, on the basis of the Warsaw Treaty, to send their armies.

Concerning Comrade Dubcek, Vinokurov said that he was a weak-willed person who had surrounded himself with people who had nothing in common with socialism. He specifically named in this connection comrades Kriegel and Smrkovsky. He also declared that Comrade Cisar was an anarchist.

Vinokurov further charged that Czechoslovak security had

been threatened, that a number of State Security members had been arrested or dismissed, and that their families had been persecuted. When contradicted, he used the following names to support his argument: Houska (former chief of the first department of the Ministry of Interior), Kosnar (former chief of the second department of the Ministry of Interior), Klima (former Deputy Minister and chief of staff of State Security), Spelina (former deputy chief of the second department). These people, he said, had been persecuted. Interestingly enough, these were almost all names of persons on whose behalf General Kotov, chief [Soviet] adviser in the Czechoslovak Socialist Republic to the Minister of Interior, had intervened with Comrade Pavel, demanding that they not be dismissed from their posts.

An important role organized by the second department of the Ministry of Interior for the benefit of the occupiers was evidently played by the thirteenth section of the second department (under its chief, Hovorka), particularly with respect to the closing down of radio stations during the night of August 20–21. Hovorka received his orders from Lieutenant Colonel Rypl. State Security members Sasek, Netik, Gibic, Bauer, and Vacik took part in these actions, and the deputy chief of the second department, Hubina, also knew about the measures that were planned and cooperated in their execution.

On August 21, 1968, at 8 A.M., on orders from Coufal (Rypl's secretary), a group of officials of the second department was formed, consisting of Beran, Simon, Burian, Mracek, Jelinek, and Kokta. This group was placed at the disposal of the Soviet adviser Mukhin. Around 9:30 A.M., the entire group, along with Mukhin and an unknown KGB member, left for the Soviet Embassy, where Mukhin met with other KGB men, particularly Vinokurov and Molchanov, who had been an adviser to the first department of the Ministry of Interior until 1962. After 10 o'clock, Mukhin asked four members of the group to guide columns of Soviet vehicles to various sites in Prague. Burian and Jelinek led a column to the Ministry of Communications, Mracek to the radio. At the special request of Mukhin, Kokta led the way to Molnar at the regional command of National Security.

At this time, Oldrich Svestka, Jan Piller, Alois Indra, and others were already in the building of the Soviet Embassy; at about 10 A.M. they were joined by former Premier Josef Lenart.

At about 10:30 A.M., a column of nineteen tanks, led by Simon, left for the Central Committee building. The column accompanied Mukhin and several other KGB members, one of whom was probably called Nalivaiko (a leading KGB official). Upon their arrival at the Central Committee building, which had already been seized, it was discovered that ten members of the regional command of the State Security in Prague, who had arrested comrades Dubcek, Smrkovsky, Kriegel, and Spacek, were already there. Also present at that time was another KGB member, who had been in Prague earlier in the year.

In the Central Committee building, the KGB men were mainly concerned with supervising the transfer of the interned comrades and with control of the entire building. In this activity, they were helped mainly by Comrade David, chief of the communications department of the Central Committee. The KGB agents also went over rosters of Central Committee officials. In this, they were said to have been helped by Comrade Kaska, an assistant of Comrade Kolder. Next to each name on the lists, Kaska wrote comments indicating whether the person in question was "good" or not.

From eyewitness accounts

Notice: From the Commander of the Allied Troops in Prague and the Central-Bohemian Region

1. In order to ensure the protection of the working people and to defend the inhabitants of Prague from the dangers connected with actions of extreme and hooligan elements, I appeal to all citizens of this city not to leave their homes between 10 P.M. and 5 A.M. unless absolutely necessary.

2. Until further notice, public meetings and other similar activities are prohibited, beginning at midnight August 21, 1968.

3. All responsible officials are directed to assure the continued functioning of economic enterprises, the regular functioning of transport, and the full operation of power plants and service enterprises for the population.

4. Because of the situation that has arisen, I consider it indispensable that radio and television broadcasting and the publishing of dailies, weeklies, and other printed matter be made subject to the approval of the relevant authorities.

I. Velichko,
Lieutenant General of the Guards

3

THURSDAY, AUGUST 22

1:30 A.M.

The meeting of some members of the Central Committee, held in the Praha Hotel, has ended.

Report by Martin Vaculik to the Extraordinary Fourteenth Party Congress on the Meeting in the Praha Hotel

In the afternoon of August 21, twenty-two members of the Central Committee met in the Praha Hotel; several more arrived during the discussion. In the evening, the meeting was joined by Kolder, Indra, Bilak, and Barbirek, who arrived under the protection of armed members of the occupation forces. The following have shown themselves to be open collaborators: Karel Mestek, Vilem Novy, Milos Jakes, Alois Indra, and Drahomir Kolder. These were joined by [Presidium member] Jan Piller, who demanded that the Central Committee adopt a resolution opposing the convocation of the Extraordinary Fourteenth Party Congress, which, he said, would aggravate the situation. He requested that delegates be sent into the regions and districts to calm the tension.

Despite the presence of the occupation officers, none of the Central Committee members present could confirm that any person or Czechoslovak authority had requested the occupation of the country by the armed forces of the signatories of the Warsaw letter.

It was not until shortly before midnight of August 20 that the Presidium of the Central Committee received a letter from the Soviet Central Committee in which the Czechoslovak side was accused of failing to uphold the agreements reached in Cierna and Bratislava. Czechoslovakia, it was alleged, had continued the polemics against the signatories of the Warsaw letter (by organizing "outbursts" in the Old Town Square and in front of the Central Committee building, as well as by the petition campaign against the People's Militia), and the Party leadership had permitted the press, radio, and television to defend General Vaclav Prchlik (who had criticized the Warsaw Pact command) and his collaborators. The letter also sharply criticized Cestmir Cisar, the Party Secretary responsible for the Czechoslovak communications media.

Thus, the leadership of our Party, as well as Czechoslovak Premier Cernik, learned about the intentions of the Soviet Communist Party only at the moment the occupation troops crossed our sovereign borders.

On August 21, the session of the Central Committee [in the Praha Hotel], in which about one-third of the membership took part, adopted a communiqué that expressed support for the part of the Presidium proclamation that appeals for calm, prudence, and order. The session [in the Praha Hotel] also confirmed that it would not allow a return to pre-January conditions and adopted the Action Program as the basis for further Party activity. In conclusion, the communiqué asks for the establishment of contacts with the commanders of the occupation troops. In Vaculik's words, the communiqué accepted the occupation of Czechoslovakia as a reality, but it failed to take into consideration the second reality—that is, the outrage and the open opposition of the Czechoslovak population to the action of the signatories of the Warsaw letter.

In addition to the communiqué [the Praha Hotel group] sent directives by teletype to Regional Party Committees. These directives, in effect, called for collaboration with the occupiers.

From Mlada Fronta, *August 23, 1968*

Leaflet of the National Enterprise Polygrafia, Prague 2

During the night we heard that four unnamed members of the Central Committee talked by telephone with Regional Party Committees and demanded the start of negotiations with the occupation troops. It may be possible to find more such men who, in uncertain times, hesitate to sign their names under official statements. Actually, this is an expression of their apprehension that the nation will condemn as traitors those who incite the people to the betrayal of the adopted goals and abandonment of Comrade Dubcek and other Party members.

Even earlier we had doubts whether comrades Bilak, Kolder, Barbirek, and Indra truly support the Action Program of our Party. There is a saying that in every piece of gossip there is a bit of truth. We appeal, therefore, to all leaders of our state, to members of the Central Committee, and to delegates to the Party Congress: Investigate and condemn actions that reek of the betrayal of freedom and socialism and that cast shame on our Party and our entire nation.

3 A.M.

A Soviet unit (including three armed cars) occupied the editorial office and printing plant of *Svobodne Slovo*.

In the Morning

A leaflet aimed against collaborators and traitors appeared.

Our Answer to Traitors

We awakened to a sombre dawn, the second day of the illegal occupation of free Czechoslovakia. This morning, apart from the courageous voice of the legal, independent Czechoslovak Radio, we heard another voice—the voice of those who, by the grace of the occupation authorities, represent themselves as spokesmen for our Communist Party.

It makes no difference whether, in the coming hours, these appeals appear under the name of Kolder or somebody else. Our only legitimate representatives are Dubcek's Central Committee,

President Ludvik Svoboda, Cernik's Government, Smrkovsky's National Assembly, and our National Front. There is only one response to traitors—the contempt of the nation and the refusal to have anything to do with them. Down with the traitors! Long live the free Republic!

Appeal to the Citizens

This morning a petition campaign begins for the release of Alexander Dubcek. Join in with your signature!

Do not form in groups, however, and do not provoke the occupiers. Our only powerful weapon at this time is dignified calm and the will to ignore the occupiers!

From a mimeographed leaflet

Report from the Children's Hospital in Prague

The orthopedic clinic of the Children's Hospital has come under fire from the direction of the Palacky Bridge. The operation theater has been destroyed, and the entire building is damaged. Children recovering from operations lie in the hallways, and it is necessary to move them to other buildings.

From Lidova Demokracie, *3rd special edition, August 22, 1968*

After 8 A.M.

A unit of Soviet soldiers entered the building of the Czechoslovak Academy of Sciences on Narodny Street.

8:55 A.M.

The editorial office of *Zemedelske Noviny* was occupied by Soviet troops.

Around 9 A.M.

Czechoslovak television resumed broadcasting.

9 A.M.

The extraordinary twenty-sixth session of the National Assembly, which was attended by 162 deputies, continued to meet (recessed at 10:52 A.M.). The Presidium of the National Assembly was assigned the task of writing a proclamation to the population.

The National Assembly of the Czechoslovak Socialist Republic, duly elected by the Czechoslovak people as the supreme organ of state power and duly convened by the President of the Republic, categorically protests to the governments and parliaments of five states of the Warsaw Pact and declares that no constitutional organ of the Czechoslovak Socialist Republic has been empowered to discuss [the arrival of foreign troops] nor has it approved any such discussions, nor has it invited the occupation troops of the five states of the Warsaw Pact.

The National Assembly categorically demands the urgent arrival of a competent and responsible political leader, or leaders, of the five states of the Warsaw Pact, who could authoritatively explain to the supreme organ of state power in Czechoslovakia the illegal acts that have taken place.

9:20 A.M.

Czechoslovak Radio announced the results of the petition in Gottwaldov for the recall of Deputy Alois Indra from his post. At least twenty thousand signatures favoring his recall were gathered. The citizens of Gottwaldov regret that Indra was ever one of them.

9:55 A.M.

The Central Telegraph office in Prague has been occupied.

10:30 A.M.

Czechoslovak Radio reported that Deputy Minister of Interior Salgovic has made contact with the occupation troops and is issuing orders for the arrest of our citizens.

10:55 A.M.

Czechoslovak Radio broadcast a demand of the North Bohemian region for a one-hour general strike today at noon.

Report on the Situation in Prague

Prague transport workers are putting transport facilities back into operation. Despite the curfew in Prague, which lasts until 5 A.M., thirty-three out of forty-nine bus lines were in operation between 5 and 6:30 A.M. Transport personnel are trying to operate on the established routes or to adjust them according to immediate needs. The streetcars began operating on some lines around 7 A.M., to the extent that the damaged trolley lines and rails and the positioning of occupation troops allowed.

Rail transport is organized as follows: From Smichov Station, trains leave for Plzen; from the Liben-Horni Station, for Pardubice; from Bubenec, for Kralupy, Most, and Neratovice; from Vrsovice, for Ceske Budejovice. Of the inner city stations, only Tesnov is in operation; trains leave from there in the direction of Lysa nad Labem, Kolin (via Nymburk), Kralupy, and Dicin. The Main Station and Center Station are under the control of the occupation troops and therefore completely out of operation.

The bus lines, too, are attempting to consolidate. Buses leave from Florence in all directions. Only the lines to Brno and Liberec are not functioning. Post offices remain closed, but the long-distance telephone office functions normally.

The hospital on Charles Square has been admitting hundreds of blood donors, so that blood supplies remain satisfactory for the time being.

From Vecerni Praha, *August 22, 1968*

Resolution of the National Enterprise Aritma, Prague

The employees of the national enterprise Aritma, Prague, have expressed their disagreement with the activity of the fractional group of the Communist Party (Bilak, Kolder, Barbirek, and Indra).

They demand the immediate and unconditional departure of the occupation troops, the immediate release of the interned constitutional and Party leaders and the immediate convocation of the Extraordinary Fourteenth Party Congress.

If the interned constitutional and Party leaders are not released by 6 P.M. today, Aritma will head the appeal of VZKG [a major steel mill in the Ostrava region] and immediately join in the general strike.

From Vecerni Praha, *August 22, 1968*

Position of Communists of the Czechoslovak Army

The response of the soldier of the Czechoslovak People's Army is known to you from the legal broadcasts of the Czechoslovak Radio. The soldiers obeyed their order and did not intervene. At the present time, they remain in their barracks and continue their weapons training. They observe passive resistance and wait for further orders from the Army Command, which has been meeting since yesterday—as we learn from unofficial but reliable sources—under the chairmanship of the Minister of National Defense, in the building of the General Staff in Prague-Dejvice.

We continue to support fully the policies pursued by Comrade Dubcek, the Government led by Comrade Cernik, the National Assembly led by Comrade Smrkovsky, and the Supreme Commander of the Armed Forces and President of the Republic, Army General Ludvik Svoboda.

We are convinced that the future direction of Party policy in this state must be determined by the Central Committee of the Party headed by Comrade Dubcek. We cannot agree that the political tasks of the Communist Party should be directed by fractional groups, and anonymous ones at that. We shall follow only the decisions passed by the entire Central Committee and by the entire Presidium. We reject the occupation of the Republic by the troops of the Warsaw Pact, and we demand their departure, because our own constitutional organs are capable of securing the building of socialism in this country. We want to discuss our position with General Ivan Pavlovsky (Commander of the Soviet occupation troops).

Colonel M. Devera,
For the All-Army Communist Party Preparatory Committee

From Vecerni Praha, *August 22, 1968*

11:05 A.M.

The military commander of the city of Prague and the Central Bohemian region, Lieutenant General of the Guards I. Velichko, issued an order forbidding people from putting up posters, forbidding public assembly, and restricting nighttime circulation in the streets. All buildings of Communist Party district secretariats in Prague are now occupied.

11:18 A.M.

The Extraordinary Fourteenth Congress of the Communist Party was opened in one of the plants of CKD in Prague-Vysocany. The Congress adopted certain basic documents expressing its position on the occupation and elected a new Central Committee. The first session of the Congress closed at 9:15 P.M. of the same day.

When the session opened, almost a thousand comrades—more than a majority of the delegates duly elected by city and regional Party conferences—were present. From Slovakia, only five comrades had so far reached Prague. Several delegates led by Deputy Premier Gustav Husak were intercepted by the occupiers near Breclav. A delegate from a Slovak region spoke on behalf of the arrested Slovak comrades. He said that all had tried to reach Prague to take part in the Congress. Thus, the Slovak delegates, too, expressed their agreement with the convocation of the Extraordinary Fourteenth Party Congress.

The Congress was opened by a member of the old Central Committee, Comrade Vladimir Kabrna. The Congress elected as members of its working Presidium all the comrades who had been interned—Dubcek, Cernik, Spacek, Smrkovsky, Cisar; the members of the Czechoslovak Government who were present, Bozena Machacova and Josef Krejci; also, Martin Vaculik, Zdenek Hejzlar, Eduard Goldstuecker, Jaromir Litera (Secretary of the City Committee in Prague), O. Matejka (Secretary of the District Committee in Prague), Marie Svermova, and two delegates from each region.

The Congress requested all members of the incumbent Central Committee to attend the session and report on their activity.

Declaration of the Extraordinary Fourteenth Party Congress
Addressed to the Citizens of the Czechoslovak Socialist Republic

Comrades, citizens of the Czechoslovak Socialist Republic:

Czechoslovakia is a sovereign and free socialist state founded on the free will and support of its people. Its sovereignty, however, was violated on August 21, 1968, when it was occupied by troops of the Soviet Union, Poland, the German Democratic Republic, Bulgaria, and Hungary.

This action is being justified on the grounds that socialism was endangered and that the intervention was requested by some leading Czechoslovak officials. However, yesterday's Central Committee proclamation, the second radio broadcast of the President of the Republic, the proclamations of the National Assembly and the Government of the Republic, and the statement of the Presidium of the Central Committee of the National Front make it clear that no competent Party or constitutional authority has requested such an intervention.

There was no counterrevolution in Czechoslovakia, and socialist development was not endangered. As was demonstrated by the tremendous confidence shown in the new leadership of the Party by Comrade Dubcek, the people and the Party were fully capable of solving by themselves the problems that have arisen. Indeed, action was being taken that was leading toward the realization of the fundamental ideas of Marx and Lenin on the development of socialist democracy. At the same time, Czechoslovakia has not breached its treaty commitments and obligations; it has not the slightest interest in living in future enmity with the other socialist states and their peoples. These obligations, however, were violated by the troops of the occupying countries.

Czechoslovakia's sovereignty, the bonds of alliance, the Warsaw Pact, and the agreements of Cierna and Bratislava were trampled underfoot. Several leaders of the state and Party were unlawfully arrested, isolated from the people, and deprived of the opportunity to carry out their functions. A number of establishments of the central authorities have been occupied. Grave injustices have thus been committed.

The Congress resolutely demands that normal conditions for the functioning of all constitutional and political authority be immediately created and that all detained officials be released forthwith so that they can assume their posts.

The situation that was created in our country on August 21 cannot be permanent. Socialist Czechoslovakia will never accept either a military occupation administration or a domestic collaborationist regime dependent on the forces of the occupiers.

Our basic demand is, of course, the departure of foreign troops. If the stated demands are not complied with, particularly if, within twenty-four hours, negotiations are not begun with our free constitutional and Party leaders for the departure of foreign troops and if Comrade Dubcek does not make a timely statement to the nation on this matter, the Congress requests all working people to stage a one-hour protest strike on Friday, August 23 at 12 noon. The Congress has also decided that, if its demands are not accepted, it will undertake further necessary measures.

From Rude Pravo, *August 22, 1968*

Letter to Comrade Dubcek

Dear Comrade Dubcek:

The Extraordinary Fourteenth Party Congress that met today sends you warm comradely greetings. We thank you for all the work you have done for the Party and the Republic. The repeated calls of "Dubcek, Dubcek" coming from our youth who carried through Prague the bloodied state flag bear ample testimony that your name has become the symbol of our sovereignty. We protest against your unlawful imprisonment and the imprisonment of the other comrades.

The Congress reelected you to the new Central Committee, and we continue to consider you our leading representative. We firmly believe that the conduct of their destinies will be restored to the Czech and Slovak nations and that you will return to us.

Delegates of the Extraordinary Fourteenth
Congress of the Communist Party

From Vecerni Praha, *August 24, 1968*

The Newly Elected Central Committee of the Communist Party of Czechoslovakia

Delegates of the Extraordinary Fourteenth Party Congress elected as members of the new Central Committee the following 144 comrades: Alexander Dubcek, Oldrich Cernik, Ludvik Svoboda, Josef Spacek, Cestmir Cisar, Josef Smrkovsky, Bohumil Simon, Frantisek Kriegel, Josef Cerny, Jiri Hajek, Libuse Hrdinova, Vladimir Kadlec, Josef Krejci, Vaclav Slavik, Oldrich Stary, Ota Sik, Vladimir Kabrna, Jaroslav Sabata, Karel Ondracek, Josef Pribyl, Bohumil Vojacek, Josef Zuda, Karel Pavlistik, Borivoj Vojacek, Frantisek Petranek, Libor Salak, Petr Klaga, Zdenek Dolezal, Olga Soukalova, Karel Mrazek, Vlado Smidko, Jiri Ploss, Josef Mara, Jaroslav Rybar, Milos Polivka, Karel Bejcek, Mojmir Hlavacek, Bedrich Kralik, Josef Hasek, Jirina Zelenkova, Jaroslav Svoboda, Jan Castecka, Zdenek Smolik, Vojtech Matejicek, Ladislav Dejl, Antonin Kabele, Rudolf Falousek, Josef Kaminsky, Rudolf Cerny, Miloslav Klinger, Vaclav Jindrich, Jaroslav Sykora, Josef Loskot, Zdenek Paulus, Josef Svoboda, Vojtech Trojanek, Bretislav Sauer, Vaclav Simecek, Jiri Stoklasa, Jan Klansky, Josef Koubek, Zdenek Kratochvil, Vaclav Tousa, Jan Jerabek, Jarmila Nemcova, Rudolf Jarolim, Miroslav Simek, Vladimir Kargel, Jaromir Frank, Josef Oldina, Jaromir Popluda, Jaroslav Falc, Josef Fiser, Zdenek Hejzlar, Antonin Hrobek, Jan Jelinek, Josef Haur, Vaclav Burian, Josef Smidka, Miroslav Galuska, Eduard Goldstuecker, Jiri Hanzelka, Josef Pavel, Evzen Erban, Jiri Pelikan, Milan Huebl, Jaromir Litera, Frantisek Pavlicek, Venek Silhan, Bohumil Broz, Jiri Judl, Karel Kosik, Josef Kratena, Zdenek Moc, Milos Nemcansky, Lubomir Sochor, Karel Vorel, Antonin Zaruba, Frantisek Vodslon, Martin Vaculik, Zdenek Mlynar, Frantisek Topek, Josef Sisovsky, Gustav Husak, Milan Hladky, Peter Colotka, Viktor Pavlenda, Josef Zrak, Hvezdon Koctuch, Ladislav Novomesky, Pavol Stevcek, Stefan Sadovsky, Maria Sedlakova, Ondrey Klokoc, Julius Turcek, Jan Valo, Kliment Nesvesky, Josef Maly, Josef Opavsky, Josef Har, Anton Jankech, Anton Tazky, Egyd Pepich, Minal Repas, Martin Dzur, Josef Skalka, Jaroslav Belaj, Jan Koscelansky, Alojz Batta, Josef Beder, Jan Pirc, Michail Faraga, Juraj Sabolcik, Pavol Varga,

Otto Pezler, Pavlina Puziova, Jan Marko, Fedor Petruna, Augustin Troeml, Jan Prochazka, Bohuslav Graca, Andrej Zamek, Bozena Machacova, Josef Boruvka. At the same time, a new 37-member Central Control and Audit Commission of the Central Committee was elected.

From Rude Pravo, *August 23, 1968*

Closing Resolution of the First Session of the Extraordinary Fourteenth Party Congress

The Extraordinary Fourteenth Party Congress met in its first session on August 22, 1968, in Prague. In spite of the extraordinary conditions, 1,192 of the 1,543 duly elected delegates have taken part in the meeting. Despite great efforts, the majority of the Slovak delegates were unable to be present; their arrival was made impossible by the occupation troops.

The Congress has dealt with the following matters:

1. an opening political declaration
2. an appeal to Communist and workers' parties of the world
3. abrogation of the mandate of the incumbent party Central Committee and of the Central Control and Audit Commission
4. election of a new Party Central Committee and a new Central Control and Audit Commission
5. adoption of an appeal to the Slovak nation
6. approval of a letter to the First Secretary of the Communist Party, Comrade Alexander Dubcek, who has been interned.

Because of the extraordinary conditions under which it met, the Congress was unable to discuss the entire agenda. It therefore declared itself in permanent session.

The Congress concluded its first session with the conviction that the entire country will grasp the seriousness of the situation, that it will support the Congress' decisions and endeavor to execute them with all the strength at its disposal.

The Impossible Has Become Reality

The first part of the Congress has come to an end.

Throughout Wednesday night and all day Thursday, delegates

arrived for the Extraordinary Fourteenth Party Congress. The
lucky ones succeeded in coming in time for the opening; others
kept arriving throughout the course of the deliberations. The
delegates from Slovakia received perhaps the warmest welcome.
One of the five Slovak delegates from Trnava, who were the first
to arrive, told me: "We had a good journey. We came in a civilian
car, but the rest of our delegation, led by Comrade Gustav Husak,
was detained near Breclav. They tried to explain that they were
not going to the Congress, but their identities were established,
and on the basis of a delegates' roster it was shown that they
were indeed delegates to the Congress." Despite all this, fifty
comrades from Slovakia eventually arrived at the Congress session. Each new delegation was welcomed with warm applause,
but at the same time one could hear calls for quiet, since every
loud noise could betray the site of the session.

It was a truly historic congress; every delegate present had
carried, as the saying goes, his skin to the market. Repeatedly one
could hear reports: Occupation troops are approaching; we must
proceed with the greatest speed. However, the pressure of time
did not prevent the Congress from carrying on its business according to the rules. Everyone was given the opportunity to
express and defend his opinion.

For many it was difficult to reach their destination. Delegates
from Brno, for example, who arrived around noon, had been
warned at a gas station in Podebrady: "Return home immediately; arrests have begun in Prague." They did not believe this
story and arrived safely. I managed to talk with delegates from
Kladno. "We are disappointed that Comrade Jan Piller is not taking part in the Congress," said Comrade Bejcek. "Especially since
he was elected by us in Kladno and it was we who nominated
him to the Central Committee. Ours is the most powerful organization in the Central Bohemian region, and except for him all of
us are here. There are even three alternates here, who have come
to take the place of three of our comrades who are on vacation
abroad."

As the election of the new Central Committee began in the
evening hours, the comrades who were prevented from coming
to the Congress were the first to be elected. They were comrades

Svoboda, Dubcek, Cernik, Smrkovsky, Cisar, Simon, Spacek, and Kriegel. Thereafter, the other members of the Central Committee and members of the Central Control and Audit Commission were elected.

The tone of the entire proceedings was calm and dignified. All delegates were aware of the seriousness of the discussion and of their great responsibility to the entire Party and all the people of Czechoslovakia.

A Trencin delegate brought a moving greeting to the Congress participants from the mother of Alexander Dubcek. Crying and worried about her son, she asked the comrade from Trencin before his departure to bring to the delegates at the Congress her greetings and her plea that they remain as courageous as they have been so far. Applauding quietly, delegates approved—eventually also by vote—a letter to Comrade Dubcek in which they sent him warm and comradely greetings and expressed their gratitude for his past work. They told him also of the young people who marched through Prague with their bloodied flag, chanting "Dubcek, Dubcek!" Finally, they informed him that they elected him to the Central Committee of the Party and that they regard him as their leading representative. The letter ends with the words: "You will return to us."

From Svoboda, *special edition, August 24, 1968*

11:50 A.M.

Czechoslovak Radio announced that several thousand people are assembled on Wenceslas Square. Trucks full of young people carrying flags pass through the square. Someone addresses the crowd near the statue of Saint Wenceslas. Six Soviet armored cars begin moving toward the statue from three directions.

Otherwise, Prague is relatively calm. The bridges remain occupied. Hradcany Castle is calm; the guard changes as usual. The tanks stationed there always move to let the guard pass and then return to their position.

12 Noon

An hour-long protest strike began in Prague.

Shortly After Noon

A special edition of *Mlada Fronta* appeared describing the occupation of its offices.

The Occupiers Have Seized Our Offices!

In the evening of August 21, Soviet occupation troops took over the editorial offices and the printing plant of *Mlada Fronta* in Panska Street. They forced us into one room and held us there at gunpoint throughout the night.

Only this morning, before 8 o'clock, did we succeed in making our way out of the occupied building of *Mlada Fronta*. They have confiscated yesterday's final special edition and prevented us from publishing the free *Mlada Fronta*.

We bring out this edition of *Mlada Fronta* determined not to cease to inform you truthfully as long as the occupation troops do not stop us. Do not believe anyone who may want to speak for a new editorial leadership of *Mlada Fronta* and collaborate with the occupation regime or our own traitors.

In 1945, *Mlada Fronta* was born in the spirit of freedom. It will never abandon or betray this ideal.

Editorial Board of *Mlada Fronta*

From Mlada Fronta, *special edition, August 22, 1968*

12:40 P.M.

Czechoslovak Radio reported that a member of the Soviet Army committed suicide near the Central Committee building.

An Authentic Story from the Tragic Days

It happened on Thursday, at a time when we still talked to them.

"Kolya, what are you doing here?"

A nineteen-year-old boy sitting on a tank barely recognized me. Never in that prehistoric time that my visit to the Soviet Union has now become did he see such horror in my eyes. Finally he recognized me.

"Kolya, what are you doing here?"

"We received our orders. We came—as friends."

"As friends—but you are shooting."

"I did not shoot."

"What will Sasha say, your sister, when you come home?"

"I did not shoot—they sent us here." He showed me the maga-zine filled with shells.

"But others do shoot. Your people shot a twenty-year-old boy. I'm sure he loved you; we all used to love you. . . . Kolya, we had peace here until you arrived. Just imagine what would hap-pen if this many soldiers drove into Kharkov. Chaos would break out even there, wouldn't it?"

A thought occurred to me: "Kolya, what do you think counter-revolution is?"

"It is when people disagree with Lenin."

"And Kolya, do you love Stalin?"

"No, he was bad."

"Novotny was equally bad. And we didn't want him. We wanted to do everything as we saw best and not according to your example. After all, yours is a large country and so things must be different than they are in a small country."

"I don't understand it, we received an order. . . . They didn't tells us the truth. . . . Why would they lie to us?"

Kolya couldn't understand. Earlier, he had spoken with dozens of other people and heard the same question: "Tell me, why did you come, why?"

I stood nearby for about half an hour, and then I saw a terrible thing happen. Kolya turned his gun on himself and pulled the trigger.

Alena

From Rude Pravo, *August 27, 1968*

1 P.M.

Soviet units finished occupying the building of the Czecho-slovak Academy of Sciences on Narodny Street.

Occupation of the Czechoslovak Academy of Sciences

During the noon hours of August 22, Soviet occupation units occupied the building of the Presidium of the Czechoslovak Academy of Sciences in Prague 1, Narodny Street 3, and brutally expelled the Academy workers. The following outrageous order was issued [in Russian] on this occasion:

I, First Lieutenant Yuri Aleksandrovich Orlov, representing the Warsaw Pact troops, order all workers and members of the Czechoslovak Academy of Sciences to cease work by 1 P.M., August 22, and evacuate all premises of the Academy of Sciences of the Czechoslovak Socialist Republic.

From materials of the Czechoslovak Academy of Sciences

Proposal to Award a Medal to Platoon Leader Guards First Lieutenant Yuri Aleksandrovich Orlov

Comrade Y. A. Orlov, while carrying out the task of occupying the building of the Czechoslovak Academy of Sciences, displayed the decisiveness, courage, and initiative of a commander, moved in at the objective from the rear, and by decisive action captured the left wing of the building. Later on, in the course of the day, he seized the entire building and organized its security and defense. While executing this and other tasks, Comrade Orlov decisively frustrated attempts by reactionary elements to conduct propaganda among Soviet soldiers and to photograph the troops and their equipment. He ceaselessly carried out educational work among his subordinates and gave them courage in the fulfillment of their tasks.

Comrade Orlov, having fully satisfied the honor of a Soviet soldier, fulfilled his international duty for the strengthening of the bases of socialism in Czechoslovakia.

I believe that Comrade Orlov deserves the Government award of the Order of the Red Star.

Davidovsky

Translated from a photocopy of the original long-hand draft

Proposal to Award a Medal to the Deputy Company Commander of a Political Detachment, Second Lieutenant of the Quartermaster Corps, Romas Jozovich Ginteris

Comrade R. J. Ginteris carried out tasks during the occupation and defense of an important objective and displayed courage. He systematically explained to his subordinates the role played by our troops during the present events. Through his political education work, he united soldiers, sergeants, and officers in the fulfillment of their assigned tasks.

Comrade R. J. Ginteris displayed personal bravery and initiative; by personal example he gave courage to his subordinates in the fulfillment of their assigned tasks, and he resolutely frustrated intrigues by imperialist agents who tried to conduct anti-socialist propaganda and photograph military objectives and equipment.

I believe that Communist R. J. Ginteris deserves the Government order "For battle merit."

Davidovsky

Translated from a photocopy of the original long-hand draft

Proposal to Award a Medal to Guards First Lieutenant Anatoly Ivanovich Grut

Comrade A. I. Grut took part in the task of seizing and securing a Moldau bridge; he acted boldly and decisively, skillfully led his team, and through personal example gave courage to his subordinates in the performance of their task. He worked ceaselessly, explaining the situation in which the Soviet soldiers found themselves. He boldly frustrated attempts of counterrevolutionary elements to provoke armed conflict between Soviet soldiers and Prague inhabitants. Under the constant pressure of moral and physical stress, he was always an example of cheerfulness, perseverance, and Party-mindedness.

Comrade Grut instilled courage in his subordinates by personal example, showed the high moral qualities of a Soviet officer, and honorably performed the tasks set by the Soviet Government and the Central Committee of the Soviet Communist Party.

I believe that Comrade Grut deserves the Government award of the Red Star.

Davidovsky

Translated from a photocopy of the original long-hand draft

In the Course of the Day

The Government of the Czechoslovak Socialist Republic met in its extraordinary second session under the chairmanship of the Minister for Consumer Industries, Bozena Machacova, and adopted the following decision.

Material resources available on the territory of the Republic, especially food and consumer goods, are here for the use of our population and our army. The Government considers the use of these resources by the occupation armies an act of violence. These resources can be handed over to the occupation armies only in exchange for receipts issued by heads of the higher occupation command units. Such receipts must at the same time be certified by the appropriate National Committee.

From Purboj, *August 22, 1968*

Proclamation of the Central Labor Union Council and the Central Committee of the Trade Union Organizations

We support unanimously the position of the legal Government of the Czechoslovak Socialist Republic, headed by Oldrich Cernik.

To give this position effective support, we ask all union organizations in factories and enterprises to establish strike committees for the defense of their plants and enterprises.

At the same time, we ask all union organizations and strike committees in the factories to preserve peace and order in their plants, to prevent all ill-considered acts, and to be prepared to support the Government's stand with a general strike, should this be necessary.

We fully support the demand for the immediate release of the detained members of the Government, especially of Premier Cernik and Minister of National Defense Martin Dzur.

In the Afternoon

We have learned that the occupation troops have reportedly issued an ultimatum demanding the appointment by 6 P.M. today, August 22, 1968, of a new government that would approve the occupation of our country and act as a willing instrument of the occupiers. The condition has been laid down that comrades Dubcek, Smrkovsky, Cernik, Kriegel, Spacek, Simon, and Cisar not be represented in this Government or the Communist Party leadership. On the other hand, according to the ultimatum, Bilak, Pavlovsky, Kolder, Indra, and Lenart must be included in the new Government and Party leadership. If this ultimatum is not met by the set deadline, an occupation regime will be formed. There is a danger that these collaborators will accept the ultimatum.

From Rude Pravo, *August 22, 1968*

3 P.M.

Czechoslovak Radio reported that posters are being put up in Prague asking the population to take part in a large demonstration on Wenceslas Square. The possibility exists that this is a provocation designed to give the occupation troops an opportunity to strike. Citizens of Prague: Do not assemble!

3:20 P.M.

The building of the Czechoslovak News Agency has been occupied, but the editors continue to work.

3:50 P.M.

A two-member National Assembly delegation was sent to the Embassy of the German Democratic Republic to deliver a letter of protest to the parliament and government of the German Democratic Republic. The deputies were received by a representative of the Ambassador, who expressed surprise that parliament was in session and protesting against the occupation of Czechoslovakia by Warsaw Pact troops. Their units were in the country legally, he claimed, since they had been invited by our authorities. When asked to name these authorities, the Embassy spokesman failed to answer. The Embassy did not accept the protest.

4:20 P.M.

There was a report from the Ministry of National Defense. The joint command of the occupation armies has issued the following order:

1. Do not disarm Czechoslovak Army units.
2. Withdraw from areas where Czechoslovak troops are stationed.
3. Withdraw from small localities.
4. In large towns, station military units in parks and in open areas.
5. Refrain from blocking buildings of state and Party organs of the Czechoslovak Socialist Republic.
6. Banks should function normally.
7. All allied troops will be supplied out of their own resources.

4:40 P.M.

The extraordinary twenty-sixth session of the National Assembly has resumed. The deputies have pledged that they will not voluntarily leave the building, and they again appealed to all deputies to attend the session.

From materials of the National Assembly

4:45 P.M.

Petitions are being circulated in the streets of Prague, demanding the departure of the occupation troops, the release of our Government, and Party leaders, and supporting the legal authorities of the state.

4:50 P.M.

Czechoslovak Radio reported that a radio reporter has just been walking through the streets of Prague. Hundreds of people are assembling in Wenceslas Square. A demonstration is supposed to begin in ten minutes. The radio requests everyone to disperse: The demonstration is an act of provocation.

Many people continue to assemble in the streets near Wenceslas Square and the nearby radio building. However, nothing serious has happened yet. There is a lot of discussion. The request for dispersal has been repeated.

5 P.M.

Citizens assembled in Wenceslas Square have responded to the appeals of Czechoslovak Radio and of members of Public Security; they have given up the plan to demonstrate and have quietly dispersed.

Wenceslas Square—Thursday, 5 P.M.

Wenceslas Square is surrounded by occupation tanks. Near the museum, they form a perfect wall. The gun barrels are aimed down the sidewalks. The faces of the soldiers are somber and hard.

At Mustek [at the foot of the Square] and on the sidewalks, the groups of people, especially young boys and girls, grow in size. Someone had spread the report in Prague that at 5:00 this afternoon there will be a demonstration in the Square. It has turned out that this report is provocation. The demonstration would have given the occupation command an excuse for harsh reprisals and, above all, a justification for their aggression. But who knows this? People are arriving on the Square in trucks bedecked with flags. The groups grow in size; the excitement mounts.

Will there be a massacre? The legal radio repeats its warnings and tells of the provocation. Many people carry big signs repeating the radio's warning. Five o'clock is drawing near.

A few minutes before 5:00, cars from the Public Security arrive on the Square. A fatherly voice intones through an amplifier: "Come on, boys, don't be silly. Disperse! Why hand the occupiers a pretext? Don't you understand what they want?"

On Jindrisska Street, a tank turret swivels as if searching for a target.

Then, slowly, unwillingly, the groups start dispersing. After half an hour, there is peace in the Square. In quiet streets, the tanks look even more threatening. They stand out as clearer proof of aggression against a free and peace-loving people.

From Rude Pravo, *August 24, 1968*

Bravo, Citizens of Prague

Yesterday's appeal for the clearing of Wenceslas Square, where a massive demonstration against the occupiers was to have been staged and which could have become a welcome excuse for declaring martial law, resulted in a display of the exemplary qualities of Prague citizens in these moving times.

Within a very short time, Wenceslas Square was completely cleared. Not a single civilian remained. Absolute silence spread over the Square, which a few minutes earlier had still resounded with noise.

The young people present were extremely disciplined and gladly helped the few members of Public Security who were there to prevent automobiles from entering the Square.

Yesterday's display on Wenceslas Square is not, of course, unique. You are fabulous, people of Prague. You are showing yourselves as patriots in the full sense of the word. With dignity, and as is proper for free citizens of the capital city, you overcome difficulties caused by the occupation. Hold out. Let us hold out. Our strength is unbreakable.

From Vecerni Praha, *August 23, 1968*

6 P.M.

The extraordinary eighty-fifth session of the Presidium of the National Assembly has reconvened (eighteen assembly members were present). The information that the President of the Republic was not recommending the dispatch of a resolution to the United Nations was discussed. A resolution of the National Assembly was prepared for publication in case martial law had to be declared. A letter to the President of the Republic was approved.

Dear and Esteemed Comrade President,

At this serious moment of our history, we want first of all to thank you for your unceasing dedication to law and the freedom of our country. We want to thank you for your firm and determined defense of the aspirations of our people for socialism with a human face, for sovereignty and independence.

We assure you once again—as members of our Presidium have done many times before—not only on our behalf, but for all the people of Czechoslovakia, of our devotion and our firm determination to pursue under any circumstances the fight for the upholding of the Constitution of the Republic, of our laws and legal order.

We promise that we shall remain faithful to you, to our legal Government headed by Premier Cernik, to our Chairman Josef Smrkovsky, to the Chairman of the National Front, Frantisek Kriegel, to the First Secretary of the Communist Party, Alexander Dubcek, and to the other heads of our supreme institutions and organs.

Conscious of our historic sensibility for the continued life of our country and acting in close cooperation with the widest strata of the Czechoslovak people, we appeal to you esteemed, Comrade President, to continue to devote your strength to our common struggle, a struggle that will enter honorably into the history of our peoples and that will always remain a bright page in the history of the world.

We warmly press your hand, wish you good health, and extend our sincere greetings to you.

> Josef Valo,
> First Deputy Chairman of the National Assembly of the Czechoslovak Socialist Republic

From materials of the National Assembly

The Parliamentary Correspondent Reports

The provisional parliament building in Maxim Gorky Square is surrounded by troops. Angry deputies demand entry into the building. After finding the responsible commander, they win the agreement to remove for two hours the tank that has barred the entrance. Afterwards, passage is barred again.

I arrived later and therefore had to find entry through a side entrance. I ascend in an absurdly small service elevator leading to the dining room. There is a surprising number of people in the labyrinthine building. Despite the extremely adverse transportation conditions, more than 170 deputies are already present.

The soldiers who, according to yesterday's reports, had entered the building, cannot be seen. Yet, I do see one after all, leaning out of the window. A woman deputy, a typically ample Slovak mother, is slowly walking away from him. "Do not pay any attention to him," she says. "I have two boys just as old as he is, who all their lives have heard only the best about them." She motioned toward the window. "I asked him how I was to explain all this to my sons. He understood and is weeping. Now he wants to be alone, to pull himself together before his commander arrives."

The largest hall of the building couldn't contain all the deputies, many of whom now crowd into an adjoining hallway. The roll call shows that the plenary session is capable of adopting valid decisions. The main point on the agenda is the proclamation of the National Assembly. The proclamation was adopted unanimously, with only Deputy Nestek abstaining. (He did not attend further meetings.)

After an exhausting day and evening of work, the deputies rest on office floors covered with their coats or whatever they can find in their suitcases. They had decided not to leave the building. They are free to leave, but there is no guarantee that they will be able to return. And the National Assembly needs as many deputies as possible, so as to be truly representative of the people.

From Mlady Svet, *No. 35, 1968*

In the Evening

The Government, under the chairmanship of its Deputy Premier, Comrade Lubomir Strougal, remained in session throughout the evening and night of August 22. Twenty-two Government members were present.

The President of the Republic informed the Government that, having exhausted all available avenues by which he had sought to achieve [the release of the interned Party and Government leaders] through negotiations in Prague, he decided to negotiate in Moscow. He therefore requested the Government to appoint two members to accompany him. To undertake this mission, the Government named its Deputy Premier, Comrade Gustav Husak, and the Minister of National Defense, General Martin Dzur. The Government was informed of the decision of the Presidium of the Central Committee of the National Front to appoint its member, Minister of Justice Bohuslav Kucera, as its representative on the President's mission. *The Government did not discuss the further make-up of the President's party.*[1] After the departure by air of the President of the Republic, the Government decided to continue dealing with current problems as they come up; it will decide about the future course only after the return of the President.

Because of the abnormal situation that reportedly has developed in the State Security, the Government, acting on the advice of the Minister of Interior, who regularly takes part in the Government deliberations, has requested Deputy Minister of Interior Viliam Salgovic to report without delay to the military office of the President of the Republic, which will immediately put him in touch with the Government.

According to Article 65 of the Constitution, the functions of the President of the Republic during his absence from the territory of the Czechoslovak Socialist Republic are assumed by the Government. The Government continues to meet.

From Free Czechoslovak News Agency reports, August 23, 1968

Commentaries on the Day by the Czechoslovak and Soviet Press

Friends, comrades, brothers—Czechs and Slovaks!

We have been on our feet since last night. We have walked through the streets of Prague. Vysocany and Liben were relatively calm. From the direction of Kbely we saw tanks, armored cars, and other Soviet military equipment heading toward Prague. Only the queues in front of food stores and a queue at the gas station on Balabenka testify to the unusual circumstances.

---

[1] Italics in original document. This is a reference to the fact that a number of conservatives accompanied President Svoboda to Moscow—apparently without authorization from any Czechoslovak Party or Government body.

This is what the editors of *Kovak* [the metalworkers' paper] at CKD Prague saw.

In the district of Prague 9, damaged pavement and streetcar islands, knocked-over light poles. There was a sad scene at the Institute of National Health in Vysocany, where ambulances were bringing the first wounded. All along the roadway in Karlin, up to Poric, we saw damaged streets and flattened streetcars. On Nekazanka Street, tanks of the occupiers had smashed dozens of automobiles, which succeeding tanks jammed into display windows and passageways. Among these automobiles were many with foreign license plates—an Alfa-Romeo from Rome, a Volkswagen from the Federal Republic, a Taunus from Vienna, and so on. Prikopy, Wencenslas Square, and adjoining streets have been ruined by the treads of tanks and other vehicles.

The worst scene is at Vinohrady, around the radio station— burnt-out houses, destroyed buses and private cars. We also saw the casualties. The hospital on Frantisek reported five dead today. An occupation tank set out to crush our news photographer, whose pictures are the ones you see most often in the pages of *Kovak,* the moment he raised his camera. The editor of *Kovak* was driven away by rifle butts from the *Rude Pravo* building, where we normally print our paper. This morning, when another *Kovak* editor tried to photograph the area of Palmovka, he was chased by an occupation soldier with an automatic rifle.

We are pressed for time, and we don't know how much longer we shall be able to continue our work. Therefore, now, only briefly, we relay the most important items from the CKD works in Prague 9.

We learn from well-informed sources that, before his arrest and deportation in a personnel carrier of the occupation troops, Comrade Dubcek smuggled out a written message in which he appealed to Prague citizens, particularly in large plants, and above all to workers of the ninth district of Prague, to hold on to their factories and remain there together, for such a concentration of strength would offer the capital city protection and a guarantee. This could be an important and perhaps even decisive force, the message concludes, which in case of need could be put to use.

According to reports we have received, the occupiers will attempt to form a new Presidium and a new government made up of collaborators. There is concrete talk about Kolder, Svestka, and Indra. For the time being, you should treat such reports as unconfirmed; but, as the saying goes, there is no gossip without a bit of truth in it. Judging by the statements of Svestka and Indra during the past few days, the information may be true. Those who participated in the meeting in the dining room of Elektro-technika will surely remember the words of Kolder, who, as early as two months ago, asked Communists not to demand an early convocation of the Fourteenth Party Congress.

During the past two weeks, we have read various articles by the editor-in-chief of *Rude Pravo*, Oldrich Svestka, that were politically regressive and that, among other things, were abusive of our workers. In the light of present developments, it has become clear what these articles and statements meant and where these officials stood and clearly stand even today. We have reason, therefore, to fear that they have betrayed us just to get into leading positions.

From the legal Kovak, *August 22, 1968*

The CKD Plant in Prague

The working people unequivocally support Alexander Dubcek and the other comrades around him, even though they do not know their fate. Lathe operator B. Tymes told us: "We would not move a finger if the occupiers tried to make us work for them. But we shall, after the departure of the armed forces of the countries, work Saturdays and Sundays, even for nothing, so as to make good the losses."

On Wednesday, August 21, the factories went silent for the entire day. On Thursday, in response to the appeal over Czecho-slovak Radio, workers in all the plants started up their machines. Thus, production was under way again, although not yet fully. At some centers—for example, at the metal-rolling plant, the coil plant of Elektrotechnika, and the turbo-compressors department of the Kompresory plant—almost all the personnel arrived at work on time. Work was under way.

From the legal Kovak, special edition, August 22, 1968

The Human Face of Socialism

We Czechoslovak Communists are building our society on the principles of Marxism-Leninism, which we want to develop creatively. However, our determination to create a highly humane and democratic socialist society, to return to socialism its human face, was not understood. In fact, it could not be understood. It had to be misunderstood, not because of concern for the world Communist movement, but out of fear that the nations of the socialist states might perceive in the Czechoslovak example a course worthy of imitation.

From Rude Pravo, August 22, 1968

Collaborators Grasp for Power

Every time the Czech nation has been struck with the tragedy of occupation there have been collaborators who lived off its misfortune. You know their names; they are the ones who would like to speak in the name of the Central Committee of the Communist Party; they are the ones who knew full well that they would fail in the forthcoming meeting of the highest organ of the Party. These political cadavers now claim a new life. Kolder, Indra, Bilak, Barbirek, Mestek, and others now curry favor with the occupiers. It is not important what position they will occupy, whether in a collaborationist government or in a dictated organ of the Party. In any case, as soon as they accept any function in any organ that has the blessing of the occupiers, they will have decided about themselves, about their character, and also about their fate.

Point to a single name of a traitor to the Czech nation from the time of the fascist occupation in 1939–45 that would not be held in contempt by all honest people. Point to a single name of a traitor who would have thrived on his lust for power. Retribution always came in one form or another. The new-fangled collaborators of our day will meet the same fate. The Czech nation has suffered too much to forget and to forgive those who in critical moments betrayed it.

Let us have no illusions and let us not think that collaborators are grasping for power in high places only. You can also find them in regional, district, and even local posts and circumstances.

Whom, in fact, should we consider a collaborator under the present complicated conditions? It is anyone who in the performance of any public function accepts directions from the occupiers or from higher collaborationist organs.

How should we deal with collaborators? In no case must we allow them to compel us to do anything or to convince us of anything. We must not execute their orders. Let them feel your contempt and show them that you are honest citizens of a free nation, which has only temporarily been caught in the vise of brutal occupation troops and in the power politics of certain Soviet political leaders.

Every occupation has come to an end and with it the collaborators. In the future, as in the past, they will find the end that traitors deserve.

From Zemedelske Noviny, *August 22, 1968*

Appeal of the Roman Catholic Bishops

At this serious time for our nations, we appeal to you, beloved brothers and sisters, to remain calm and prudent, not to allow yourselves to be provoked to acts inconsonant with your Christian convictions, and to call with faith upon the Lord to bestow freedom and peace on our country. We stand firmly behind the legal representatives of our people, and we assure them of our unshakable support and solidarity.

> Roman Catholic Bishops of the Czechoslovak
> Socialist Republic

Report by Tass on the Situation in Czechoslovakia [2]

As reported earlier, anti-socialist forces are trying to disturb normal life in the country and create complications by stirring up nationalistic passions and hostility toward the healthy, patriotic

[2] Distributed in Czech translation as a leaflet by the occupation armies.

forces of Czechoslovakia, which are devoted to socialism and to the fraternal countries that came to the aid of the Czechoslovak people.

Hostile elements, trying at any cost to aggravate the situation, are committing grave crimes. Thus they arrested Oldrich Svestka, the editor-in-chief of *Rude Pravo,* who happens to be a member of the Presidium, and published a special issue of that newspaper in which they attacked the Soviet Union and other socialist countries. Comrade Svestka was released from captivity by Soviet troops.

The counterrevolutionary forces, particularly in Prague, are resorting to dangerous actions. In the center of Prague, they have staged an act of sabotage: They burned four Soviet armored personnel carriers and set fire to neighboring buildings. These saboteurs are also trying to put out of operation communication and transport facilities and to interfere with the distribution of food in the city.

The counterrevolutionaries have activated previously set-up illegal radio transmitters and printing presses. The slanderous fabrications and falsifications devised by the counterrevolutionaries and transmitted in this way are taken up by imperialist propaganda, which is trying to pass them off as an expression of the official position of Czechoslovakia and its public opinion.

The groundless attempt by some Western powers to bring up "the question of Czechoslovakia" before the U.N. Security Council should also be viewed in this context. On August 21, the Czechoslovak Minister of Foreign Affairs pointed out that this attempt is groundless, stressing that Czechoslovakia will not agree to a discussion of this question in the United Nations because relations between Czechoslovakia and other socialist countries are decided by these countries themselves within the framework of the socialist community.

❖   ❖   ❖

The numerous meetings, resolutions, and letters by working people of the Soviet Union and other socialist countries reflect the complete approval of the measures taken in defense of socialism in Czechoslovakia. These measures are also receiving the loyal support of many Communist and workers' parties, the working people, and leaders of progressive forces.

Some statesmen in several bourgeois countries are beginning to take a realistic position. Of course, the imperialist quarters, which were counting on tearing Czechoslovakia away from the community of socialist states, cannot resign themselves to the collapse of their hopes. They are continuing to create around the Czechoslovak events an atmosphere of tension and political hysteria. The ruling circles of Bonn are especially noteworthy in this respect. They are raging and thus involuntarily reveal their intentions regarding the activities of counterrevolutionary forces in Czechoslovakia.

On the whole, throughout August 22 the situation in Czechoslovakia was calm. Nevertheless, anti-socialist forces in Prague continued their subversive activities, trying to spread tension and uncertainty among the population. Illegal radio stations and counterrevolutionary leaflets continue to be used for this purpose. Incendiary posters containing slanderous attacks on prominent Czechoslovak Party and Government leaders, as well as on allied troops, have been put up in some Prague districts. Cars with loud-speakers transmitting illegal radio broadcasts have appeared in the streets.

Illegal radio stations and publications are spreading falsifications of the lowest kind. Certain officials are directly aiding them in this. Thus, for example, Ota Sik, Jiri Hajek, Frantisek Vlasak, and Stefan Gasparik announced that they would discharge Government functions "outside Czechoslovak territory," which, as a matter of fact, no one has authorized them to do.

Everyone who holds dear the cause of socialism in Czechoslovakia will firmly reject the pretensions of bankrupt politicians and those who back them to speak in the name of the Czechoslovak Socialist Republic.

According to reports coming from Czechoslovakia, the soldiers of the allied armies are helping with honor, dignity, self-discipline, and awareness of duty their class brothers—the working people of Czechoslovakia—to uphold the cause of socialism and dispel the threat to the security and sovereignty of the Czechoslovak Socialist Republic.

In the streets and squares of towns and villages, one can often see soldiers and officers of the allied armies hold friendly discussions with the population, reply to numerous questions, help correctly evaluate the political situation, and help explain the noble goals pursued by the armies.

From Pravda, *August 23, 1968*

4

FRIDAY, AUGUST 23

12:30 A.M.

The Presidium of the National Assembly resumed its extraordinary eighty-fifth session. It adopted a proclamation addressed to the Slovak National Council.[1] It was decided to ask [National First Deputy Chairman] Comrade Valo to deliver to the President of the Republic a recommendation that under no circumstances should he leave the territory of the Republic.

From documents of the National Assembly

To the Slovak National Council

Dear Comrades: .

On this occasion, we are sending you our sincere, brotherly greetings. We beg you to consider that we should remain together and united in our fight against the occupation of our country, in the fight for freedom and independence, so that we shall remain faithful to the principles of socialist law, so that we shall faithfully serve the interests and needs of our peoples.

To defend the development of a socialist Czechoslovakia, to cultivate the welfare of our nations, does not mean that we should betray President Ludvik Svoboda, Comrade Dubcek, Comrade Cernik, Comrade Smrkovsky, Kriegel, Husak, Spacek, Cisar, and other legal representatives of our leading organs.

Long live the brotherly cooperation of the Czechs and Slovaks!

[1] Given at 2:14 A.M. to Czechoslovak Radio for transmission.

Long live a united, federalized, and free socialist Czechoslovakia!

Presidium of the National Assembly

From documents of the National Assembly

8:22 A.M.

The Presidium of the National Assembly resumed its continuing extraordinary eighty-fifth session. There was again discussion of the move to oppose the departure by the President of the Republic. (The President had taken a different stand and promised to report to the National Assembly after his return.)

From documents of the National Assembly

Meanwhile, before dawn, the Central Committee of the Communist Party of Czechoslovakia, which was elected at the Extraordinary Fourteenth Congress of the Party, ended its first meeting and issued a communiqué.

1. The Central Committee of the Communist Party of Czechoslovakia, elected by the Extraordinary Fourteenth Party Congress, met in its first session together with the Central Control and Audit Commission, in the night hours of August 22, 1968, and elected the following members to its presidium: comrades Alexander Dubcek, Josef Smrkovsky, Oldrich Cernik, Josef Spacek, Frantisek Kriegel, Bohumil Simon, Cestmir Cisar, Ota Sik, Venek Silhan, Vaclav Slavik, Libuse Hrdinova, Vojtech Matejicek, Vladimir Kabrna, Zdenek Hejzlar, Jaromir Litera, Eduard Goldstuecker, Bohumil Vojacek, Milan Huebl, Zdenek Moc, Vaclav Simecek, Gustav Husak, Josef Zrak, Anton Tazky, Stefan Sadovsky, Peter Colotka, Julius Turcek, Viktor Pavlenda, and Andrej Zamek.

2. The Central Committee unanimously elected Comrade Alexander Dubcek as the First Secretary of the Central Committee.

3. The Central Committee elected Presidium member Comrade Venek Silhan as Secretary of the Central Committee and authorized him to direct the Presidium of the Central Committee during the absence of First Secretary Comrade Dubcek.

4. The plenary of the Central Committee adopted, for the immediate future, political and organizational measures to cope with the serious political situation in the country.

5. The Central Committee, the only legally constituted leading organ of the Party in the period between sessions of the Congress, requests all lower Party organs to carry out their activities exclusively in accordance with the directives of this legal Central Committee and its Presidium.

Declaration of Slovak Delegates to the Extraordinary Fourteenth Party Congress

Early morning on Friday, after considerable difficulties, a number of other duly elected delegates from Slovak districts arrived in Prague to attend the Extraordinary Fourteenth Party Congress. After obtaining basic information and meeting members of the new Central Committee, they signed this declaration:

The undersigned duly elected delegates to the Extraordinary Fourteenth Party Congress, who arrived late because of transportation difficulties, have been informed of the discussion of the Congress by Presidium member Comrade Litera and request to be considered as duly participating in the Congress.

> Ottakar Pezlar (Svidnik), J. Gula (Spisska Nova Ves), Karol Jarek (Nove Zamky), Choma (Kosice), Luptak (Zvolen), Jan Marejka (Cadca), Tamas (Kosice), Stefan Chovanec (Cadca), Pozgay (Detva), Viktor Roth (Michalovce), Medel (Zvolen)

From Rude Pravo, *August 24, 1968*

6:15 A.M.

Czechoslovak Radio announced that [Slovak] General Samuel Kodaj [a critic of rapid reform, who resigned his National Assembly seat in July] was one of those who, after the occupation, declared himself for Dubcek and denounced the occupation.

6:30 A.M.

Czechoslovak Radio broadcast an interview with National Assembly member Comrade Polednak, who said the Party had no reason to go underground. A new Central Committee has been elected, he pointed out. Asked whether parliamentary discussion can influence the situation in a decisive way, he responded by saying the situation was very complex and not under our control. These are not our tanks and our troops. The National Assembly considers it its duty to do everything to remove these "abnormalities," if one can use such a gentle expression.

In the Early Morning

Czechoslovak Radio broadcast an order by the commander of the occupation troops in Prague imposing a curfew on Prague citizens between the hours of 10 P.M. and 5 A.M. during the night of August 23–24.

8:20 A.M.

Czechoslovak Radio reported that there is an unceasing stream of resolutions from all parts of the Republic demanding neutrality for Czechoslovakia.

Neutrality?

I am not a politician, know little of military affairs, and would find it very difficult to express an expert opinion on demands so frequently voiced since last night that our country be declared neutral.

I know only this: The historical experience of our nation has for many years created pre-conditions for such a psychology. The thing people want least is to wage war. They know that any armed conflict in Europe would sweep through us. They know why the Warsaw Pact is so concerned about our western border. They know that our country is no more than a military area in which would be staged—in the event of a world war—the first destructive confrontation.

Can we wonder at demands for neutrality?

Since the founding of the Republic, Czechoslovakia has had a strong army, but with the exception of fighting abroad [during World War II], it has never been allowed to use it. Every time we want to mobilize the army for our defense, the act of mobilization itself would threaten our very national existence.

Something occurs to me now that must indeed have occurred to the majority of those who demand neutralization: For years we have built up and maintained an army; then, when the time arrived for which an army is built up, we have behaved as a neutral state. Involuntarily, under duress—and therefore also without the advantages of a neutral status.

I don't know whether neutralization would be the right solution, either in general or at this particular moment, whether it would be the right solution militarily and politically. In the last three days, however, it is not a question of either a pacifistic mood or cowardice or an abstract discussion, it is just a simple expression of despair over our position.

When people call for neutrality *de jure*, it amounts to neutrality *de facto* because they realize this is the kind of neutrality that is paradoxically forced upon us again and again by the pressure of history.

From Literarni Listy, *August 23, 1968*

8:25 A.M.

Czechoslovak Radio broadcast an appeal to all mailmen and newsstand operators to be on the lookout for *provocateurs* and not to disclose to anyone lists of subscribers to various publications.

8:45 A.M.

Czechoslovak Radio broadcast a statement by the President of the Republic.

Yesterday, that is on August 22, 1968, I had discussions with representatives of the Soviet Union in Prague on how to solve the situation created by the entry of Soviet and other troops on Czechoslovak territory, especially on how to restore the functions of the constitutional organ of the Czechoslovak Socialist Republic. When these discussions did not produce a satisfactory result, I asked, in the morning hours, members of the Government who at this time are still at Hradcany Castle, to give their consent to direct talks with the highest representatives of the Soviet Union. This morning, the Ambassador of the Soviet Union expressed a positive attitude of the Soviet leadership to such talks.

The following people will accompany me for the talks: Husak, Dzur, Piller, Bilak, Indra, and Kucera. We shall inform the National Assembly of our trip.

Dear citizens, I want to thank you for your support and trust, and I ask you to give further support to my next approach. I urge you to maintain calm and restraint and to help, through your attitude of awareness, create favorable conditions for the coming discussions with Soviet representatives. We hope that we shall emerge from this situation, which threatens tragic consequences for our people and our country, with honor and assure you that we are continuing on the path of a democratic development of our socialist homeland in the spirit of the January plenary meeting of the Central Committee. We expect to return home this evening and immediately after our return to inform the constitutional organs, as well as you, dear citizens, about the talks.

9:20 A.M.

Czechoslovak Radio reported that this morning a reliable person from the office of the President telephoned to say that the President would like the public to know that his trip to Moscow was being made at his own initiative and that he had not signed any decree establishing a collaborationist government.

Information by Telephone from Comrade President Ludvik Svoboda

At this time, the President of the Republic is leaving, or has left, by plane for Moscow. He is being accompanied by two or three members of the Government, two or three members of the new Central Committee, his son-in-law [Milan Klusak, former Czechoslovak Ambassador to the United Nations], and Dr. Novak, head of the office of President of the Republic. The President has expressed the wish that all Czechoslovaks know that this trip is being made at his own request. He declares that he has resisted pressure and believes the discussions will lead to good results. He assures everyone that he has not signed proposals to establish a collaborationist government.

From Obrana Lidu, *August 23, 1968*

9:30 A.M.

President of the Republic Ludvik Svoboda and members of his party left by plane for Moscow.

11 A.M.

The Streets of Prague

There is still no streetcar traffic downtown, but automobiles are crisscrossing in all directions. The streets are full of people wearing the national colors on their clothes. The cars carry signs saying: "Return Dubcek." Buildings display portraits of the President and the First Secretary of the Party. A short time ago, the legal transmitter of the municipal committee of the Party broadcast an appeal to intercept automobiles with registration plates AE 4001 and ABA 7119 because they are en route to arrest our representatives. This appeal, distributed in handwriting and even on mimeographed sheets, can be seen on every house I am passing. Boys have pinned copies of the appeal to their backs. In the Square of the Republic, Soviet tanks are still stationed. The barrels of their guns are aiming at the bridge. Nobody talks to the Soviet soldiers any more. The people are passing by and pay no attention to them. But you can see everywhere written in large letters in the Russian alphabet: "Go home!" "Don't shoot at us!" Tanks are patrolling the state bank. A very appropriate poster there reads:

> There is no need for a Russian tank
> To defend our state bank.
> What little is still there
> We can defend ourselves.

One man in front of the Ministry of Transport claims he witnessed the interception of car AE 4001. He says it happened near Perla. The youths react quickly, deleting the number from their posters and filling in others as they are announced over the radio.

I missed the usual lines in front of food stores. Instead, there was a long one in the park next to the Children's Home. Thousands were signing a petition to have Czechoslovakia declared neutral.

Passing cars dump stacks of special editions of the papers, proclamations of the new Central Committee, and lists of its members. Voluntary newsstand helpers are picking them up and handing them out to passers-by.

I don't know who has organized the youth, but its total unselfishness is without precedent. In the morning, new appeals are being posted: to leave the streets between noon and one o'clock. Prague is to become a dead city. We are declaring a one-hour general strike.

Wenceslas Square is full of discussion groups. The debate is a disciplined one. Here, too, nobody pays any attention to Soviet troops, except several youths who approach the tanks and hang posters on them. "Go home! Return Dubcek!" A very young soldier, sitting on top of a tank, calls for his officer, who is pulling off the posters, and in a tired gesture shrugs his shoulders. Do the occupiers feel any shame? They do, obviously. Their eyes are always on the move, trying to avoid looking at the faces of the people around.

Noon is approaching, and the Square is slowly emptying. People don't need orders; it is a discipline from the inside. From the direction of Narodny Street, one can hear people shouting: "Neutrality, Dubcek, Svoboda!"

It is noon. All over Prague, sirens are wailing. The general strike is on. At 12:35 there is shooting. Unfortunately, it is not the first time.

From Politika, *first issue, August 24, 1968*

10:57 A.M.

The continuing extraordinary twenty-sixth session of the National Assembly resumed (interrupted at 12:08 P.M.). Present are 170 assemblymen and three members of the Czech National

Council. From the agenda: a report of the discussions between National Assembly First Deputy Chairman Valo and the President of the Republic on the attitude of the National Assembly to the President's trip to Moscow. Unanimously approved was an expression of thanks to radio, television, and newspaper personnel.

From documents of the National Assembly

Proclamation of the National Assembly on the Work of Radio, Television, and Newspaper Personnel

All members highly appreciate the unusual initiative and activity of radio, television, and newspaper personnel and thank them in their name and that of all Czechoslovak people for their unselfish, patriotic, heroic work, which the grateful people of this country will never forget.

Thanks to you, a mighty patriotic movement is spreading, our backbones are being straightened, our determination to resist occupation and to face up to the traps laid by traitors and cowards is getting a firm hold.

Your selfless work, as well as the resolutions, decisions, and other expressions of the united will of our people and its organs, which you make known to us, are a tremendous help to us, the legal representatives of the people of Czechoslovakia, in our work.

Once again, heartfelt and sincere thanks. Once again we reaffirm our common slogan: We believe you, trust us!

> National Assembly of the Czechoslovak
> Socialist Republic

From documents of the National Assembly

11 A.M.

Czechoslovak Radio reported that the Karolin [one of the oldest buildings of Charles University in Prague] has been occupied.

Scene from the Streets of Prague

From the heart of occupied Prague Friday morning, one can get a view that symbolizes the current picture of the country, invaded by foreign troops. Soviet trucks and armored cars, spiked threateningly with the barrels of automatic rifles and machine guns, are bombarded by angry looks. Why have you come? What do you want? These are questions that can be seen from the looks of every one of our citizens, from every gesture of clenched fist. They can also be heard in every one of the groups that gather around the military vehicles of the occupiers. The Soviet soldiers for the most part keep quiet or cite higher orders. Many try to argue: Your government invited us . . . . They cannot understand that the nation has decided not to identify itself with the pitifully small group of traitors whose names are posted on every corner. On Thursday, I witnessed a nerve-shattering scene: a young boy showing a Soviet soldier the bloody, bullet-ridden remnants of a newspaper, a souvenir of a friend who died under fire from the aggressors. "This is your work." The Soviet soldier lowered his head.

From Lidova Demokacie, *4th special edition, August 23, 1968*

In the Morning

Czechoslovak Radio announced that the occupation troops had seized the Bartolomejska Street police station.

11:35 A.M.

Czechoslovak Radio reported that an occupation television service is using channels one and seven, but our television is preparing broadcasts on channel three.

12 Noon to 1 P.M.

The one-hour general strike, called by the Extraordinary Fourteenth Congress of the Communist Party of Czechoslovakia. Some reports said the employees of certain plants wanted to go into streets during the strike. Announcers on Czechoslovak Radio warned: "Do not enter the streets; do not give any cause for conflict; do not leave your plants. Don't listen to people like Kolder, Bilak, and others. Ignore the occupation forces."

How the Strike Was Carried Out

From the National Museum, a line of young people marches down Wenceslas Square. They are holding hands and shouting: "Evacuate the streets!" Behind them there is only the empty, wide space of the Square. The sirens begin to wail; car horns join them. The soldiers in tanks look around. They don't know what is going on. They are scanning buildings on either side, watching the windows. Some of the tanks are closing their hatches. The machine guns and cannon are turning around, looking for targets. But there is no one to shoot at; nobody is provoking them. The people have begun a general strike, as proclaimed by our Communist Party.

All of a sudden Wenceslas Square is empty; only dust, papers, posters rise up in the wind. All that is left are tanks and soldiers. Nobody around them, none of our people.

At 1 P.M., Wenceslas Square begins to fill up again. People are clapping hands and shouting: "Dubcek, Svoboda!" From Mustek [the foot of the Square] up to the top comes a stream of those who minutes before showed their self-discipline in the strike. The general strike showed how the young and old, the men and women, think: We are behind Svoboda and Dubcek; we support the new leadership of the Communist Party.

From Rude Pravo, *August 24, 1968*

How Propaganda Is Made

On Friday, August 23, 1968, at noon, the one-hour strike began. All over the capital sirens wailed. Prague citizens, acting with discipline, evacuated the streets. There were no people, not even in front of the *Rude Pravo* publishing house on Porici. But inside the building were the forty members of the occupying authorities who seized the editorial offices and the printing plant Wednesday.

A few minutes after noon, two armored Soviet transports showed up and Soviet soldiers opened fire at windows in the *Rude Pravo* building. Windows and even walls inside from street level to the fourth floor are scarred by bullet marks from hundreds of shots. People watching from shelters did not understand why they were doing this. But everything became clear when a Soviet cameraman appeared on top of one of the armored vehicles and began to take pictures of the action. Next week Soviet movie-goers will be shown a newsreel about a fight with counterrevolutionaries in Czechoslovakia. This very film is going to tell people how the revanchists or imperialists attacked the building housing the central publication of the Communist Party. And, looked at from the other side, it will be the truth. It was, indeed, an imperialistic attack.

From Politika, *No. 2, August 28, 1968*

The General Strike

At noon, all plants and other places of work stopped working, with the exception of those that are providing direct services for the population. In the railroad depot Praha-Vrsovice, there is an unusual quiet. Surrounded by a circle of steam engines, under a tall smoke stack decorated with the sign "Friendship, not occupation," railroad workers are discussing their latest resolution. Naturally, they, too, are against the occupation. They also know, however, that the people expect more of them. We shall never allow the railroads to be used for helping the occupation, even if they use force. Every one of us knows a lot of ways of crippling traffic. We shall never move occupation troops on our lines except when we know that they are going home and when we get orders from people whom we fully trust. We shall not transport anything that might harm our republic—such as ammunition or similar cargo. Each one of us has the duty to see to it what is being carried in the cars. There is talk about a train containing jamming equipment against our radio stations. It will never pass through here.

Precisely at 1 P.M., the engineers climb back into the cabs and pull the whistle to signal the end of the strike. Answering signals come from other factories; sirens sound all over the town.

In the Vysocany Praha plant, a strike committee was set up before the Central Council of Labor Unions called for one. The general strike has been approved by all labor union sectors one hundred per cent, including, of course, the signatories of the [pro-Soviet Auto Praha factory] letter published [in July] by Moscow *Pravda*.

From Prace, *August 23, 1968*

2:30 P.M.

Czechoslovak Radio broadcast a report about a decision of the Central Committee to remove Oldrich Svestka as editor-in-chief of *Rude Pravo* and replace him with Jiri Sekera. Nominated as deputy editors-in-chief were comrades Zdislav Sulc and Emil Sip.

In the Afternoon

In the afternoon, a delivery van from the Prague Bakeries drove by the building of the Ministry of Interior in Letna. Without any reason—unless we consider it a crime to display the Czechoslovak flag—the truck was fired on by occupants who had seized the building.

From Svoboda, *August 25, 1968*

According to the municipal statistical office, the presence of the occupying powers has cost us more than 200 million Czech crowns [$28 million at the official exchange rate; more realistically, $12.5 million] in losses to the gross national income. Every additional day, we shall lose 65 million crowns more [$9 million officially; more realistically, $4 million] in Prague alone.

The heaviest losses—the lives of our citizens—have not yet been accurately ascertained. The estimates are more than three hundred wounded and about twenty dead. It is impossible to translate into figures the enormous damage to the national economy as a result of the ruthless behavior of the occupying powers. The figures we have cited are only partial, reflecting the disruption of our economic and social life.

From Vecerni Praha, *August 24, 1968*

5 P.M.

Czechoslovak Radio announced that the Czechoslovak News

Agency is calling on all employees not to accept any directives from the Agency's Director General, Miroslav Sulek. In the first hours of the occupation, Miroslav Sulek produced an anonymous document aimed at justifying the occupation. It is to the credit of the Czechoslovak News Agency employees that this document was not used in transmissions either inside Czechoslovakia or abroad. The same document was later broadcast by [the Soviet news agency] *Tass*.

5:25 P.M.

Czechoslovak Radio reported that it is expected that there will be arrests during the night. An appeal has been issued to paint over or remove street signs and number plates on houses, to render illegible name plates on apartments, and to repaint highway direction signs throughout the country.

Streets Without Names

Already on Thursday night we have seen many street signs painted over, also direction signs on the main arteries and highways. After noon on Friday, the city was flooded with leaflets calling on citizens to remove, or at least paint over, street signs as well as the signs on important offices and plants. There was a lightning reaction to this appeal. Prague streets have lost their names!

From Prace, *August 23, 1968*

A City of Anonymity

Who came up with the wonderful idea? After the legal radio station "Praha" appealed to them late Friday, hundreds of thousands of people destroyed corner street signs and number plates on houses. In some places, even name plates of apartment residents don't exist any more. Vodickova Street and Charles Square have ceased to exist. Prague names and numbers have died out. For the uninvited guests, Prague has become a dead city. Anyone who was not born here, who has not lived here, will find a city of anonymity among a million inhabitants: a city in which the occupiers will find only appeals of all kinds, in Czech and in the Russian alphabet. We have seen signs on highways saying: "Moscow—1,800 kilometers." Prague is defending itself against tanks, artillery, and occupation troops. And without bloodshed. Against collaborators who, by helping to arrest innocent people, are trying to make the nation nervous. Therefore, let us follow the slogan: The mailman will find you, but evil-doers won't! Bravo Prague and other cities that followed and follow its example!

From Lidova Demokracie, *5th special edition, August 24, 1968*

Condemnation of the Occupation by the Signers of the Letter Addressed to the Soviet Embassy on July 16 from the Auto Praha Plant

The signers of the Auto Praha letter yesterday expressed their attitude on the occupation of Czechoslovakia in messages to the Soviet Embassy and to the highest institutions of our Party and state. They pointed out that in their earlier letter [in July, to the Soviet Embassy], which was published by *Pravda* in Moscow, they wanted to express the idea of friendship between our nations but that the letter was not quite suitably phrased. They added: "We have watched the entry of Warsaw Pact troops into our territory with the deepest indignation and disappointment. This act is in deep contrast with the principles of friendship among socialist states. The illegal occupation of our country by Warsaw Pact troops is for us, who have always had warm sympathies for the Soviet Union, a deep moral disappointment."

In conclusion, they have asked that the occupation armies immediately leave our territory and that compensation be paid for all losses caused by the occupation. They expressed full support for the democratically elected leaders of our state, President Ludvik Svoboda, Premier Oldrich Cernik, National Assembly President Josef Smrkovsky, and First Secretary of the Central Committee of the Communist Party of Czechoslovakia Alexander Dubcek.

They pressed a demand that their new letter also be published in the Moscow *Pravda.*

From Prace, *August 24, 1968*

I Accuse

The undersigned hereby accuses Alois Indra, Vasil Bilak, Drahomir Kolder, Vilem Novy, Milos Jakes, and other unknown persons of suspicion of, and complicity in, murder and inflicting bodily injury.

The above named are suspected of having called in a foreign power, which by its acts caused the death on August 21, 1968, of Zdenek Prihoda, born on November 27, 1941, and domiciled in Prague 2; Milan Kadlec, born September 26, 1947, and domiciled in Prague 6; and another unidentified young man. Autopsy on all three was carried out by the Institute of Criminological Medicine in Prague 10.

Furthermore, heavy bodily injury has been inflicted on more than sixty-five persons, who were treated on August 21, 1968, by Dr. Polak in the Vinohrady Hospital. Their names are available in the files of the hospital.

Dr. Milan Jaros

From Vecerni Praha, *August 27, 1968 (Dated in Prague, August 23, 1968)*

Appeal to the Office of the General Prosecutor

Comrade Prosecutor General:

We request you to initiate immediately, under the appropriate laws of the Czechoslovak Socialist Republic, prosecution of those who have betrayed their homeland, who have collaborated and are collaborating with the enemy against the legal government of Czechoslovakia, the National Assembly, and the President of the Republic, and who have participated and are participating in the enemy occupation.

The purpose of this appeal by the citizens to you, Comrade Prosecutor General, is to announce the names of those traitors about whom we know: Kolder, Bilak, Indra, Svestka, Piller, Jakes, Mestek, Hoffman, Sulek, Rigo, Novy, Rytir, Lenart, Salgovic, Rezek, Rypl, Kozuch, Hubina, Klima, Spelina, Beran, Bokr.

Citizens, remember their names!

Away with the occupiers, death to the collaborators!

From Student, *an undated first special edition, probably August 23, 1968*

To All Students of the World

I am a Czech student, twenty-two years old. As I am writing this proclamation, Soviet tanks are stationed in a large park under my windows. The barrels of their guns are trained on a Government building decorated with a huge sign: "For socialism and peace." I remember hearing this slogan ever since I was able to grasp the meaning of objects around me. But only during the last seven months has this slogan slowly acquired its original meaning. For seven months, my country has been led by people who wanted to prove, probably for the first time in the history of mankind, that socialism and democracy can exist side by side. Nobody knows where these people are now. I don't know whether I shall ever see or hear them again. There is much that I don't know. For example, how long will it take the Soviet troops to silence free radio stations, which are telling the nation the truth? I don't know, either, whether I shall be able to finish my university studies or meet again my friends from abroad. I could carry on and on like this, but somehow everything seems to be losing its original value. At three o'clock in the morning of August 21, 1968, I have opened eyes on a world entirely different from that in which only six hours before I had gone to sleep.

You will think, perhaps, that the Czech people have behaved like cowards because they did not fight. But you cannot stand up to tanks with empty hands. I want to assure you that Czechs and Slovaks have acted as a politically mature nation, which may be broken physically but not morally. This is why I write. The only way you can help is: Don't forget Czechoslovakia. Please help our passive resistance by increasing the pressure of public opinion around the world. Think of Czechoslovakia even when this country ceases to be sensational news.

From Student, *undated first special edition, probably August 23, 1968*

Killing Children

The occupation of Czechoslovakia by forces of the Soviet Union and other socialist regimes dependent on it is now sixty-three hours old. Eternal shame should cling to those who have used their arms against the defenseless Czech and Slovak people and who have not even balked at killing children! One of these killings, which stand out like an exclamation point, occurred in Prague during the night from Thursday to Friday on Palacky Bridge. There, a young boy was shot by the occupation army because he refused to hand over copies of *Svet v Obrazech* [an illustrated magazine], which he was distributing to the people.

Occupiers! Your mothers and fathers will one day be ashamed of you from the depths of their souls!

From Zemedelske Noviny, *August 24, 1968*

A Sad Night

I am sure the events of the last eight hours will leave lasting scars on the memory of us all. For me, it will be the memory of a thoroughly rain-soaked man on the run because there was no place for a Communist newspaperman who loves truth, freedom, and his country to think in peace.

And so we wandered through the streets. My first stop was one of the local police stations. There, men in uniform clustered around the radio listening to the latest news. On the wall hung a picture of Alexander Dubcek: Their political sympathies were clear. The oldest, a major, told us what a blow the occupation by Soviet troops was for him. He was forty-seven years old and had lived through two tragedies like this. His hair was gray. I was proud when I saw how he was sending his boys out to patrol Vinohradska. "In the beginning," he explained, "we were full of self-pity. Now all that is left is anger and disgust and, unfortunately, a complete impotence to do anything." These were the parting words of the major.

As I went out again to continue my wandering through the streets, rain began to fall. The street signs had disappeared. The houses had no numbers. Traffic signs were painted over. Some, made of glass, were broken. Then I saw a Soviet occupier on Prikopy Street walking along with a Czech girl. The street was empty. The girl, in a dark blue dress, was telling him something in Czech, and he, an automatic rifle on his back, was listening. And they walked together down the wet Prague street.

More rats will crawl out of their holes, more collaborators and traitors will appear. Let us be united in these very difficult times when we still don't know what happened to our legal representatives. The world is with us.

From Vecerni Praha, *August 24, 1968*

The Hour of Truth

We should never forget that in these moments there have appeared in our midst politicians who have sold out to the occupiers. If we call them traitors, it does not mean very much. Let us regard them as virus that entered our body and will again leave it in the process of convalescence. Politicians of the type of Indra, Kolder, Bilak, Hoffman, and Lenart will find a handful of followers at all levels. It is a handful that means nothing in a nation of fourteen and one-half million.

On the day of the occupation of our country, a meeting took place in one of the offices of the Central Committee of the Czechoslovak Physical Training Association. Three men took part in the meeting, and their unusually serious problem was to seize positions that may become vacant. One of the three explained it in an interesting way: It is essential to prevent dishonest people from occupying these positions. Therefore, he said, one must reconcile himself with the situation and seek possibilities of filling these positions. Two of the three officials of the Physical Training Association declared with malicious joy that they had nothing to be afraid of because in recent months they had taken care not to identify themselves prominently with the new trend in the country. Only those should be afraid, they said, who shouted, who—together with rotten intellectuals—brought us to our situation today and became victim of Zionistic schemers. Take pity, please, on this last silly declaration. We have not all been born with the same I.Q.

But let us consider the main problem. The present situation will, indeed, provide an excellent possibility for moving up, getting an office, occupying a position, ruling: at all levels—in the physical-training movement, anywhere from sections and units, up to the Central Committee. But those who think like the three should be reminded of certain facts. Let us suppose their stomachs are strong enough to withstand general ostracism and that they have enough courage to spend the rest of their lives in the company of fourteen and one-half million enemies. Let us suppose that they consider their career more important than basic values that make life what it is: honor, law, decency. Then they should consider one thing: Occupiers come and go. The first occupation of our country lasted three hundred years, the second only six years, and we are all convinced that the time graph in this case will decline even faster. Occupiers come and go: The nation, the people, however, remain. And the people don't forget! It will be well to know one, two, ten, twenty, and a hundred years from now who passed the test of this hour of truth and who did not. If anyone thinks of his career more than of the honor and interests of his country, let him think now of his career one year, two, ten, or twenty years from now.

From January through August of this year, we have been acting in a humanistic way. We have kept in office even those who we knew could betray us. Next time we won't make the same mistake.

From Ceskoslovensky Sport, *August 23, 1968*

Foreigners with the Tricolor

The man spoke French and English, but he was an Italian. We were standing on the corner of Old Town Square with two patrolmen. He was showing us his passport and asking where his visa could be extended.

"Go home," we told him. But he said he could not very well do that. Until now he has always been a friend of the Soviet Union, a member of the Communist Party of Italy. Now he must stay and see everything so that he can tell the people at home how it really was.

"Right now I cannot really think. I have seen young people walking down the street, and all of a sudden, drrrrrrrrr, they fell down, and there was blood. Members of the Communist Party of Italy don't think the same way as these Soviet Communists, and yet we are really in the same party. I don't know."

In the streets of Prague there are Frenchmen, Englishmen, Germans, and other foreigners who wear our tricolor in their lapels. We are grateful to them for being on our side.

From Mlada Fronta, *August 23, 1968*

Hoodlums Are Still on the Loose

There are still individuals who are trying to take advantage of the abnormal situation. Late in the evening, some people broke into the self-service restaurant Jizera on Wenceslas Square. The police seized three youths with bags full of loot, including the till. The police also arrested their ten accomplices.

From Lidova Demokracie, *5th special edition, August 24, 1968*

Commentary by a Special Correspondent of Pravda

Somewhere in Prague yesterday, a secret gathering took place, convened by rightest revisionist elements who called it an "Extraordinary Congress of the Communist Party of Czechoslovakia." Illegal radio stations have broadcast hastily concocted decisions of this meeting and the composition of the "new leadership," which consists largely of people known for their revisionist and publicly voiced counterrevolutionary views. Illegal printing plants have published these "documents," and the Yugoslav news agency *Tanjug*, which has assumed the doubtful role of a publicity agent for this enterprise, is distributing them abroad. How did it actually come about that this gathering, which throws a shadow on the good name of the Party, was convened? It happened like this. Soon after the January, 1968, plenary of the Central Committee of the Czechoslovak Communist Party, rightist revisionist forces took advantage of the temporary weakening of Party leadership and started an offensive against the healthy elements of the Party under the slogan of "democratization of the society." Their aim was to take over the leadership of the Party. The original plan was to call a congress of the Party only next year. But one day, everything changed: A decision was imposed on the Party to convene a congress on September 9, 1968. There was little time left before the congress. Its program included questions of primary, vital importance: the current situation, a reorganization of the state, approval of new regulations of the Party, and others. But those who wanted to seize leadership of the Party and force upon it a new line—which would betray Leninism, as the current events have shown—were not much bothered with preparations for discussing these questions. For them, only one thing was important: to call a congress as soon as possible and dictate their will so as to forestall any possible unmasking of their dirty plans.

All means were employed to make sure that the revisionist elements would have a majority at the congress. Among the delegates elected for the congress, only 17 per cent were workers. The delegates also included people who made no secret of their inimical attitude to the basic tenets of Leninism—for example, the authors of the counterrevolutionary proclamation "Two Thousand Words." [2]

The decision of the fraternal parties to give the working class and the Communist Party of Czechoslovakia immediate help in its fight to preserve and strengthen the foundations of socialism spurred the rightists to speed up their plans. They wanted to give an appearance of legality to their designs, through which they wished to remove mercilessly the healthy forces of the Party and create an antagonism against the fraternal parties and people of the socialist countries.

Already, on August 21, illegal radio stations broadcast an appeal to the congress delegates to come immediately to Prague. Typically, they were told not to come to the building housing the Central Committee of the Party but to meet at secretly agreed to places.

This secret gathering took place yesterday. We have facts to prove its illegal character. Nobody checked the credentials of the participants. The delegates of the Communist Party of Slovakia

[2] Written in June by novelist Ludvik Vaculik and signed by seventy liberal intellectuals and workers, this document advocated strikes and other public pressures to prod the Dubcek Government into speeding up the pace of reform. The Party leadership formally dissociated itself from this document on the grounds that its liberal demands went too far.

were not present—even the organizers announced that there were
"only a few people" from Slovakia in attendance. They did not
even consider it necessary to maintain the appearance of congress
discussions—listen to reports, carry on a debate, and so on. Everything was done with lightning speed: Resolutions were adopted
to achieve a break from the fraternal parties and countries, calling
for resistance against their armed forces, which had come to help
the Czechoslovak people. Illegal radio stations were broadcasting
lists of people elected to the Central Committee and its Presidium. These lists show eloquently that what happened was an
anti-Party conspiracy to remove from the leadership of the Party
its best and most faithful sons and substitute for them political
adventurers who are capable of anything.

On August 21, the illegal radio stations and press stepped up
the frenzy of attack on those leading members of the Central
Committee who had remained faithful to Leninism. One member
of the Presidium, Comrade Oldrich Svestka, was seized by in-
furiated anti-Party elements in the editorial offices of *Rude Pravo*.
Posters showing a gallows were displayed in Prague, threatening another member of the Presidium, Comrade Vasil Bilak. The
campaign was directed against other leading members of the
Party.

Who then is attempting to pose as leaders of the self-appointed
Central Committee? They are well known. Among them is
Cestmir Cisar, who has proved his betrayal of Leninism by a series
of public statements. There is Ota Sik, whose revisionist views
in the field of economy are equally well known. Now he is working hard abroad as one of the directors of the rightist forces.[3]
There is [Writers Union Chairman] Eduard Goldstuecker, who
in recent months made many anti-socialist statements in Czechoslovakia and abroad. With these are persons who are so far not
so well known but suspect all the same—for example, a certain
Venek Silhan, until now an inconspicuous director of a building
institute, who suddenly emerged as the man "empowered to carry
out the functions of the First Secretary of the Central Committee."
These men were hiding behind the backs of others and waiting

[3] He was vacationing in Yugoslavia at the time of the invasion.

for the right moment. Now they have been fully unmasked as enemies of the Party and of the Czechoslovak people. They are trying to use their key positions to undermine the foundations of socialism. This is shown quite convincingly by the first acts of Silhan, to which we shall refer later.

These men, who now try to pretend that they have been authorized to take over key positions in the Party, have also made sure that they have appropriate assistants. Among them are, for example, Frantisek Kriegel, Vaclav Slavik, and Milan Huebl, who have shown themselves as able organizers of the rightist forces; Zdenek Hejzlar and Jiri Pelikan, who furiously campaigned against Party cadres in the radio and press; Josef Pavel, who in the 1950's participated in bloody persecutions against innocent persons and now proclaims himself as a protector of democracy in the function of Minister of Interior and who fled as soon as the troops of the fraternal countries approached Prague. Then the social democratic misfit Jan Jelinek, chief editor of the notorious *Mlada Fronta;* Jan Prochazka, whose anti-socialist and anti-Soviet views have on many occasions been subjected to criticism in the press of the socialist countries; and finally authors of the counterrevolutionary "Two Thousand Words," Oldrich Stary, Jiri Hanzelka, and others. There are "members of the Central Committee" like Josef Boruvka, in whose office—in the Ministry of Agriculture—we have today found a secret cache of arms. Shots were fired against Soviet troops from this building.

These are the facts. They show that, through the activities of anti-socialist forces, the Communist Party of Czechoslovakia has gotten itself into a complicated situation. A section of the Party still strongly defends the positions of Marxism-Leninism and of the proletarian internationalism, socialist progress, and basic interests of the people. This section has for a long time been subjected to a furious attack and moral terror by the anti-socialist forces. Representatives of this healthy section could not even properly use the mass media of information in order to give lie to the stream of abuse that has been directed at them. The other section of the Party gave in to a demagogic speculation about past mistakes carried out by political adventurers and in the resulting confusion has lost its true orientation until finally it began to abandon gradually the positions of class revolution. The political adventurers took advantage of this and ruthlessly tried to seize leadership of the Party. The "decisions" of the secret gathering, which has proclaimed itself as an Extraordinary Congress of the Party, cannot, of course, be taken seriously. Men who now call themselves "members of the Presidium," especially the notorious Cisar, who through the illegal radio thanked those who "elected" him, cannot be considered as legal leaders of the Party. They have thoroughly unmasked themselves by using these undignified methods.

If anyone had any doubts, these should definitely be removed by the self-invited Silhan, who has been "empowered to carry out the functions of the First Secretary of the Communist Party." Around noon, Western radio stations and news agencies distributed Silhan's "proclamation," first broadcast by the illegal radio in Prague.

In this "proclamation," Silhan said today that "the Central Committee had expressed itself in support of neutralization of Czechoslovakia." This formulation of neutrality means that Czechoslovakia should leave the Warsaw Pact. Six minutes later, the "free Prague radio" broadcast a list of factories, military units, and representatives of the civilian population all over the country that allegedly have signed resolutions demanding neutrality for Czechoslovakia.

Jiri Hajek, the escaped Foreign Minister, who, by the way, was also included in the "new Central Committee" and who at this time was on his way from Yugoslavia to New York, commented on Silhan's statement. He said the idea of neutrality interested him, but he did not think it was "realistic." Two hours later, Silhan, who must have realized that he was proceeding at a rather fast pace, again spoke through the illegal radio. He "corrected" himself to say that the "formula of Czechoslovak neutrality had not been endorsed by the Congress" because "neutrality in itself does not guarantee the inviolability of the country." "In itself does not guarantee . . ." How is one to understand that? Doesn't it mean, perhaps, that it was not enough for the participants of the secret gathering to leave the Warsaw Pact and enter neutrality but that they are requesting membership in NATO? Be that as it may, Silhan added that what was needed now was a "deep change in the relationship among socialist countries." All this feverish activity, of course, has no practical value. Czechoslovak Communists, devoted to the cause of socialism, will not permit such suspects as Silhan and his company to take over leadership of the Central Committee and do as they please. As it is, their activities have all too long remained unpunished. Now that these men have unmasked themselves, the Communists will know better with whom they are dealing. Calling the secret gathering, which has illegally adopted the name of a congress, constitutes an open attack against the Party. But the Party will not die. Healthy forces will manage to revive it. And again it will win the deserved glory of one of the fighting units of Marxism-Leninism and of the world Communist movement.

From a mimeographed translation distributed by the occupation forces

5

SATURDAY, AUGUST 24

6:20 A.M.

Czechoslovak Radio broadcast that Gustav Husak has reported
from Moscow that comrades Dubcek, Smrkovsky, and Cernik,
who were brought to the Soviet capital on August 22, are also
taking part in the negotiations.

8:00 A.M.

The continuing extraordinary eighty-fifth session of the Presidium of the National Assembly resumed. The session lasted, with
an intermission, until 12:50 P.M. From the agenda: reports on the
situation in Prague and in the regions; Friday's general strike and
spontaneous strikes; Government measures; activity of parliamentary committees; cooperation with the Slovak National Council; discussion of the demand for neutrality.

From National Assembly documents

The National Assembly Continues

The Presidium of the National Assembly met with representatives of the National Committee of Prague, Lord Mayor Ludvik
Cerny and his deputy. It heard their report on some urgent
problems of the life in the capital city. Until the situation is
normalized by, above all, the departure of foreign troops and the

return of comrades Dubcek, Smrkovsky, Cernik, Kriegel, and others to their posts, both organs consider it necessary to coordinate their joint measures primarily in the sector of food supply, transportation, health, and in the preparations for the opening of the school year. The representatives of the National Committee of Prague reaffirmed that they regarded as the only bearers of state power Cernik's legal government and Smrkovsky's National Assembly.

All National Assembly committees were also in session to consider a specific program of activity in the given situation. The number of deputies present is increasing daily. Deputies from Slovakia keep arriving. There are 196 deputies present, among them 47 from Slovakia.

When the committee deliberations ended, delegations of deputies were dispatched to industrial and agricultural enterprises and state institutions, and a delegation was sent to the Slovak National Council.

The Presidium of the National Assembly also evaluated the question of losses in the national economy. The damages caused by the occupation affect primarily our society. For this reason above all, the National Assembly Presidium repeats that it does not consider it a suitable solution to protest by strikes, since work stoppages can only hurt the economy.

Later, the National Assembly Presidium issued an instruction that all persons who would follow orders of the occupation units or orders other than those consistent with the laws of the Czechoslovak Socialist Republic or directives of legal state organs presented by the respective ministers should be dismissed from the prosecutor's offices.

From Zemedelske Noviny, *August 25, 1968*

Decision of the Czechoslovak Government: Viliam Salgovic Dismissed

In its Saturday morning session, the Government adopted the following decision: On the basis of a report by the Interior Minister on the activity of State Security and in view of the fact that Deputy Interior Minister Salgovic failed to present himself to the Government to report on his activities, the Government recalls him from the post of Deputy Minister until his activities can be investigated. All orders issued by him and measures taken by him since August 20 are hereby declared invalid. The Minister of Interior has personally assumed the direction of State Security.

From Rude Pravo, *August 25, 1968*

Order of the Minister of Interior

On the decision of the Czechoslovak Government of August 24, 1968, Deputy Interior Minister Colonel Viliam Salgovic has been relieved of his duties, and all decisions issued by him since August 20 contrary to the laws of the Czechoslovak Socialist Republic are invalid. In order to assure the performance of all tasks of the Ministry of Interior, I am personally assuming the direction of State Security.

1. I am recalling the chief of State Security of the Prague region, Bohumil Molnar, and am relieving him of his duties effective immediately. The interim chief of State Security for Prague will be appointed by the commander of the Regional Guard, National Security Corps in agreement with the Party organization.

2. I am recalling the deputy chief, second bureau, headquarters of State Security, Lieutenant Colonel Josef Rypl, and the chief of the seventh section and am relieving them of their duties effective immediately. The vacant posts will be filled by the commander of State Security headquarters in agreement with the Party organization.

I am also ordering the commander of State Security headquarters and his deputies to maintain an orderly performance of duties in accordance with the laws of the Czechoslovak Socialist Republic and with the Action Program of the Party and thus assure the restoration of a good reputation of all sectors of the Interior Ministry in harmony with post-January developments.

3. Cadre measures arbitrarily carried out since August 20 by the former Deputy Interior Minister Colonel Salgovic in the first administration of the Ministry of Interior are invalid. I order the duly appointed leading officials of the first administration to

resume their posts without delay and to assure an orderly performance of duties in this sector.

4. I order the commanders of State Security headquarters and administrations to request the respective military prosecutors to institute criminal proceedings against those State Security members who have committed punishable acts in connection with the forcible measures in our country. At this time, so grave for our nation, the Government of the Czechoslovak Socialist Republic appreciates the attitude and the self-sacrificing efforts of the members of the police. I call on all police as well as on members of all other units of the Interior Ministry to henceforth obey only the orders of their superiors in accordance with the laws of the Republic and with the instructions of the legal government of the Republic.

I order all police and workers of all units of National Security, in addition to the regular performance of their duties, to assist with every means and with all efforts the legal organs in assuring the accomplishment of all complex tasks in this extraordinary situation.

Josef Pavel,
Minister of Interior

From Prace, *August 26, 1968*

10:00 A.M.

Czechoslovak Radio reported that, in the morning hours, a rotation of the originally assigned forces of the occupation armies began.

In the Morning

The Presidium of the City Committee of the Communist Party met in Prague.

Report on the Meeting

The Presidium stated that one of the conditions of its normal activity is the freeing of a member of the newly elected Presidium of the Central Committee of the Communist Party and the leading secretary of the City Committee of Prague, Comrade

Bohumil Simon, from the internment in which he has been held since the arrival of occupation forces in Prague. In the course of the session, therefore, a delegation of the Presidium of the City Committee of Prague was dispatched to the Soviet Embassy with an urgent request that Comrade Simon be released and enabled to resume the direction of the Prague city organization.

The delegation was stopped by a cordon of Soviet military posts surrounding the Embassy building. When the delegation requested an interview with Soviet Ambassador Chervonenko, the Soviet attaché, A. M. Pershin, appeared in front of the building and told the delegation the following: The Soviet Embassy knows nothing about the internment of Comrade Simon. As an office of diplomatic representation, the Embassy is in no position to conduct a search for private persons, and it knows nothing about Simon's being held by military units. To the amazement of the entire delegation, he recommended that the delegation take its request to the Czechoslovak Public Security. The delegation nevertheless demanded that the Soviet Embassy undertake everything possible for the finding and freeing of Comrade Simon.

Shortly after the delegation returned to the City Committee's session, attaché Pershin telephoned and gave the Presidium the following information:

1. The Soviet Embassy is doing everything in order that Comrade Simon be found, released, and enabled to resume his duties.

2. He asked that Comrade Simon's family be assured that he is all right and told not to worry about him.

3. He promised that as soon as the Soviet Embassy receives additional information, he shall immediately inform the Presidium.

From Rude Pravo, *August 26, 1968*

Saturday Morning in Prague

There were military actions on Wenceslas Square, Old Town Square, Charles Square, near the radio building, in the vicinity of the Central Committee building, on the Smichov side of the Palacky Bridge, and near the Letna Tunnel, while smaller incidents took place in other locations. The following buildings are occupied: the City Committee, the Regional Committee, and the District Committees of the Party, the Czechoslovak State Bank and its branches in Prague districts 1 and 9, the Commercial Bank, and the Trades and Investment banks. The Main and Center Railroad stations are also occupied. Of the Post Office facilities, the occupiers have seized the City Telephone Center, the City Telegraph Center, the Central and City Communications Administration, and the City Telecommunications Administration. Editorial offices of Prague dailies and some printing houses, for example, the Svoboda enterprise, the Czechoslovak Press Agency, the Czechoslovak Academy of Sciences, the Writers Union, the Faculties of Philosophy and Law, and the Journalist Center. The Ministries of Interior, Foreign Affairs, Foreign Trade, and Defense and the Presidium of the Government are also occupied. Occupation units are also in the Pankrac Prison and in the radio and television buildings. All important communication links and bridges as well as the branches of the Benzina National Enterprise at the Ruzyne and Kbely airports are occupied.

From Lidova Demokracie, *5th special edition, August 24, 1968*

11:25 A.M.

Czechoslovak Radio broadcast a speech by acting Party First Secretary Venek Silhan. He thanks everyone for the support given to the Central Committee and to the Extraordinary Fourteenth Congress of the Party. He thanks all institutions that made available funds, communications, housing, and so on. The Central Committee is now expecting the return of the delegation from Moscow. President Svoboda has sent word from Moscow that, until the delegation returns, no measures should be taken that might make the Moscow negotiations more difficult.

In response to a reporter's question about the situation of the Party workers Silhan replies that most of those in Prague have reported for work under the new Party leadership. Almost all have placed themselves fully at the disposal of the newly elected Central Committee. A number of groups are already at work preparing analyses and propaganda materials. Discussing economic problems, Silhan explains that these extraordinary days will result in tremendous economic losses, which must be overcome. No one is going to give us anything. The grains, hops, and so on will have to be harvested. Some surveys of the harvest in the regions have already been made. We have lost a great deal, but at the same time we have gained something—the patriotism of the people.

11:45 A.M.

Czechoslovak Radio reported that three television antennas are being installed near the Soviet Embassy.

12:00 Noon

An announcement was made by the Office of the Prosecutor General and by the chief Military Prosecutor of the Czechoslovak Socialist Republic:

On the basis of reports, broadcast by the radio, about arrests of our citizens by State Security organs and about prisoners being released from the Pankrac Prison by Soviet organs, the Office of the Military Prosecutor has conducted an investigation and established that as of 12:00 noon on August 24, 1968, no member of the Czechoslovak armed forces had been arrested by members of military counterintelligence. Similarly, no member of military counterintelligence has witnessed any arrests of civilian citizens. A parallel investigation of State Security organs established no arrests of citizens of our state by official organs of State Security. It was established, however, that, in addition to the leading officials of the state, three leading officers of State Security, Lieutenant Colonel Jankrle, Lieutenant Colonel Formanek, and Major Pesek, were interned by organs of the Soviet command. The Office of the Military Prosecutor is taking steps for the release of these officers. Investigations in the Pankrac and Ruzyne prisons has established that, except for a few criminal elements, no citizen of ours has been placed in these jails. No one has been released, either, with the exception of persons whose term of punishment has expired.

From Free Czech news agency report number 26, August 27, 1968

12:10 P.M.

Czechoslovak Radio revealed that a report is being spread in Prague that Alexander Dubcek has been sentenced to death. It is probably a provocation aimed at inciting people to react violently against the occupiers, who could then massacre them.

12:20 P.M.

Czechoslovak Radio reported that the occupiers are searching all automobiles coming into Prague; they are looking for printed matter.

12:40 P.M.

Czechoslovak Radio reported that Soviet helicopters have been flying over Prague all morning looking for clandestine radio transmitters.

12:40 P.M.

Czechoslovak Radio reported that occupation commanders have made it possible for Viktor Pavlenda [a Slovak Party official] to communicate with Gustav Husak in Moscow. Husak said that he, along with Dubcek, intends to take part in the Congress of the Communist Party of Slovakia [scheduled for August 26]. Their return therefore should be soon.

1:10 P.M.

Czechoslovak Radio reported that a helicopter is continuously flying over Prague dropping leaflets with the proclamation issued by the five governments.

1:30 P.M.

Czechoslovak Radio started broadcasting in "relays." Regional stations came on the air in a regulated sequence.

Shortly After Noon

On Saturday, after lunch, the Czechoslovak Government received the following information from Moscow: President of the Republic Ludvik Svoboda and the delegation reportedly consider the negotiations thus far as constructive, with the prospect of a mutually acceptable solution. The President of the Republic and the delegation are demanding the release of interned officials so that they may fully perform their duties and restore the activity of constitutional organs. The other side is reportedly accepting this with understanding. Further details would be premature at this hour.

From Mlada Fronta, *2nd special edition, August 25, 1968*

1:50 P.M.

Czechoslovak Radio reported a shooting this morning on the Liben Bridge between members of the Bulgarian and Soviet armies.

Afternoon

An interview was held with Zdenek Hejzlar, a new member of the Presidium of the Central Committee:

Question: How do you evaluate the situation and the mood of the people at this moment?

Answer: First of all, I see an almost total unity in evaluating the tragic situation in which our country has found itself as a result of the occupation. Our people are unequivocally condemning this occupation, which only a wholly incredible hypocrisy can represent as assistance by fraternal countries, and they leave no one in doubt as to their attitude. The very fact that it has not been possible to form a collaborationist party or state grouping and that therefore the declaration of the "allies" about somebody having invited them into our country is clearly revealed as an untruth is an irrefutable proof of this. The attitude of our people is marked by deep indignation over the violation of sovereignty and brutal intervention in the internal affairs of the country. Naturally, in the attitude of total resistance against the occupation, there occasionally appear some nervous, extremist views that do not always proceed from a sense of the reality of this day, whether they are, for instance, well-meant attempts at mass rallies or demonstrations or even certain political slogans; but such extreme appearances are not dominant. It is of course necessary to warn against them, because they sharpen internal tensions and then lead to dangerous clashes with occupation forces, causing needless losses in matériel and lives.

Question: What is going to happen with the comrades who have been interned?

Answer: The freeing of the illegally interned state and Party officials, their return to their duties and the free exercise of these duties, as well as an immediate restoration of freedom to all state and Party organisms, are, in my opinion, pre-conditions to any further negotiations. No one can at this time speak on behalf of Czechoslovakia without Dubcek, Svoboda, Cernik, and Smrkovsky, because the people will not recognize any other representatives.

Question: What is most encouraging at this moment?

Answer: I believe that it is the determination of our people to achieve full sovereignty for their state again. Liquidating the current state of affairs, however, is not going to be a simple or short-term affair; it is going to require considerable discipline and awareness among the ranks of our citizens. It is probably not going to be as simple as people would wish or as our sense of justice would require.

Question: What else would you like to say to the people?

Answer: That they should believe that it is unthinkable that, in the twentieth century, in Europe, and in a country such as ours, an occupation regime can be established in the name of socialism. The events within the Party, especially those surrounding the Extraordinary Fourteenth Party Congress, are in my opinion historic events. The Party is thereby completing the post-January stage of an absolute break with Stalinism and progressing to a really Czechoslovak socialist policy. If, despite the tremendous complexity of the situation, the new Central Committee can maintain the position of the Party at the head of the people that has been achieved since January, it has the possibility of creating a really new, popular, and democratic policy to a degree unmatched by any other Communist Party anywhere.

Question: Do you believe that non-Party people are passing the test of civic maturity in their relationship to the Party?

Answer: Undoubtedly. This tremendous identification of the

Party and the people and the fact that, at this moment, there are no differences between Party members and non-Party people is proof of it. I believe that Party organizations should, without delay, start accepting new Party members, particularly from among the young people, that they should be accepting, without any formalities, all those who want to join the Party of Dubcek, Cernik, Smrkovsky, and others whose names they have written on their banners. The Party should remember that what it needs in all its organizations is to recruit all those who are today fighting for state sovereignty and for a uniquely Czechoslovak brand of socialism.

Question: Is it not against Party statutes to recruit new members "on the spot?"

Answer: I believe that an extraordinary situation calls for extraordinary measures.

From Zemedelske Noviny, *August 25, 1968*

2 P.M.

Czechoslovak Radio reported that the Presidium of the Central Committee requests that this report be transmitted: The Presidium, in agreement with the views of those Slovak delegates who have not been prevented by the occupation forces from attending the Extraordinary Fourteenth Party Congress, asks all Slovaks not to yield to disorienting reports about a postponement of the Slovak Communist Party Congress. It is considered important that the Slovak Party Congress take place under any circumstances and without delay.

3:20 P.M.

Czechoslovak Radio broadcast a report by Viktor Pavlenda on his telephone talk with Gustav Husak [in Moscow]: They are proceeding in the spirit of the mandate of the Slovak Communist Party Presidium. They are striving for an honorable solution dictated by reason and by the interest of our nations. He requests that we support their efforts by our common sense. They shall return tomorrow (that is, today, Pavlenda adds) with good results.

3:25 P.M.

A transmitter of the Central Committee broadcast an appeal to all organs of the People's Militia in Czechoslovakia: Whereas it is necessary to make certain that the People's Militia shall not be misused against the interests of the Czechoslovak working people, the Presidium of the Communist Party Central Committee and the main staff of the People's Militia are issuing the following instructions for all units and staffs of the People's Militia. For the time being, perform your tasks in civilian clothes. Maintain continuous close contact with your Party organs and follow exclusively the instructions issued by them.

In the Afternoon

The First Press Conference of Our Government—Under Gun Barrels

The Government Presidium building is blockaded, tank guns are aiming at the building from all sides, guns stand in firing positions in the little park at Klarov. The Government Presidium is blockaded, but the Government is functioning. Twenty-two ministers meet, hold discussions, make decisions, report to the parliament on their activity, maintain contact with the new Party leadership. Since Thursday, our Government has exercised some presidential powers, too, since the President is outside of the territory of the Czechoslovak Socialist Republic. His stay [in Moscow] is being extended. People are getting concerned, and newsmen are clamoring for information. And so, on Saturday afternoon, the first press conference took place, literally under gun barrels. The informants are Ministers Vaclav Vales and Stanislav Razl. Some answers: Because of the situation, the Government is actually functioning as a real government rather than merely directing individual departments. If this style of work could be carried over to normal times, it would be marvelous. The Internal Trade Minister, Oldrich Pavlovsky, attended only one of the meetings. On Thursday, he excused himself because of his wife's illness. On Friday, without an excuse, he failed to appear. Internal Trade is thus under the direction of the first

Deputy Minister. One member of the Government is in constant contact with the parliament; sometimes he even sleeps there. Minister Peter Colotka is in Bratislava, which is very expedient these days since it assures contact with Slovakia. Members of the Government are firm in their attitude. No one has retreated from the adopted positions. Josef Pavel has not been arrested; on the contrary, he has also taken over the State Security sector, which was run until now by his deputy Salgovic, who cannot be reached at present and has been relieved of his duties. Members of Security in Prague are behaving splendidly. The Prosecutor General has been attending the Government sessions since Friday. He reports that since Tuesday no one has been arrested for political reasons, and it is untrue that the occupation forces have released some people from the Pankrac Prison. On the most important matter [negotiations in Moscow], unfortunately, information is scanty. A reliable communication link has been assured through our Ministry of Foreign Affairs, and mildly optimistic reports are coming in from Moscow. But it is clear to everybody that the talks are tremendously difficult. Jan Piller, Vasil Bilak, and Alois Indra are not part of the official Government delegation in Moscow. The Government does not know who delegated them. No information has been received through official channels as to whether anyone else has joined the delegation on the spot, and it is not known whether the reports about comrades Dubcek and Cernik taking part in the negotiations are true. The Ministers would like to believe it is so, as they would like to believe the announcement that Dubcek is going to attend the extraordinary Congress of the Communist Party of Slovakia. The occupation forces tried to negotiate with the Lord Mayor of Prague, but he refused to see them. The Government hopes that the President will return soon. Should the agreement be intolerable or humiliating for us, should the Government reject it or should it abdicate, there is no choice but to face the prospect of an occupation regime.

From Politika, *No. 2, August 26, 1968*

3:35 P.M.

Czechoslovak Radio reported that the telephone center was occupied yesterday, and the *Rude Pravo* building was shot at. On the night of August 23–24, members of occupation forces were tearing down posters and, under the protection of armored transport vehicles, were putting up the proclamation of governments participating in the occupation of our Republic. In the first two days—that is, on August 21 and 22—there were 307 wounded and 18 dead in Prague. Of that number, 10 died in hospitals. Big industrial enterprises are not functioning, but today, Saturday, part of their work force has reported for work. Food-supply enterprises are functioning, but bakeries and dairies are asking for volunteers for the second and third shifts. The situation in the supply of meat and fats is worse. In the outlying districts, agricultural cooperatives are helping by bringing in potatoes. There are cases of occupation forces confiscating food supplies that are being distributed. Production enterprises furnish means of transportation for the distribution of food. According to an agreement with the occupation forces, it will be possible to transport food supplies at night, but the vehicles will have to be marked accordingly. City transportation was also restored yesterday. This morning, streetcars were already providing transportation in the center of the city.

Report on the Situation in Prague

Prague changed overnight. The occupiers were tearing down slogans, posters, and appeals to the citizens. To no avail! New ones were up by morning. Prague is like one huge poster. "Occupiers go home!" And still another change occurred in Prague during the night. On the suggestion of Czechoslovak Radio, all street and building signs were torn down. Instead, inscriptions appeared on walls: Dubcek Avenue and the like. Such inscriptions can also be seen on a main thoroughfare in Liben. Prague has simply been transformed into Dubcek Avenues. Let the occupiers, traitors, and collaborationists find their way! They have signs to guide them! In the vicinity of the Soviet Embassy, in Pod Kastany Street, a Soviet tank recklessly rammed a small passenger car full of people, totally demolishing its front section. The passengers of the car were seriously injured in the collision. Newly pressed phonograph records with the statement of the Extraordinary Fourteenth Party Congress were already available in Prague on Saturday morning. According to a report from Prague hospitals, 328 Czechoslovak citizens have been treated so far, 8 of whom have succumbed to their injuries. Most of the injuries were gunshot wounds.

From Svoboda, August 25, 1968

In the Afternoon

The commander of the occupation forces in the city ordered a curfew between 10 P.M. and 5 A.M.:

Order of the Soviet Military Commander of Prague and the Central Bohemian Region No. 3

Anti-socialist forces are trying to disturb normal life in Prague and create complications in the city, aiming at fomenting nationalist passions and hostile activity against the fraternal nations who have come to aid the people of Czechoslovakia. Hostile counterrevolutionary elements that are trying to sharpen the conflict at any price are resorting to dangerous and provocative actions and are committing grave crimes. Members of the Soviet Army have been murdered and tanks set on fire. Diversionists are trying to disturb communications, transportation, and the food supply for the population. In order to stop the provocative action, I order the commanders of army groups and their detachments to take the most decisive measures against persons who attempt to attack members of the allied armies.

During the Day

Yesterday, the Central Committee Presidium held talks with members of the Government Bohumil Sucharda, Vladimir Kadlec and Miroslav Galuska. A complete identity of views was reaffirmed in this session. Similar talks took place with representatives of the National Assembly, which is in continuous session and where almost two hundred deputies are present by now. [Former Minister of Agriculture] Karel Mestek, described in posters in Prague streets as an outright collaborationist and traitor, sent a letter to the National Assembly dissociating himself from the occupiers. Mestek writes in his letter that he will retain his dissenting opinions, because of which he did not sign the first National Assembly proclamation, but that he opposes the occupation. This statement can be regarded as a sign of a split among the collaborationist forces.

The Central Committee Presidium calls on the workers to think it over well before they decide to strike. Strikes must have a well-thought-out political character if they are to have effect in the public opinion. Strikes that only result in economic losses have no political impact, and the occupiers don't mind them.

The Presidium further stated that the work of the Party apparatus is being consolidated under the leadership of Martin Vaculik, who has the full confidence of the Presidium.

Reliable reports were received from Bratislava that the traitor Salgovic, the former Deputy Minister of Interior, had been seen there accompanied by members of the Soviet secret police.

The occupiers threaten to take over the railroads if they do not operate properly. They also threaten to paralyze our army unless it behaves as an inseparable part of the Warsaw Pact. Our position is that the railroads must serve our needs. As far as the army is concerned, it too is subject exclusively to Czechoslovak legal organs and is guided solely by the interests of our people.

To inquiries from the public as to why General Vaclav Prchlik [1] is not a member of the new Central Committee [chosen by the Extraordinary Fourteenth Party Congress], we can announce that General Prchlik enjoys the full confidence of the Party leadership. The Extraordinary Fourteenth Party Congress has not ended, and General Prchlik is one of the first candidates in the event that the Central Committee is further augmented.

From Zemedelske Noviny, *August 25, 1968*

Scenes from the Streets of Prague

An occupation vehicle is being driven through Sokolovska Street, and an officer is throwing out little leaflets. He turns

---

[1] Early in the summer, Prchlik—head of the Communist Party's Defense and Security Affairs Committee—was denounced by the Kremlin for his open criticism of the Warsaw Pact command structure. In July, as a concession to Moscow, Prchlik was dismissed from his post.

around, waiting to see if anyone will pick them up. Some people do pick them up, but, rather than read them, they burn them. The vehicle drives on.

❖   ❖   ❖

There is a long queue in front of a food store on Dejvice Square. An old automobile drives by. A large bundle of freedom newspapers flies out of the window. The queue surges forward. In an instant, everybody is reading. A car belonging to the occupiers stands nearby. Suddenly it starts moving, and the officer in the back seat also throws newspapers at the people in the queue. The people tear them up, trample them, throw them into garbage cans.

❖   ❖   ❖

In front of the National Assembly building, two Russian soldiers behind their tanks. Dirty, tired, maybe hungry, too. An elderly gentleman passing by started talking to them. He said he used to know some of the brave Russians who had brought freedom to Prague in 1945. "We used to invite them to our homes, we gave them food, we did all we could for them. But we don't want you! You have come uninvited, unwelcome!" The soldiers don't know how to reply anymore; maybe they too would rather be in their own home town, asleep in their own beds. Will it be soon?

From Prace, *special edition, August 24, 1968*

6:40 P.M.

The continuing extraordinary eighty-fifth session of the National Assembly Presidium resumed (recessed at 7:28 P.M.).

7:30 P.M.

The continuing extraordinary twenty-sixth session of the National Assembly resumed (recessed at 8:30 P.M.). Present were 179 deputies.

The session of the National Assembly has lasted for four days already. The National Assembly building is surrounded by foreign troops, but the deputies are not leaving; they have imposed on themselves a house arrest. Acting on the summons by the Presidium, almost two hundred deputies from all over the Republic have reported in, a fifth of them from Slovakia and an almost two-thirds majority guarantees the validity of any decision. The session is taking place in a hall that is not very large, so that all deputies cannot get in, many of them filling the adjacent corridor. Telephone conversations are usually conducted on a first-name basis because the lines may be tapped. On the first night, the deputies slept on the floor of their offices; for the following nights, they were able to get blankets and, more important, field cots for the women. Machine gun salvoes rattle under the windows of the National Assembly building at night. Supplies in the dining room are satisfactory, but deputies from distant places have problems with their laundry. The men have solved the shaving problem by pooling the available razors. Information about what's going on in the Republic and in the world is provided mainly by transistor radios and by special editions of newspapers and magazines.

Neither the gun barrels aimed at the National Assembly windows nor the threat of arrest will force the deputies to capitulate. The permanent session is to continue until some solution to the aggression is found. Resolutions of confidence are piling up on the Presidium tables.

From Politika, *No. 2, August 26, 1968*

10:45 P.M.

Czechoslovak Radio broadcast the following message from the President of the Republic [who was still in Moscow]:

Dear Fellow Citizens:

First of all, I want to ask all of you to accept heartfelt greetings from all the comrades accompanying me. I told you before my departure that I expected to return that same evening and to report to you on the results of the negotiations. I want you to know that I would not stay one minute longer in these difficult moments if it was not urgently required in the interest of our socialist republic. Immediately after our arrival in the Kremlin, we started our discussions with the leading representatives of the Soviet Union. We considered it essential that comrades Dubcek, Cernik, and Smrkovsky should also take part in our negotiations. I can announce to you that these comrades are already, along with us, taking part in the preparations for further negotiations. And that is also the reason we have extended our stay in Moscow. I am turning to you again, dear fellow citizens, in my own name, in the name of comrades Dubcek, Cernik, Smrkovsky, and the other comrades present here, with a request to remain calm, thoughtful, and confident. Go responsibly about your work in the factories, in the fields, in all places of work. Such a loyal attitude on your part will be the best support you can give us in our further negotiations.

> Ludvik Svoboda,
> President of the Czechoslovak Socialist Republic

Statements of August 24, 1968

Proclamation of the Presidium of the Central Trade Union Council to All Workers

The Presidium of the Central Trade Union Council expresses its total support for the President of the Republic Ludvik Svoboda, for the Cernik Government, for the National Assembly and the National Front headed by comrades Smrkovsky and Kriegel.

The Presidium also supports the Central Committee of the Communist Party of Czechoslovakia headed by Comrade Dubcek. It demands with the utmost determination that the constitutional officials and the duly elected Central Committee of the Communist Party of Czechoslovakia be allowed to resume their activity and that peaceful life in our country be restored as soon as possible—without the presence of the occupation forces.

Appeal of the Presidium of the Central Council of Czechoslovak Trade Unions to Aleksandr Shelepin

Esteemed Comrade Shelepin:

We are turning to you, the Chairman of the All-Union Central Council of Soviet Trade Unions, in the gravest hour of our nation.

In the night of August 20 to 21, 1968, our country was, without reason and without the knowledge or assent of the President of the Republic, the Government, the National Assembly, or the Central Committee of the Communist Party of Czechoslovakia, occupied by the military forces of the Soviet Union, the German Democratic Republic, the Bulgarian People's Republic, the Polish People's Republic, and the Hungarian People's Republic. It happened at a time when all our people firmly believed in the assurances of Soviet statesmen, given at Cierna nad Tisou and at Bratislava, that the sovereignty of our socialist state is fully guaranteed. However, a tragic mistake occurred: events took place that could have unforeseen effects on the international workers movement, the world of socialism and Communism, on the friendly and fraternal relations of our peoples.

That is why, in this grave hour for our country, we are turning to you and, through you, to the Soviet trade unionists and to the workers of the Soviet Union with an urgent appeal: Demand an immediate withdrawal of the Soviet Army and of the forces of the German Democratic Republic, the Polish People's Republic, the Bulgarian People's Republic, and the Hungarian People's Republic from the territory of the Czechoslovak Socialist Republic, so that our constitutional officials, duly elected by the will of the people, can resume their posts and the affairs of our nations revert to their own hands!

Declaration by the University Committee of the Communist Party

On behalf of the Communist Party organizations of the universities in Prague, we solemnly declare that we fully support the decisions of the Extraordinary Fourteenth Congress of the Party and the new Central Committee elected by the Congress. We categorically demand that comrades Dubcek, Cernik, Smrkovsky, Spacek, Kriegel, Simon, and the other interned comrades be immediately allowed to resume their Party and constitutional offices and to exercise their duties without interference. We firmly support the President of the Republic, Comrade Svoboda. We refuse to recognize any other officials, imposed by anybody or self-appointed, and we shall not follow their instructions or statements. We demand that the occupation forces of the Warsaw Pact armies immediately leave the territory of the Czechoslovak Socialist Republic.

From Student, 3rd special edition, August 25, 1968

The Soviet Union Doesn't Belong in the Olympics

The forcible occupation of Czechoslovakia is so utterly contrary to the humanitarian mission of the Olympic idea that the Soviet Union has lost any right to participate in the nineteenth Olympic Games in Mexico.

Emil Zatopek,
Meritorious Sports Champion

From Rude Pravo, August 24, 1968

To the Citizens of Free Socialist Czechoslovakia

Remain calm and prudent. Our only weapon is the strength of ideas. Our weapon is the conviction that truth shall prevail. Today and in the future, under whatever circumstances, refuse to support any attempts of the occupiers to form traitorous institutions in this state. You hear nothing, you see nothing, you know nothing, you say nothing. Help each other and stand together. Ostracize the traitors, ostracize their families. Do not help them.

We have no way of communicating with you. The building of our union has been seized by the occupation forces. The workers of our editorial offices have been dispersed. Therefore we ask anyone who can use a typewriter: Make copies of this brief leaflet and distribute them among the people.

Union of Czech Journalists

From an undated printed leaflet, probably August 24, 1968

A Commentary of the Day

Should we trust [Presidium member] Jan Piller?

He was against the convocation of the Extraordinary Fourteenth Party Congress. He did not show up at the Congress. In the Presidium, on that critical night before the occupation, he failed to adopt a decisive position. But let us also consider this: He sent word to the Congress that he was negotiating for the release of Comrade Svoboda and others. And he went to Moscow with the President. But Alois Indra went too.

Should we trust Comrade Piller, or should we not?

As of now, we are not accusing him of treason. But of temporizing, yes. Therefore we shall reserve our attitude. If he proves us wrong with his deeds, we shall be glad to apologize.

From Svoboda, *August 24, 1968*

A Strange Occupation

I think this is the most peculiar occupation ever known in history—an occupation in which so many occupation soldiers have tears of sorrow and shame on their faces. I personally witnessed a scene in Opletalova Street in which a tank crew refused to obey an officer's order to disperse a crowd of people. I saw how a young soldier started to cry when an old woman asked him: "Does your mother know that you, her son, have murdered peaceful people?" However, let us not think, because of such episodes, that the occupation soldiers would somehow hesitate if they were ordered to start firing at us with all their weapons. Certainly not; for a soldier, an order is an order. And so, let us just show them again and again that they are unwelcome guests here, that they are our enemies, maybe our mortal enemies, today. Therefore, let them eat only what they brought along themselves; let us give them nothing to drink, let us not show, even by the slightest gesture, any momentary pity over their situation.

From Czechoslovak Radio, August 24, 1968

The Political Fiasco of the Occupation

The occupation of the Czechoslovak Socialist Republic by the armies of five Warsaw Pact countries has entered its fourth day, and although we are still unable to judge all its aspects and consequences at this moment, some partial conclusions can be drawn.

The military intention of the occupying powers has been accomplished, but the same cannot be said of the political side of
the matter. Every occupation force needs a domestic political
force to appear in its support at the moment of the military
intervention. Three full days have passed since the day of the
occupation. But to this day the occupation powers have been
unable to announce the names of the "leading politicians" who
allegedly invited them in this country. It is a total political fiasco.

From Lidova Demokracie, *5th special edition, August 24, 1968*

"Brothers" with Peasant Faces

On the twenty-fourth, at a quarter to ten in the evening, a submachine gun salvo sounded in Podoli, in front of the waterworks,
which has been held by Russian soldiers ever since the beginning
of the occupation. In a little while, a boy with blood all over his
body ran into the nearby inn and collapsed there. On the road
near the waterworks, a car was standing. In it were two other
boys in a puddle of blood. When Public Security reached the
spot, the car was already empty, and eyewitnesses were only
able to say that the wounded had been taken to the Thomayer
Hospital, that the car had been hit by shots fired by one of the
occupiers patrolling the road, and that the name of the boy who
collapsed in the restaurant was Karel Sarka.

The Public Security commander and his men went to the waterworks. At first, the Russians didn't want to let him in. Then one
of the occupation soldiers aimed an automatic at his back and
led him through a cordon of armed men to his commander. Still
under the barrels of their guns, our commander started his investigation. He learned that, allegedly, the guard on the road had
attempted to stop a car of the Zuk type by waving a lighted
flashlight but that the driver had reacted by increasing his speed
and switching on the high beams. Supposedly, only four shots
had been fired, and the car had gone on for several dozen yards
before it stopped against a pile of gravel. The two boys who had
remained in the car after Sarka's departure had been searched,
and the occupation officer said he had some documents in his
hands proving that the passengers of the car had harbored coun-

terrevolutionary intentions. However, he refused to hand over the documents. He also refused to give his name to our commander or the name of the man who had fired the shots. With that, the hearing ended, and our commander was led outside, again under the barrels of the Russian automatics.

The two boys who had remained in the car after the shooting died on their way to Thomayer Hospital. Karel Sarka survived with wounds on both hands. Before he was operated on, he was able to tell our policemen that the two dead boys had not been distributing leaflets with him but that he had only picked them up on his way. He himself had borrowed the automobile from the Podoli ice depot and had been on his way back with it. The police were permitted to continue to investigate the case, but only because it was registered as car theft.

I saw the car. It had been towed to the ice depot. It stands there, covered with a tarpaulin. The first thing I noticed was the tires. They were full of air, not shot through. Obviously, the occupiers did not even try to stop the car; they just went ahead with murder. Their version about trying to stop the car by waving a lighted flashlight seems dubious too, for the shots came from in front of the car. The windshield is gone. On the front seats and under the pedals are little crystals of glass and blood. The autopsy of the bodies showed how the boys were shot: first from in front, then from the left side, and finally from the back. One of the dead boys was hit twice in the chest; the other one was hit directly in the eye. The rifleman aimed well and had no scruples. He obviously did not mind that he was killing children. Too bad that he could not read the blood-drenched leaflet left on the floor of the car. I know that there are outspoken leaflets to be seen in Prague, but this one spoke about the spring, about kisses and flowers and peace. The first of the dead boys was seventeen. He was blond, around 5 feet 9 inches tall; he wore a knit jacket with a black leather front, a blue shirt, dark pin-stripe trousers, black underpants, and dark sandals, one of which was left in the bloodied car. The other boy, hit in the eye, was about fifteen, blond, thin, about 5 feet 6 inches tall, wearing a pair of blue jeans manufactured in Czechoslovakia and a dark plaid sweater. In his pockets were found a Japanese-made pencil, five keys with a Yugo-auto pendant. A one-peso Uruguayan bank note was found on his body.

World, tremble with helpless terror, with desperate anger, with revulsion and shame for murders! In Prague and in Czechoslovakia, they are shooting at children! They are murdering children! Let us remember: All the dead, all the wounded, all of them, all are victims of the occupiers! They would not have died, they would not have been wounded, if we had not been occupied! The right is on our side! It is our right to do anything and everything, literally everything, to show our resistance. And if we are being reasonable and not doing everything, that is our business our prudence! But we cannot and must not admit, by a me thought, by a single word, that someone is to blame for his own death. Then we could go right ahead and say that the citizens of Prague who fell during the May Revolution were fools and that no one would have been hurt if they had only let the Germans alone. Prudence and common sense are good weapons, but they can also be, and sometimes are, expressions of fear. Let us separate the one from the other! Let us realize that we are afraid, let us realize it and admit it. There is nothing wrong in that. The greater will be our courage then and the clearer our reasoning.

They are the occupiers, and they are shooting at us. No one has invited them, and they are nothing but murderers. Murderers of defenseless children! Shame on them!

From Literarni Listy, *special edition, August 28, 1968*

Statement by Frantisek Graus

There are always moments in history when every man must decide how to behave and whether he is ready and willing to defend, with his whole self, justice against despotism, humanity against brutality. One can perhaps resist anything, escape anything, except one's own conscience; that is something a worthy man can never escape, and it will mercilessly condemn everyone who would collaborate. If it seems for a moment that brute force can prevail, it is a passing impression. Never yet has it been possible to silence truth permanently, to stop evolution, even when the mightiest occupiers tried it with the most brutal means. I shall never recognize any occupation of the Czechoslovak Socialist Republic, any injustice, or backwardness. I fully support the Extraordinary Fourteenth Congress of the Communist Party, our legal Government, and its authorized representatives.

> Frantisek Graus, Ph.D.
> Ordinary Professor, Faculty of Philosophy, Charles University; Corresponding Member of the Czechoslovak Academy of Sciences

From Czechoslovak Historical Magazine, *special issue, August 24, 1968*

The Fourth Day

Today, Saturday, August 24, is the fourth day of the occupation.

What have the occupiers succeeded in? Breaking the world Communist movement. Breaking Czechoslovak-Soviet friendship. Turning world public opinion against themselves.

What have the occupiers failed in? Breaking and crushing the Czech and Slovak people. Finding a sufficient number of collaborationists and traitors who would be willing to serve.

> Staff of the Czechoslovak News Agency

From Free Czechoslovak News Agency reports, August 24, 1968

Politics

Leonid Brezhnev, you were supposed to have been a worker once. Today you have lived to see the day when it can be written: Brezhnev is Hitler. When did you cease to be an honest man? Was it at that dizzying moment when your fingers touched power, when you smelled its aroma and it was yours, when you reached for a whip and it started moving by itself, when you said a word and people started to move?

When did you cease to be an honest man? Was it at that time or was it only at the moment when you committed the act that so many times since the beginning of the world has been ascribed to Judas?

It may not matter to you, but somewhere in Europe there are several million people who hate you!

From Student, *2nd special edition, August 24, 1968*

6

SUNDAY, AUGUST 25

In the Night of August 24–25

The Soviet occupiers, using force, entered the building of the Ministry of Transport on Prikopy Street in Prague. They were purportedly looking for arms, but in fact they were destroying technical equipment. They shot and wounded Comrade Kolda, who was on duty at that time. Another employee succeeded in escaping. Kolda, who almost bled to death, was taken to the Bulovka Hospital.

Czechoslovak Radio reported that members of the Soviet State Security entered the building of the Czechoslovak Ministry of Foreign Affairs in Prague. Covered by a strong military occupation unit, they searched all offices, so that at this moment the Ministry of Foreign Affairs is unable properly to carry out its function.

2:30 A.M.

The continuing extraordinary eighty-fifth session of the National Assembly Presidium resumes.

Declaration of the Presidium of the Central Committee of the Communist Party of Czechoslovakia

Comrades:

Last January, after many years, our Party obtained new leadership, accepted its Action Program, and launched a policy that has been supported by a vast majority of the people. We began to try to bring about a socialism that would truly have a humane face, as Comrade Dubcek has repeatedly said.

Today, our fatherland is occupied by the armies of certain Warsaw Pact members. The blood of the Czech and Slovak people was needlessly shed. Tanks are now blocking the road to the policy by which we wished to strengthen socialism. What must Communists do today in order to be able in the future to continue the policy that began in January?

Comrades, let us put aside all that has been dividing us. Let us put aside petty disputes. Let us concentrate all the efforts of all Communists on the main problems of today:

1. Let us demand without delay that comrades Dubcek, Cernik, Smrkovsky, Kriegel, Spacek, and Simon assume their posts in the Government, the Party, and the National Front.

2. Let us not recognize as a representative of the Party anyone who does not have a democratic mandate for his post. In the central organs of the Communist Party, this means anyone who has not been given a mandate by the Extraordinary Fourteenth Congress of the Party.

3. Let us demand a complete departure of the foreign armies of the Warsaw Pact, which is being violated by the presence of the armies on the territory of the Czechoslovak Socialist Republic.

4. Let us warn against any provocation. The blood of our people is most precious property, and anything that might lead to its needless shedding must be effectively prevented.

5. Do not leave the ranks of the Communist Party even if the worst happens, even if brutal force were used to suppress all that is guaranteed by our Constitution, the laws of the Republic, and the by-laws of the Party. Let there be in the ranks of the Party the greatest possible number of honest people, for if the Party remains strong at the bottom, it will be able later to bring forth again capable political leaders who can lead our nation from the situation into which it was thrown by superior force.

Comrades, the alliance of socialist countries and the unity of the Communist and progressive movement in the whole world cannot be achieved through force but only through confidence, cooperation, and mutual assistance given where the socialist country or Communist Party really wishes it. It is in this sense that the leadership of the Party, mandated by the Extraordinary Fourteenth Party Congress, understands all the basic documents of the international workers movement, including the joint declaration of the six parties issued at Bratislava on August 4, 1968. This very declaration is, however, being violated by the armed action taken against our country by its other signatories.

It is a tragedy that, under the slogan of giving assistance to our Party, a situation was created that threatens to destroy all trust in socialism, in the Soviet Union, in the ideals of the Communist movement. Let us defend these ideals in the name of the movement. Let us do everything in our power not to lose the confidence of the people, so that socialism will continue in this country to be the product of voluntary activity.

From Rude Pravo, *August 25, 1968*

Interview with Czechoslovak Minister of Culture and Information Miroslav Galuska

Question: The world continues to be interested in knowing whether any Czechoslovak organ really did ask the Soviet Union for help.

Galuska: No help, especially no military help, was requested from the Soviet Union or any other of the states whose armies have occupied this country. I repeat again: The Government has declared that the occupation of Czechoslovakia is illegal.

From Rude Pravo, *August 25, 1968*

7:35 A.M.

The continuing extraordinary eighty-fifth session of the Presidium of the National Assembly resumed (adjourned at 8:12 A.M.). From the agenda: draft of a letter for the delegation to Moscow; a delegation appointed to take up the letter with the Presidium of the Central Committee and with the Government;

conditions in which the Government works; Soviet General Ivan Pavlovsky's failure to keep his promise.

From documents of the National Assembly

Morning Session of the Czechoslovak Government at Prague Castle

At its Sunday session, the Czechoslovak Government took note of the assertion of certain official news agencies of some socialist states that civilian cars with arms for the forces of counterrevolution are moving in the streets of Prague. The Government rejects this assertion and states that the purpose of the assertion is only to provide pretense for further reprisals of the occupation armies. The Government also takes note of the fact that so far the commander of the occupation forces has not kept the promise he gave to President Svoboda concerning the relinquishment of Government buildings and the securing of the activities of Government organs. In fact, during the night from August 24 to August 25, the occupiers entered ministries and Government buildings, disarming units of the People's Militia. With respect to the conduct of the occupiers, the Government instructed our Ministry of Foreign Affairs to lodge a protest with the occupation governments against their armies' behavior toward civilian population.

From Svoboda, *August 26, 1968*

Aide-Mémoire *of the Ministry of Foreign Affairs*

As instructed by the Government of the Czechoslovak Socialist Republic, the Ministry of Foreign Affairs hereby communicates to the Embassy of the Union of Soviet Socialist Republics the following:

The Government of the Czechoslovak Socialist Republic must state that so far the promise given to the President of the Republic Ludvik Svoboda by General of the Army Ivan Pavlovsky, commander of the armies that occupied the Czechoslovak Socialist Republic, has not been kept, the promise being that the disarming of Czechoslovak units would immediately stop, the areas where units of the Czechoslovak Army are stationed would be vacated, all towns and villages would also be vacated, and in cities units would be stationed only in parks and other places where they would not interfere with traffic. Further, according to this promise, the occupation and blocking off of buildings of all state organs of the Czechoslovak Socialist Republic and of all organs of the Party should have ceased immediately. The release of banks and all other buildings necessary for the normal economic activity of the country should have been effected and effective steps taken to achieve a situation in which the occupation forces are supplied only by their own means and from their own sources. It was promised at the same time that the occupation forces will avoid the use of arms against the population.

The Government of the Czechoslovak Socialist Republic must urge the fulfillment of the promises communicated directly to the President of the Republic, because failure to carry out these fundamental steps is conducive to increasing the atmosphere of tension for which the full responsibility cannot but be borne by the occupation forces.

A matter of particular concern is the fact that even the elementary principles of humaneness are still being ignored in dealings with the population, whose lives continue to be threatened.

The Government of the Czechoslovak Socialist Republic urgently and emphatically expects the steps in question to be taken without delay.

In the Morning

Czechoslovak Radio reported that a majority of the workers employed by CKD reported today for a shift that we call "Dubcek's Sunday." Office workers turned up, too, and when they have nothing to do in their offices, they help out where necessary. All plants and shops of CKD report calm and order; plants with all the important equipment are securely in our hands. Important posts are being manned continuously. Members of the People's Militia are on duty and stand guard over us.

9:45 A.M.

Czechoslovak Radio reported that, at 9:45 A.M. today, while on duty at Palacky Square, Sergeant Jaroslav Beran was detained by Soviet soldiers and taken away to an unknown place. The city headquarters of the Public Security protested against this illegal act, so far without result.

10:03 A.M.

The continuing extraordinary eighty-fifth session of the Presidium of the National Assembly resumed (adjourned at 10:48 A.M.). From the agenda: joint letter to the President of the Republic (recommended to be withheld from publication in Czechoslovakia for the time being); news about the situation in Prague and about the military-security arguments of the occupiers; news about talks with representatives of the Slovak National Council; meetings of National Assembly members from each province suggested.

From documents of the National Assembly

In the Course of the Morning

The open letter of the Chairman of the Czechoslovak Academy of Sciences, academician Frantisek Sorm, to the President of the Academy of Sciences of the Soviet Union, Mstislav Keldysh, was published.

Dear Comrade President:

This is the fifth day of the unwarranted, illegal, forceful occupation of our country by the armies of the five members of the Warsaw Pact. The occupation took place against the will of all our legitimate constitutional authorities, including the President of the Republic, the National Assembly, and the Government of the Czechoslovak Socialist Republic. The political, economic, and cultural life of our beloved country has been paralyzed and disrupted; the number of casualties of both dead and wounded Czechoslovak citizens, as well as immeasurable economic losses, mount daily. Both sides are becoming increasingly more nervous, and this may lead to a catastrophe of immense consequences.

The whole of our people was aghast and revolted by the occupation. This act of force, which is probably without parallel in the history of mankind, is being unequivocally rejected by our people. The people cannot see how an independent state—moreover, a socialist state—can be subjected, without any warning and against the will of all the people, to a military occupation by those whom they had presumed up to that point to be their true friends and allies. The sincere love and fraternal relationship of the Czech and Slovak people toward, especially, the people of the Soviet Union—feelings rooted in the traditions of centuries—are now being quickly transformed into feelings of sorrow and even hatred, which might last for decades or more. And not only that: We are observing with profound sadness how Soviet soldiers, young boys who do not know what is happening, do not understand the expressions of indifference and repugnance with which they are being received by all the people of our country. In their minds and hearts, too, are growing feelings that will have a long-term impact on the relationship between our nations.

I would like you, Comrade President, to realize that the information about the situation in our country, and especially about the position of both the nations in this country, that is being given to the Soviet public is quite erroneous and does not correspond to the truth. The military occupation has unified all our people, regardless of their political opinions, into a monolithic whole that rejects the occupation quite spontaneously. As an indication of this unity, the National Assembly, which was properly elected in 1964, has been in continuous session under inconceivably difficult conditions since the beginning of the occupation. In spite of these harrowing conditions, the session is attended by two thirds of that body. They have unanimously condemned the occupation as an act of force and demand an immediate departure of the occupation armies, as well as the release of all interned representatives of the Government, the Party, and the National Assembly.

The occupation has had a painful effect on our sciences, too. The building of the Czechoslovak Academy of Sciences, where you, among others, were received as our guest of honor, was needlessly occupied by the Soviet Army; the members of the Academy and the employees who were in the building were driven out under the muzzles of submachine guns. Our schools of higher education are also under military occupation.

Dear Comrade President, I declare, with full responsibility as a member of the National Assembly, as a long-time member of the Party, as a public official, and as a scientist, that there was no danger of counterrevolution in our country and that we have always been strong enough to put down any excesses that might have occurred here. In the name of friendly relationships between the scientists of the Soviet Union and the scientists of my country, I am asking you to exert your influence so that our country can be rid of the shackles of occupation and continue building socialism here in the interest of all the countries of the socialist camp, as well as in the interest of the victory of socialist ideas in the whole world.

Frantisek Sorm

From documents of the Czechoslovak Academy of Sciences

10:56 A.M.

The continuing extraordinary twenty-sixth session of the National Assembly resumed (adjourned at 11:37 A.M.). Present were 193 members. The text of the letter to the President of the Republic was approved unanimously.

To the President of the Czechoslovak Socialist Republic Ludvik Svoboda, Moscow

Dear Comrade President:

The whole country and all our people, with full confidence in you, are eagerly and impatiently awaiting the results of your negotiations in Moscow.

We consider it necessary to provide you with information about the situation in the country since your departure.

Our people resolutely reject the occupation as illegal, unconstitutional, and groundless and demand the departure of the occupation armies.

The National Assembly and the Government of the Czechoslovak Socialist Republic are in continuing session under difficult conditions. They fully back the demands and opinion of the people. The Extraordinary Fourteenth Congress of the Communist Party elected a legitimate, new Central Committee and Presidium and, at the same time, expressed full confidence in comrades Dubcek, Smrkovsky, Cernik, Kriegel, Spacek, Simon, and others. The resolutions of the Congress are supported by the whole Party and all the people, as demonstrated by the hour-long general strike on August 23, 1968.

All the organs mentioned above have so far succeeded, with the aid of the means of communication, in maintaining a relative calm in the country—in spite of the fact that the editorial offices and printing shops of periodicals, as well as the radio and television, are occupied by foreign armies. Already two attempts have been made to occupy the transmitting station at the Ministry of Foreign Affairs, which is our only link with our embassies and other offices abroad and also our only link with you.

This is the situation in which our nation is now living through on this, the fifth day of the occupation. The tension continues to increase as a result of casualties and material losses. Taking Prague only, there have been about thirty dead and over three hundred wounded up to Saturday. The casualties are on our side. The neighborhood of Prague Radio is heavily damaged. Calm is being maintained and confrontations avoided only with the utmost effort. The activity of elected organs is being restrained, civil freedoms and rights are being emasculated. Arrests take place, and not a day or night passes without shooting being heard in the streets of Prague. The shooting is initiated on any pretense or excuse. During last night, the foreign armies searched all central offices. In some cases, arms of the People's Militia were confiscated, and in the building of the Ministry of Transport arms were used.

The occupation organs have so far failed in gaining the support and cooperation of the population. This failure heightens their nervousness. The National Assembly and other organs of the country possess evidence of acts of force. We emphasize that we do not consider it normal that there should be a lack of communication between ourselves and your delegation in Moscow about the contents of your negotiations in Moscow.

The economy falters. The difficulty of supplying the population increases. It is actually impossible to be out in the streets of Prague after 10 P.M. Public transportation does not work. Rail transport is disrupted. Air links are nonexistent. Import and export falters. The supplies of coal are approaching the minimum limit. All this is a consequence of the occupation regime.

A dangerous factor is the growing fatigue and nervous tension of the occupation armies and of our population. The tension on both sides has now increased as a result of the unforeseen extension of your stay and the stay of other officials out of the country.

Dear Comrade President, aware of the fact that no written report can fully portray the atmosphere in the cities and the spirit of the people and concluding from the reports of [the Soviet news agency] *Tass* that Soviet organs are being informed quite distortedly and unobjectively, we consider that a necessary pre-condition of your further negotiations is for you to be more fully and precisely informed about the real state of affairs.

We therefore recommend that information be given to you by a special consultative group composed of representatives of the Central Committee, the National Assembly, and the Government, whose presence in Moscow you could urgently request.

We are also submitting for your consideration the suggestion that your negotiations be interrupted temporarily and for a brief period and you return to Prague along with comrades Dubcek, Smrkovsky, and Cernik. You could use the short interval to become better acquainted with the situation and to consult with the appropriate organs.

We are sending to you, dear Comrade President, our cordial greetings and assurances of full confidence.

> J. Valo,
> Presidium of the National Assembly
>
> V. Silhan,
> Presidium of the Central Committee
>
> L. Strougal,
> Government of the Czechoslovak Socialist Republic

From documents of the National Assembly

After Noon

Czechoslovak Radio reported that, at 11:00 A.M., while crossing the Sverma Bridge, a truck of the Robur type was shot at. The ricocheting bullets wounded two boys. One of them, twenty years of age, was wounded seriously. The bullet entered the liver. He is being operated on at this moment. The other boy was wounded lightly. At Old Town Square, some boys were talking with Soviet soldiers. One of the officers started shouting at a boy and pulling him toward the statue of Jan Hus. The boy tried to resist and was subdued by a blow to the nape of the neck. He fell down and remained lying on the grass, and only at 12:45 was he released by the Soviet occupation soldiers.

At the morning meeting of the National Committee of Prague, liaison officers of the occupation armies stated that anyone caught writing slogans or putting up posters at night will be fired at.

Czechoslovak Radio reported that the Prague city headquarters of Public Security was occupied. Seven Soviet officers remained in the building.

12:10 P.M.

Czechoslovak Radio broadcast a notification to National Committees:

According to an order of the Minister of Defense, signed on his behalf by the chief of the General Staff, members of the Czechoslovak Army are to assist National Committees and other legal organs of the state. These organs may therefore call on the representatives of our army for assistance.

12:35 P.M.

Czechoslovak Radio broadcast a protest of the professors and students of Charles University against the occupation of the university.

12:40 P.M.

The continuing extraordinary eighty-fifth session of the Presidium of the National Assembly resumed (adjourned 1:32 P.M.).

The question of taking a stand on neutrality was discussed.

From documents of the National Assembly

12:50 P.M.

Czechoslovak Radio reported that this morning Soviet units confiscated the weapons of a unit of the People's Militia at the Higher Political School in Prague. The arms have been laid out in the yard, and the Soviet units are now photographing them. The pictures are evidently intended to serve as evidence of counterrevolutionary preparations in Czechoslovakia.

Time Not Given

Czechoslovak Radio reported that today the occupiers trucked away the arms from the armory of the People's Militia at the Central School of the Communist Party at Veleslavin. They also resolved to do the same thing this morning at 9:15 at the House of Electric Power Production at Narodny Street. The level of political education in the Soviet Army is attested to by a conversation a reporter had today with a group of freshly arrived Soviet soldiers and one officer. We are alleged to have two million anarchists in this country, and the Soviet troops will not go away until they eliminate them all—which is, after all, in our interest. When the reporter remarked that we have a right to our own freedom, she was answered as follows: You are dependent on us, we give you coal and oil. We liberated you, and that's something you cannot make up for—ever. And so far, just in the night from Friday to Saturday, you shot and killed seven of our soldiers.

Objections by the reporter to the effect that we could hardly have killed anyone with bare hands were answered by repeated references to the arms found near Sokolov.[1] Sokolov is the place name in the Republic that they know best of all.

[1] In July, the Soviet Union gave considerable publicity to an alleged "Sudeten revanchist" and "counterrevolutionary" cache of U.S.-made arms discovered at the Czech town of Sokolov near the West German border.

1:30 P.M.

Czechoslovak Radio broadcast news about the situation in the Pankrac Prison. Only those who have completed their sentences were released from the prison. The building is located in the so-called first zone of protection, so that the occupiers were not allowed to enter the area of the prison. Dangerous criminals were transferred to a place where there is no danger that they might be misused.

2:00 P.M.

Czechoslovak Radio reported that a train of the occupiers carrying jamming equipment was halted at Lysa nad Labem. The cargo is being reloaded into helicopters of the occupiers and transported to an unknown destination.

3:05 P.M.

Czechoslovak Radio reported that representatives of the Soviet State Security are trying to establish contact with organs of the military counterintelligence corps. They are asking their assistance, which, however, our people positively refuse to give. One of the latest specific cases is reported from the garrison at Mlada. Organs of the military counterintelligence corps refuse to talk with members of the Soviet State Security in the absence of witnesses. Always, when such talks take place, representatives of the political organs of the Czechoslovak People's Army are present.

Communiqué on the Saturday and Sunday Session of the Presidium of the City Committee of the National Front in Prague

The Presidium of the City Committee of the National Front in Prague associates itself fully with the thousands of declarations and resolutions issued by all the organizations of the National Front and insists on a full and free development of the activities of all legal political and state organs in the city, in the districts and places of work, without any limitations imposed by the occupation armies. We welcome the declaration of the Extraordinary Fourteenth Congress of the Communist Party, and we support fully the newly elected Central Committee and its Presidium headed by Alexander Dubcek. We insist on an immediate release of all the interned functionaries, including comrades Smrkovsky, Kriegel, Simon, and others. We appreciate greatly the brave and proud attitude and selflessness of all the Prague people, especially the youth and those who at this time unhesitatingly prove in a thousand ways their patriotism, their love for the capital city, their political maturity, and their heroism. We are communicating the greetings of the people of Prague to all who work in the mass communication media for providing us all the time with inexhaustible sources of moral strength.

There are indications, particularly a number of incidents last night, that the occupation regime in the city is becoming harsher —which is in contradiction to the assurances and promises given by the Soviet occupation command. This is causing us grave concern. In this connection, the City Committee of the National Front again calls on the citizens of Prague to retain discipline in the factories, transportation, commerce, and supplies. Even though the Soviet occupation organs state that no restrictions have been instituted in Prague, we are warning the citizens, in light of the events of last night, that they should leave the streets of the city between dusk and dawn and thus avoid exposing themselves to possible reprisals of the occupation armies. We are calling on the management of enterprises and on labor unions to adjust working hours in such a way that the employees would not be exposed to unnecessary risks on their way to and from work. Continue to secure the inviolability of your factories and shops and ensure undisrupted operation mainly in the enterprises of the food industry and in the supply organizations of the city.

We also call to your attention the fact that distributing leaflets, printed materials, and posters during the night involves a danger of severe reprisals by the occupation armies.

Continue to act toward the occupation armies as you have so far: Ignore them. Our chief weapons remain calmness, discipline, and levelheadedness.

From a mimeographed leaflet

4:14 P.M.

The continuing extraordinary eighty-fifth session of the Presidium of the National Assembly resumed (adjourned at 7:47 P.M.). The discussion of neutrality and of how to make the position on this matter public was continued. The telegram to the President of the Republic was approved. The internment of Bohumil Simon, member of the Czech National Council, was protested and the protest distributed to the Czechoslovak Radio. There was further discussion of the economic situation.

From documents of the National Assembly

Scenes from the Streets of Prague: A Sunday in August

The sun shines as if it wished to shake out the largest possible number of warming rays from its garments. It gilds the streets, the façades of buildings, the uneven surface of the river. Prague's first Sunday of the occupation.

The free, legal radio passes on news items like the baton of a relay-race to transmitters all over the country.

From time to time, the air is stirred up by the buzzing of a helicopter dropping the leaflets of the occupiers; rifle shots resound through the streets: sounds and noises that have no harmony with a Sunday's serenity. Exactly at noon, as if nothing had happened, the radio broadcasts the bells of a clock tower and a Sunday poem. But this poem is not one that was selected at random to suit a Sunday of serenity. It is a poem we heard many years ago. A poem by a great poet and an honorable Czech. A poem composed in the darkest times that rings true today. A warning and a challenge.

"Think of the hymn!" [2]

The Sunday goes on. The shop windows have been transformed into a huge public reading room, with graffiti, both serious and angry, posters, curt messages, notices, even humor.

Thank God, even humor. Rhymes and slogans that cheer up

---

[2] Probably the old Czech patriotic hymn that begins: "Do not fear the enemy, / Do not count their numbers."

the saddened faces of the passers-by. There is even laughter, and that is good, because laughter is a great thing. It shows that you're on top of the situation, that you have grasped its absurdity, that you don't get intimidated. Humor has unmasked half-truths and the hypocrisies of Pharisees, who kiss your cheek just before they betray you. Humor unmasked them just as surely as the "allied" gun on Wenceslas Square that hit Cechie, the symbol of Bohemia, on the ramp of the National Museum, directly in the heart.

From Zemedelske Noviny, *August 27, 1968*

6:00 P.M.

Czechoslovak Radio reported that leaflets signed by our representatives appeared in Prague. This is a fraud of the occupation armies!

6:03 P.M.

The continuing extraordinary twenty-sixth session of the National Assembly resumed (adjourned at 6:48 P.M.). A position on the demand for neutrality was approved.

From documents of the National Assembly

Statement of the National Assembly on Demands for Neutrality

The National Assembly again associates itself, as it already did in its resolutions of August 22 and 23, 1968, with the statement of the Government of April 28, 1968, and with the Action Program of the Communist Party, which unequivocally affirm Czechoslovakia's membership in the socialist community. A declaration of neutrality would be legally ineffective.

A unilateral declaration of a state's neutrality does not bind any other state to respect that neutrality. A permanent neutralization is possible only on the basis of agreements with all interested states. It follows clearly from this that any declaration of neutrality would have no legal validity and could not be carried out.

Explanation of the Position Taken

In today's divided world, neutrality is not a means to secure the sovereignty and independence of our socialist republic, notwithstanding the fact that a unilateral declaration of independence has no legal effect. Neutrality itself has never assured national and state sovereignty to any state. From the point of view of international law, a state's declaration of its neutrality is insufficient and in our international situation would be quite inappropriate.

A declaration of neutrality of the Czechoslovak Socialist Republic would be a unilateral act that would not obligate any other state to anything. A really valid and binding neutrality could be established only if it were accepted, recognized, and guaranteed by all powers, in the first place by the Soviet Union.

To call for neutrality is therefore legally quite ineffective and cannot help us. On the contrary, in the present situation it is politically incorrect and harmful. The National Assembly therefore rejects the appeals and demands for neutrality, which may be sincere—let us not belittle them—but which have not been thought through and are unwise.

The National Assembly of the Czechoslovak Socialist Republic, in line with resolutions already adopted on this matter, takes the position that the general requirement is for the following fundamental demands to be met:

1. Full, undisturbed, and sovereign execution of their state function must be made possible for all properly elected and appointed constitutional and political organs of the Czechoslovak Socialist Republic that have the full confidence of the Czechoslovak people and for their rightful constitutional and political officials, most immediately for those who have been illegally interned—namely, First Secretary Dubcek, Chairman of the National Assembly Smrkovsky, Premier Cernik, Chairman of the National Front Kriegel, Chairman of the Czech National Council Cisar, Spacek, and others.

2. Combat operations and the use of combat techniques and equipment must cease, and the withdrawal must take place of

the occupation units of the five member states of the Warsaw Pact, which are now on the territory of Czechoslovakia and which we consider to be occupation forces in the full sense of the word.

The National Assembly considers the fulfillment of these elementary requirements to be a necessary precondition for the normalization of state and economic life. It is a basic precondition for the renewal of all the fundamental values that ensue from the Republic's position as a sovereign and equal, and thus also firmly anchored, part of the whole socialist commonwealth of states and nations.

The National Assembly, along with the constitutional organs of our Republic, acting within the limits of its possibilities, urges that on the question of neutrality we do our duty and reject it as ineffective.

From documents of the National Assembly

6:15 P.M.

Czechoslovak Radio reported that approximately eight hundred members of the occupation powers have landed in Prague today in civilian clothes. They are furnished with forged Czechoslovak passports and speak fluent Czech and Slovak. They are said to be members of the Soviet State Security, and they are being assigned to various cities. About forty are already in Bratislava.

Late in the Afternoon

On Sunday, representatives of the Communist Party met with leading editors and reporters of our free press, radio, and television. Acting First Secretary of the Party's Central Committee Venek Silhan and Central Committee Presidium member Zdenek Hejzlar informed the newsmen about important aspects of the present situation.

The attention of the newsmen was focused primarily on the trip of President Svoboda to Moscow and on the negotiations now taking place there. These negotiations have been unexpectedly extended. Complications arose, and there is no certainty as to when they might end because representatives of the occupation countries are now taking part in them as well.

Our reporter, who was present at this press conference, asked whether the Central Committee of the Communist Party is prepared for various contingencies at the close of the negotiations after the President returns home.

Silhan answered as follows: "We shall not accept any agreements that would prevent the effectuation of the Communist Party's Action Program of this year, restrain our civil freedoms, or bar us from continuing with the reforms that were initiated in economic and political areas."

From Mlada Fronta, *1st extra edition, August 27, 1968*

6:20 P.M.

Czechoslovak Radio broadcast the following statement by Venek Silhan at the Communist Party Central Committee Press Conference:

The negotiations [in Moscow] in which the President of the Republic is taking part have been considerably protracted. Originally, it was expected that they would last about a day or two, but now it is the third day, and no one knows for sure whether the negotiations are drawing to a close. If the reports that we have turn out to be true—namely, that Ulbricht, Gomulka, Zhivkov, and Kadar were invited to Moscow—then we can expect that, first, the negotiations will be more difficult and, second, that they might be extended for another day.

7:15 P.M.

The Central Committee transmitter broadcast the following news item: Traffic at the civilian airport at Ruzyne has practically ceased. Only aircraft belonging to Aeroflot land and take off. In addition to returning Czechoslovak tourists, airplanes from Moscow bring more members of the Soviet State Security. The latter change their clothes at the airport, taking off their civilian clothes and putting on civilian clothes of Czechoslovak manufacture. They have cards identifying them as members of our Public Security as well as other cards identifying them as Czechoslovak citizens, in addition to large amounts of money in new banknotes.

7:30 P.M.

Czechoslovak Radio broadcast an interview with the Minister of Interior Josef Pavel. Moscow radio is spreading lies about Minister Josef Pavel, who was elected a member of the Central Committee at the Extraordinary Fourteenth Congress of the Party, lies to the effect that he fled abroad and so on. Czechoslovak legal free radio conducted the following interview with him on August 25, 1968:

Pavel: As you see, I am no apparition. I'm sitting here with you in Prague; we are looking out of the window onto the street where Prague citizens are walking. Up there in front, you see runners who bring me messages, which are evaluated here, and then the runners leave again to pass on my orders, either in writing or by telephone. As you can see, I cannot telephone from here. I want to tell you that this is not the only place where I work. I have a number of work places like this, and I keep shifting from one to another all the time.

I assure you that I sit in the Government, I take part in all the work connected with my function as a member of the Government, and I accept full responsibility for the decisions of the Government, too. You can see that I do, in fact, run security.

Question: What would you say about the work of the Security Forces in the present complicated situation?

Pavel: You are right that it is a very complicated situation, which makes the work of our Security Forces extraordinarily difficult. If I should sum up my opinion on the work of Security, I would begin with Public Security. That is the uniformed part of the service. Its members work very well, and here the law is not being broken. They give assistance to our citizens, they protect them against arrest, they help to distribute leaflets, they support our radio and television and give false information to the occupiers. I am very satisfied with them.

A somewhat more complicated situation prevails in State Security, which has been tainted and some of whose members, it seems, have taken part in unlawful activities. People should be careful here. They should watch out for these men so that they cannot do them any harm. However, I do ask our public not to harm unnecessarily men purported to be enemies without this being proven. I am afraid that new wrongs might be perpetrated. I promise those members of State Security who are being in any way wronged that I will carry out an investigation of everything when I get back into the building of the Ministry of Interior.

Report from Prague's Streets

The night falls over the city. The streets are deserted. Only the treads of the occupiers' tanks pound the hardened asphalt. Searchlights wander around walls and windows as if they were looking for something that has eluded them for six days.

I'm moving through the network of pathways in the plant of CKD. In the foundry, cranes are buzzing under the roof; this is one of the few places where life is full of activity at this hour. People do not talk, but every so often they spit and hiss out, "the sons of bitches." Sons of bitches, swines, and even cruder, more fitting terms. I stop by an arc-oven spewing flames and talk to the man who has been working the oven for twenty-four years and who has been a member of the Communist Party for twenty-three years. He presses my hand, clenches his fist, and shouts that the people who committed treason are not human beings at all, that they have never meant well for the workers. Dubcek should have put them all behind bars in January so that they couldn't do any harm. Put them behind bars or strip them of their positions. Why did he coddle them? Why did he trust them? I know Dubcek's a fine man and has a heart of gold. But the workers would have forgiven him that trespass against democracy. And the Russians should get the hell out, he shouts very loudly again and his swearing mingles with the howling of the oven.

It's a still August night. I wrap myself up into a sleeping bag on the ground. Next to me is a young man, a delegate to the Extraordinary Fourteenth Party Congress. Where is Antonin Kapek [General Director of CKD and a Presidium candidate member], I ask him. Kapek is a traitor, he mumbles half asleep. Don't bring up Kapek, voices call from all sides.

For them, Kapek has ceased to exist. But what is one collaborator and traitor against honest men? Here, in the eleven plants of the CKD, there are over twenty thousand honest men.

From Mlada Fronta, *1st extra edition, August 26, 1968*

Message from Vice-Chairman of the National Assembly Marie Mikova

On behalf of all the female members of the National Assembly, I send a message to our Czechoslovak women and mothers. We women can best demonstrate our firm position by working in our jobs and preventing economic setbacks, which would threaten our standard of living. There are tanks in front of the National Assembly building. It is not easy to communicate with newsmen. This message, in effect, is being smuggled out.

From Rude Pravo, *August 25, 1968*

Open Letter from the Officers of the Prague Garrison

To officers of the occupation armies on the territory of the Czechoslovak Socialist Republic:

The perfidious occupation of our fatherland in which you have participated represents a gross violation of the sovereignty of an allied socialist state—an act that is without precedent in the history of the socialist revolutionary movement. The occupation also constitutes a gross and unwarranted insult to the Czechoslovak People's Army, to all Czechoslovak soldiers and officers—your former comrades and brothers in arms.

Our army has been fully capable of protecting the country from any potential enemy at all times. It has been unprepared for only one eventuality: for a blow in the back from its own friend and allies.

You came at night, you pounced on a country that was asleep and on an army that was turned to face the enemy on the western border. You denied to a full-fledged member of the Warsaw Pact, to the Czechoslovak People's Army, its most sovereign and unalienable right—to defend the security, sovereignty, and freedom of its own country.

While we are free, we walk by you and look at the mess you have created in our country in the few days that you have been here, and we feel bitter. Our hearts burn with the heavy insult and with the feeling of being betrayed by those we considered to be our combat comrades in life and death and who are now giving us "a lesson in friendship and assistance" by their coarse and nonsensical conduct in the streets of our cities and towns.

Socialism and Communism are served very, very poorly by those who impose by means of bayonets their concepts of socialism and Communism on another nation.

Whether you like it or not, your posture in our country is that of an aggressor!

Be done with this shameful assignment, which is incompatible with the honor of an officer of a socialist army!

Go back home! Ask your own commanders and state representatives that you be withdrawn from the territory of the Czechoslovak Socialist Republic.

From Rude Pravo, *August 25, 1968*

Letter of Czechoslovak Sportsmen to the International Olympic Committee

Dear Mr. Chairman:

As you certainly know from the official proclamation of the Czechoslovak Government and National Assembly of August 21, 1968, armies of five countries have invaded the territory of the Czechoslovak Socialist Republic and have occupied it. Czechoslovak constitutional officials have protested against this occupation, which has taken place without their knowledge or approval, and they demand an immediate withdrawal of the foreign armies from our territory. This act, which is in gross contravention of international law and of the Olympic idea of peace and friendship among nations, seriously threatens the participation of the Czechoslovak Socialist Republic in the Nineteenth Olympics. This act has the effect of excluding the sportsmen of the five countries from the Olympic games because their countries have not kept faith with the Olympic ideals or with the United Nations' general declaration of human rights. Dear Mr. Chairman, the Czechoslovak Olympic Committee asks you and the Executive Council of the International Olympic Committee to take this

letter into consideration and act on it; at the same time, it asks
you to request members of the International Olympic Committee
from the five countries to call on their governments immediately
to terminate this act of force and violence.

From Ceskoslovensky Sport, *August 25, 1968*

9:45 P.M.

On Sunday, August 25, at 9:45 P.M., the Government received
the following message [from Moscow]:

Dear Fellow Citizens:

We send you cordial greetings on behalf of the whole delegation.

The negotiations have been continuing today and will go on
into the night. We know that you are thinking of us. And we are
thinking of you. We appreciate your coolheadedness, which is of
great help to us here. We ask you to keep it up.

Once more, many greetings, and we are thinking of all of you
at home.

> Yours,
> Svoboda, Dubcek, Cernik, Smrkovsky, and
> the others.

From Vecerni Praha, *August 26, 1968*

Prague—A City Unbowed

It's a pleasurably warm Sunday afternoon in August with a sky
of light blue. I'm standing on Jungmann Square and reading a
poster colored in red. An armored car patrols from one end of
Narodny Street to the other; the submachine guns in the hands
of the soldiers are ready to be fired. A young fellow wearing
glasses goes on reading the news to a small crowd. Every so often
he looks at the group of people who are listening to him and says:
"You see, folks, it's all right, I can still speak." Over his head hangs
a white board with this written on it: "We ask citizens to tell us
if they see anybody spying on us or to hand the collaborator over
to Public Security. Thank you."

Life moves in a sort of rut. People in their Sunday best are out
strolling. Some even push baby carriages. Lovers hold hands.

Little groups of grown-ups hold lively conversations, exchange slogans and write them down, swap leaflets. And on every corner there is a curt notice: Report dead and wounded to telephone number 38 20 45.

On Wenceslas Square at about 2 P.M., the occupiers tried to play the collaborationist radio station over the public address system, but as soon as the first few words were heard, the people in the Square responded by whistling until the ears of the occupiers must have hurt. They tried several times but eventually gave up. A citizen commented: "It was to be an educational program about Novotný, but it didn't come off."

The Sunday in an unbowed city is now dissolving in dusk. People are hurrying home. On Jirasek's Bridge some people are patiently trying to explain to several soldiers that we would be very happy if they left. The Ivans had just received a fresh edition of *Pravda*, and now they are confused. They see and hear one thing, then read a different version in the paper. They mumble something about illegal radio stations. They say they would be very glad to go home as soon as everything is normal again.

As I write these lines, I hear firing from the center of Prague and heavy vehicles moving in nearby streets.

The fifth night of the occupation: Prague is dark and quiet. An unbowed city.

From Reporter, *No. 35, August 26, 1968*

Politicians and Compromise

Politics has often been called the art of making compromises. Undoubtedly, the question of compromise will now come up again. The mere fact that our leaders are forced to negotiate constitutes a compromise, for the invasion and occupation of the country could have been sharply rejected. But the force of tanks, airplanes, and rockets can be very persuasive. The Soviet leaders responsible for the aggression are dealing with our state and Party officials, some of whom were kidnapped and taken to Moscow; others flew there "voluntarily." This doubtful "voluntariness" points up the negotiations' character of compromise.

However, a more serious question arises—namely, what to

negotiate about. And here our representatives face a serious dilemma. Should they offer too little to the aggressors, the latter will stop negotiating with them; should they offer too much, their own people will view them as traitors and will refuse to recognize the results of the negotiations. But does a middle way exist? Can the huge Soviet Union in its present shameful hour demand anything less than treason? Is there anything that could conceivably come about that could still be called a compromise? [3]

We all realize that our "allies" have painted themselves politically into a corner. But the situation is quickly coming to a head. While a relatively small compromise was good enough in the first few days, tomorrow the worst treason may not suffice. Consequently, every compromise is useless, even harmful. All a compromise would do is to disrupt today's admirable unity of the nation.

The peculiarity and extraordinariness of our present situation rest in the fact that circumstances do not allow any political compromise. If only every Czechoslovak would understand that there is no political way out, then perhaps our "allies," the occupiers, would see it, too. It is not our turn now; and our Warsaw Pact partners are in the unenviable position in which there is no move by which they could win the match. They have only two alternatives—to admit, sportsmanlike, that they have lost, or to kick the chessboard. Kick it with brutality but at the same time with complete impotence, for the greatest power is now the same as the greatest powerlessness.

From a mimeographed copy of Slova Svobody

Lessons of These Days

The fraternal military assistance rendered by the five countries of the Warsaw Pact to their class brothers in Czechoslovakia has quickly driven all the reactionary and counterpopular forces in our country back into their lairs, and this has made it possible for the Czechoslovak people at last to speak up absolutely freely, openly, and without unnecessary scheming. The military inter-

---

[3] One of the most perceptive passages in the book, this paragraph spells out in precise terms the dilemma faced by the Czechoslovak leadership in the wake of the Warsaw Pact invasion.

vention can be clearly called aggression, the disposition of foreign troops on our territory can be called occupation, the shooting of the citizens of the occupied country can be called murder. All this has unified the people and the two nations of the Republic to an unprecedented degree and has pointed up national character-istics that we didn't even suspect we had. Also, it has given us a number of lessons.

Perhaps the most remarkable lesson for both sides is the Czechs' realization that the Slovaks do not wish to break up the Republic, and the Slovaks' realization that without the Czechs their life would be a tragedy. We find evidence of this in every news item, and we are touched by it deeply. I submit that this should be forever borne in mind, especially by us Czechs.

Those who have been pretending to be our friends and brothers, protectors and saviors, succeeded in one stroke in accomplishing the impossible: to cancel and surpass Munich; to change the fifteenth of March, 1939, into an idyllic episode; and to erase May, 1945.

From a mimeographed copy of Slova Svobody

Lenin, Wake Up!

That is the slogan one sees most often on the walls of Prague's houses. But there is a next installment to it, too: "Brezhnev had gone mad!"

Prague is covered with posters. No matter that the Soviet occu-piers (believe me, this term is difficult to write down, but it is, unfortunately, descriptive) are tearing down the signs from the windows of buses (which came out into the streets this morning with signs saying "UN: SOS") and from shop windows in the center of the city, which have been turned into huge display areas for the posting of notices.

The well-known Czech humor, to which we have always taken recourse when we needed help, is evident everywhere. Written in Czech and Russian: "Ivan, go back home quickly: Your Natasha is going steady with Kolya. Love, mother." "We have lost five allies, but the whole world is with us now!" says another.

A helicopter belonging to the occupiers is flying over the city and dropping leaflets. Our Government and leaders of the Communist Party are said to have asked for help against counter-revolution. Who asked? They name no names. And so the leaflets are quickly thrown into sewers or torn up or burned.

By the way, overnight, Prague has lost street signs and often house numbers also. Last night, when arrests were expected, the city was on alert. It rained without let-up, but boys (sometimes quite young boys) were out to take down the street signs and house numbers, to paint over or tear down signposts, and to see to it that the only people who find their way around the city are those who are supposed to.

Prague, then, is on its feet. Today, the name-day of Saint Anna, is the fifty-fourth anniversary of the outbreak of the First World War and of Schweik's expedition, in a wheel chair, "against Belgrade." [4] Schweik, in the good sense of the word, can be found in the streets of today's Prague.

From Rude Pravo, *August 25, 1968*

An Interview

She is tired, she hasn't had enough sleep, she is dejected.[5] Asked if President Svoboda left for Moscow yesterday of his own free will and without coercion, she answers: "I am sure of it. He telephoned me to say that he would be back in Prague by evening and would call me up right away." It is now morning and the President of the Republic, Ludvik Svoboda, has not yet called.

Are you afraid?

"Yes. But I don't believe he would give in to any pressure. I believe he will live up to everything he said in his statement before he left. I've known him for a long time. He's a man of extremely good character. I trust him. I know how profoundly he was affected by this attack on our Republic by the Soviets and their allies."

Do you think President Svoboda went to Moscow expecting a favorable outcome or in order not to leave anything untried?

[4] See Book I, Chapter 7, of Jaroslav Hasek's *The Good Soldier Schweik* (New York: New American Library, Signet Classics, 1963).

[5] The person interviewed is not named in the text, but sources in Prague identified her as Svoboda's wife.

"He's known them well since his experiences in Russia during World War II. Before he was named Hero of the Soviet Union, he was put up before a Troika Court, which usually meant the death sentence. He got out of that because he kept telling them the truth about himself, because he didn't say—no matter how they pressed him—that he was an anti-Soviet agent. He didn't let them intimidate him; he stuck it out, and in the end he gained their respect. I'm sure that he is no more likely to compromise now.

"He will not give in to pressure. He kept informed about the unprecedented unity of our nations in these days. At first, he was anxious because there wasn't much news from Slovakia. But I know that he was aware that some units in Slovakia declared that they were ready to go into the mountains, in case the occupiers refused to leave our country."

Is there any truth to the story that the President was put under house arrest?

"The castle [Hradcany Castle, the presidential residence] was hermetically sealed by tanks and artillery. However, he could move freely within the area of the castle. He was not restricted there. He could move between the castle and his villa at Jeleni Prikop. And the same applied to his family."

How do you know that?

"He called the evening of August 20. He asked how I was. I said I was watching television. He said he was going to bed; he had had enough for the day. But at one o'clock in the morning, his secretary suddenly called and said they were at the Central Committee of the Party and I should brace myself. First I thought something had happened to the President. No, not that, he said. But I can't let you go to sleep without telling you: The Soviets are occupying us. All I could say was, 'What sort of condition is he in?'

"The secretary answered that the President was pale and disturbed and that he was not a cheerful sight at all. I couldn't go back to sleep. At a quarter to seven in the morning, that was the twenty-first of August, the President himself telephoned me. He said I shouldn't worry, he was all right, feeling good, that his son-in-law [diplomat] Milan Klusak and his daughter were with him and he could lean on them. During the course of the day, he called me up three more times and said something to the effect that he was in the castle because shells were coming down in the courtyard of the villa at Jeleni Prikop.

"On August 22, in the morning, he told me that he planned to take an inspection tour through Prague. He wanted to take three cars decorated with the flag of the President. But then the plan wasn't carried out because his family and the secretary feared for his safety. He also told me that, in the afternoon, he was to meet with Soviet General Pavlovsky and Soviet Ambassador Chervonenko.

"Later on, he told me that he talked with them from 11:30 A.M. to 2:30 P.M. and that the talks were inconclusive. Consequently, he considered it necessary to talk to the highest Soviet officials. Then at about nine o'clock in the evening his secretary called me and said that a group of comrades from the Central Committee had come to see the President. The secretary said that sitting next to the President on one side was Kolder and on the other Bilak and behind him was his son-in-law. Also present was the President's doctor, because Ludvik Svoboda had high blood pressure at that time.

"At about 11 P.M., the secretary called again and said that other members of the Government were waiting to see the President. I sleep only a little, almost not at all. When the President called me later on—it was shortly past midnight, in other words it was August 23 by then—he told me that the talks had finished and that he was getting ready to go to Moscow.

"I wasn't anticipating that. My reaction was to ask him how he felt. He said that he felt as well as could be expected. About six o'clock in the morning he called again to say that the situation was changing. He said he had reports that a new government had been appointed without his approval, and that he would not go to Moscow. Then, at ten minutes to eight, he told me he was going to Moscow after all. He had had a long talk with Ambassador Chervonenko, who had evidently told him that they were willing to negotiate. He told me that he was going with three members of the legal Government, three members of the legal Central Committee, his son-in-law, his secretary, his personal guard, and his physician.

"He said that they would be taking off at 9:30 A.M. and that he would not call again until his return in the evening. Then some doctors we know called to say he should not eat or drink anything and should watch out for drugs. I told this to him through the secretary, who said he would see to everything. He was said to be leaving in good condition. I could tell that, too, when he telephoned me. His voice was sharp as usual, soldier-like."

From Mlada Fronta, *August 25, 1968*

The Nation Will Never Forgive the Traitors

A black cloud has descended on Prague, and we live in sadness and sorrow. An artillery piece is pointing at the National Theater. The Academy of Sciences is surrounded by armored cars, and armed occupiers are guarding the entrance of the building of the Czechoslovak Writers Association. In the street you see a car with a sign saying, "They occupied Charles University!"

They act just like the previous occupiers—sometimes worse, in fact. They shoot at ambulances, they press the trigger of the submachine gun without being attacked.

And still, they will be increasingly more impotent. They are in a foreign country, and hate cannot be changed into friendship by machine guns.

Our only defense in these awful days is to stick together. We are bound together by resistance, by the knowledge of the truth of Dubcek, Svoboda, Smrkovsky, Kriegel, by the truth of all of us. We are bound together by the blood shed by our brothers and sisters, by the posters of resistance in the streets, by the street signs that were painted over, by the flags at half-mast, by the tricolor band in the button-hole. We must be bound together by anger against collaborationists, traitors; although we are powerless to act against soldiers, we must act against the traitors. The river that flows between the steep banks must not be dammed by our own mud. It is our river, and we must clear it ourselves. Only, for God's sake, watch out for the innocent as you act. The license plates of cars are shaky evidence; they could be mistaken, and innocent people could be victimized.

We must fight the collaborationists systematically and effectively with the assistance of the honest individuals in State Security who know the traitors in their own ranks. The fewer they are, the better for all of us.

Only that nation which defends itself in times of adversity as best it can deserves to be free. We have been proving our desire for real freedom and democracy every day since January of this year. We continue to prove it in these hours as well.

Czechs and Slovaks go arm in arm, unbroken, unbowed. One thing is clear today: These wonderful peoples have passed the test with flying colors. They may be humbled, they may be silenced, but they cannot be defeated. Barbarism cannot permanently prevail over civilization, especially not over advanced and cultured nations.

We have but one choice: to stick together.

We have but one hope: that we cannot lose.

From Vecerni Praha, *August 25, 1968*

7

MONDAY, AUGUST 26

Early in the Morning

Latest News from Sokolovo

About 70 per cent of the employees showed up for work this morning [at this machinery works in Prague], and more kept arriving all the time. It all depended on the connections people could make. It was all right if you were coming from downtown Prague, from Pankrac, Letna, Dejvice, or Stresovice, but those living in Garden City or in Strasnice were worse off.

It is estimated that enforced work stoppages in enterprises all over the Republic cost over 65 million crowns a day. This is something we cannot afford under any circumstances, and so every minute is precious. Not even the interruption of work on the locomotive of the CME-3 type is a good thing. Let us not forget that this machine has the designation T-669 in the Czechoslovak-type series and can be fully utilized in the Czechoslovak railway network. And the T-478.1s are also waiting for willing hands.

The Sokolovo works cafeteria became a target of some sharp-shooting last night. The reason: A passer-by refused to light a cigarette for an occupation soldier, and when the Sokolovo men refused him too, the crazy man fired a salvo at a wall. Obviously, the psychological warfare we are conducting against the occupiers is working. But let us be careful that no more blood is shed.

The people's trust in the Communist Party is growing constantly these days. More and more people are applying to join the Party. The Sokolovo works committee secretariat was asked for three application forms, two of which—requested by students —have been forwarded to the district University Committee of the Communist Party.

At the Compressor plant, almost 100 per cent of the employees showed up for work. As far as Sunday's "Dubcek shift" is concerned, the mobilization instructions came too late, and only about 40 per cent of the regular shift showed up at the plant.

The ROH [Revolutionary Trade Union Movement] works committee at the Compressor plant has established an information center. Someone is permanently on duty at the radio receiver, and news bulletins are issued twice daily. It certainly cannot be said that our factories are cut off from the world. When people are at their places of work, they can hear the voices of the legal Czechoslovak stations, which are fed into the public-address system.

Statement of the Communists of the Main Administration of State Security

Because some reports contrary to the facts have been broadcast over the radio in recent hours, and in response to inquiries by some enterprises about the real attitude of members of State Security, Communists of the main administration of State Security are issuing the following statement:

1. The All-Unit Committee of the Communist Party in the main administration of State Security in Sadova Street declares again that it stands fully behind the legitimate Czechoslovak constitutional and Party organs and that it is guided in its work solely by the orders of Minister of Interior Josef Pavel.

2. In order to be able to follow these orders, members of the State Security main administration shall not leave the building until they are so ordered by Minister Pavel or until they are driven out by force. We call upon State Security members in other facilities to follow our example and thus maintain their freedom of action. For the information of the public, we want to explain that the position of the members of the State Security

main administration in Sadova Street is not easy, because this facility is surrounded by occupation soldiers supported by tanks and fast-firing cannon. Occupation soldiers are also patrolling inside the building. The promise given by the commander of the occupation forces to President of the Republic Ludvik Svoboda has not been fulfilled in this case·either. The internment of the arrested members of the State Security main administration continues in spite of the fact that resolute steps have been taken with the occupation units for their release.

3. Members of the State Security main administration assure our citizens that they fully dissociate themselves from the numerically negligible handful of traitors who are serving the occupiers outside of this building; they reaffirm that they shall never become untrue to the people of this country and that they are ready to fulfill all duties according to their oath of service. In conclusion, we are turning to the workers of the radio and of the press with the request that they consider the sometimes untrue or half-true views and statements of individuals as anonymous and treat them as such. Only the legitimate Party and state organs are authorized to take positions on behalf of State Security.

From Rude Pravo, August 26, 1968

9:00 to 9:15 A.M.

Czechoslovak Radio broadcast the events of a fifteen-minute demonstration during which all the sirens in Prague sounded, bells rang, and automobile horns sounded. The demonstration apparently frightened the occupation troops. At the main railroad station, Soviet officers with drawn pistols threw themselves on an engineer and tried to force him to stop the locomotive whistle. During the demonstration, a young woman was shot at Klarov. She was taken to a hospital, but she died.

10:07 A.M.

The continuing extraordinary eighty-fifth session of the Presidium of the National Assembly resumed (recessed at 12:25 P.M.). From the agenda: reports on the attitude of the world trade union movement to the events in our country; a review of the situation in the enterprises; approval of the proclamation of the National Assembly, the Government of the Republic, and the Central Trade Union Council to all working people; reports on Government measures; approval of the draft proclamation on the anniversary of the Slovak national uprising; assurance of permanent communications with Slovakia.

From documents of the National Assembly

10:40 A.M.

Do Not Leave Me, My Son

The funeral parlor of the Strasnice crematorium is a place of last farewells. But this is no ordinary funeral: This life had been destroyed by violence. It was a life that had barely begun. Zdenek Prihoda, one of the first victims of the occupation, was twenty-seven years old. I am using the word "occupation" without an adjective, although it deserves all that expresses brutality, inhumanity, condemnation of a terrible deed. Proof? There are many at hand, but here is one to speak for them all—the death of Zdenek Prihoda. He carried no flag in his hand. He was not handing out leaflets. He was doing nothing to provoke a submachine gun. On the first day of the occupation, he was sitting quietly on his motor bike at the end of Vinohradska Street, waiting for an occupation truck and two armored vehicles to pass him. He did not live to see it; the last vehicle did not pass him by in peace. Its driver decided to kill. Brutally and recklessly, he shot the young man, a brother to two brothers and a sister, the son of a widowed mother. Deliberately, eyewitnesses say. Then he sped away.

So many people, so much pain, so much despair over a thwarted life could not find room in the Strasnice funeral parlor. Foreign newsmen, tears in their eyes, could only say: "We have never seen anything like it." The strains of the Hussite hymn were followed by reminiscences of the victim—an honest, straightforward man who had never done anybody any harm in his whole life. He had graduated from the Industrial Arts Academy, but because he was critical of the life presided over by Novotny, he was not accepted at the university. So he put on working-man's overalls and was a member of the Armabeton [heavy construction] brigade, and that is how death caught him. A group of young people, weeping, forced their way into the hall; they were carrying a Czechoslovak flag and a banner reading: "We are coming to bury the victim of your 'liberation.'" In the name of students, workers, friends, Czechoslovak mothers whose children had fallen in the streets of Prague, the speakers swore that we would never forget these days and their victims. "I last spoke to you a week ago in Rybalkov Street [named for a Soviet commander who helped liberate Prague in 1945]. It will never bear that name again!" This oath of one of the speakers is sure to be fulfilled. And then the mother's heart-rending voice mingles with the strains of the national anthem: "Do not leave me, my son. . . ."

From Zemedelske Noviny, *August 27, 1968*

Before 11 A.M.

Czechoslovak Radio reported that the Presidium of the Central Committee of the Communist Party of Czechoslovakia summons the Central Committee and the Central Control and Audit Commission for a plenary meeting in Prague on Tuesday, August 27, 1968. Leading workers of the Regional Party Committees will attend the session.

11:40 A.M.

Czechoslovak Radio broadcast a message by President Ludvik Svoboda from Moscow.

Before Noon

Report on the Meeting of the Czechoslovak Government

A Government session took place on Monday morning. An appeal by the Ministry of Finance was issued for an immediate payment of wages and retirement benefits. It was announced that the Minister of Power Industry, Josef Korcak, has returned from Moscow. He had been attending talks in Moscow that began before the occupation of our country. The Minister expressed his agreement with the attitude of the Party and of the Government in the present situation.

From Zemedelske Noviny, *August 27, 1968*

Protest of the Czechoslovak Government to the Council of Ministers of the Soviet Union

The Government of the Czechoslovak Socialist Republic is turning to the Government of the Soviet Union with an urgent request for immediate and effective measures against the inexplicable and nonpermissible acts committed by members of the Warsaw Pact armies who have occupied the Czechoslovak Socialist Republic.

These acts have gone so far that the lives of the peaceful population and even of members of the Czechoslovak Government are threatened without reason. Specifically, on August 25, 1968, at 9:45 P.M., Minister of Heavy Industry Josef Krejci, Minister of Transportation Frantisek Rehak, and Minister of Mining Frantisek Penc came under fire while returning from the Government session in the Prague castle.

In a mockery of human relations, the Minister of Transportation was actually told that shots had been fired from his car, although no one in the car had a weapon. Such incidents were occurring directly under the Prague castle a few hours after a meeting in which the Soviet Ambassador in Prague promised closer cooperation with the legal Government in easing the consequences of the occupation of Czechoslovakia by troops of the five Warsaw Pact countries. These examples can serve to show you the atmosphere in which the population of our capital city is living.

The Government of the Czechoslovak Socialist Republic therefore urgently requests the Council of Ministers of the Soviet Union, in awareness of its responsibility, to immediately draw the necessary consequences from these facts.

At the same time, the Government of the Czechoslovak Socialist Republic is turning to the Council of Ministers of the Soviet Union with the request that it order its military forces to vacate public buildings, particularly the building of the Presidium of the Government, in order that the Government obtain at least the minimum basic conditions for its activity, which has been rendered virtually impossible. The release of the building was promised on Thursday, August 22, by General Pavlovsky to President of the Republic Ludvik Svoboda.

From Rude Pravo, *August 27, 1968*

Report on the Situation in Prague

On Sunday night, the streets of Prague were empty again. The capital city remained a city without lights, without street signs and house numbers—an anonymous city for the hated aliens. Their provocations were expected. Reality surpassed expectations.

In Prague-Podoli, the occupiers shot up a civilian automobile, allegedly because, as a Soviet officer stated, the vehicle disobeyed a guard's order to halt. Public Security has established that the vehicle was shot through four times and that the inside was stained with blood and brain tissue. Four gravely wounded persons were brought into the Thomayer Hospital from the area of the Podoli Sokol Hall. Three of them have died, and the fourth is in serious condition. One of the dead—a boy of fifteen or sixteen—had been shot in the eye, and the back of his skull was crushed. An act of "heroism" of the Soviet lads that will not surprise anyone anymore. According to unconfirmed reports, several cases of rape occurred in Prague. Women: Avoid any contact with the occupation soldiers. Do not leave your homes after dark!

This morning at nine o'clock, bells and sirens were sounded throughout the Republic—a protest of the citizens of a sovereign state against a forcible occupation, against barbarism and the brute force of the occupiers. The wail of the sirens mingled with the majestic tolling of church bells. The Bishop of Ceske Budejovice, Dr. Josef Hlouch, called upon all the clergy of his diocese to support the negotiations of our statesmen in Moscow by the tolling of these bells. In the streets of Prague, even the cars of foreign visitors sounded their horns. The whole world is protesting, but Radio Moscow reports: "The progressive public opinion of the world approves our measure." We have no doubt that many listeners in the Soviet Union believe this because they have no opportunity to hear the other side.

The Soviet occupiers are sitting on their tanks. They are tired, cold; some are hungry. The looks on their faces are grim, but if you happen to see a more intelligent face, you can clearly see that they are confused, too. Many of them have realized, for the first time in their lives, that they are being lied to.

It is Monday morning, the sixth day of the occupation. Prague is less of a dead city now because it is daylight. The night belongs to the occupiers, to their helpless rage; the day belongs to the people of Prague. New posters and inscriptions nullify the night work of the occupiers, who were, in vain, trampling on every piece of paper with any writing on it. The shops are filling up, streetcars and buses are operating, citizens go about their work. They are working for themselves, not for the occupiers. The Soviet rulers thought they were sending their troops among a herd such as they are accustomed to seeing at home. They have been badly disappointed, and more disappointments are in store for them.

From Lidova Demokracie, *8th special edition, August 26, 1968*

1:00 P.M.

Czechoslovak Radio reported the Ministry of Education announcement that the school year will begin on September 2.

The National Assembly Reporter Reports

Underneath the placard "Shaving gear," another public notice has appeared: "Hair drier." Washrooms have also been placed at the disposal of women deputies; they take turns in groups of three. But personal comfort is a secondary matter.

We are plagued by tension. The medical service has several kinds of pills handy: calm-down pills, pep-up pills, sleeping pills.

It is inhuman the way the Moscow talks are dragging on. When the President was leaving, he promised to be back that same evening, and he has been there for four days now. But we are glad that Dubcek, Cernik, Smrkovsky, and the other comrades are with him.

In our voluntary internment, we hunger—for the printed word. Every bundle of a special edition of a newspaper or magazine is gone in a few seconds. Transistor radios can be heard at all times, on dining-room tables, in the halls.

After the rush of meetings, the plenary session of the National Assembly takes place in the evening. Although a group of delegates to the Congress of the Slovak Communist Party has left for Bratislava, there are 201 deputies present. After an evaluation of the domestic and international political situation, after the Government report on the state of the Moscow talks, and after the approval of a proclamation on the anniversary of the Slovak national uprising, five special commissions have been appointed: Security, Health, Information, Cultural, and Purchasing.

Measures are being taken for a prolonged stay in the building.

After the meeting, a movie of the first day of the occupation, made by television workers, was shown. Then a [full-length Czechoslovak] color film, *Capricious Summer*. After the showing, around midnight, I met [former Defense Minister General Bohumir] Lomsky over a wash bowl. He was shaving, naked above the waist. We discussed the National Assembly. I confess that I used to have some strong reservations about it, but the deputies have now shown themselves in the best light. Some of them who tried to appear as progressives, such as Miroslav Sulek, have betrayed our cause openly, while others who were criticized for their conservative attitude are playing a great role these days. For instance, General Samuel Kodaj has demonstrated great courage and decisiveness as a commander in Slovakia. The same goes for Martin Vaculik, who has taken over the leadership of the Secretariat of Dubcek's Central Committee. And there are more deputies like these. In our conversation, General Lomsky expressed a thought that may have been missed by the public: This National Assembly was elected four years ago, the deputies being selected by the methods used at that time, and so it is the only institution no one can accuse of being a tool of the counterrevolution or of being illegal.

From Mlady Svet, *No. 35, 1968*

1:10 P.M.

Czechoslovak Radio broadcast a protest by members of all Communist Party works organizations of the Czechoslovak Power Plants Prague, Central Management, against the confiscation of weapons of their unit of the People's Militia from a sealed and guarded armory at 1:30 A.M. on August 26, and against the seizure of weapons of other People's Militia units.

2:30 P.M.

Czechoslovak Radio broadcast a report by the Deputy Director of the Czechoslovak State Bank. This morning, a group of Soviet officers arrived at the bank and requested the management to agree to an exchange of rubles for Czechoslovak currency. The management of the State Bank rejected their demand as contrary to Czechoslovak regulations. Thereupon, the State Bank was seized by the occupiers. The workers of the State Bank informed the Government and the National Assembly of the situation.

3:08 P.M.

The continuing extraordinary eighty-fifth session of the Presidium of the National Assembly resumed (recessed at 4:30 P.M.). From the agenda: reports on the over-all military and political situation in the country; some broader aspects of the occupation of the Czechoslovak Socialist Republic.

3:15 P.M.

Czechoslovak Radio reported that Jiri Lukas [a Novotnyite editor], who has been working with the collaborationist television, was expelled from the Czechoslovak Communist Party at this morning's meeting of *Svet Sovetu* [*The Soviet World*, magazine of the Czechoslovak-Soviet Friendship Association].

4:00 P.M.

Czechoslovak Radio reported that the Government is calling a meeting of the chairmen of Regional National Committees for 3 P.M. on Tuesday, August 27, to discuss the situation and further measures.

In the Afternoon

Plenary Session of the City Committee of the Communist Party in Prague

In opening the session, Secretary of the City Committee, Engineer J. Kotrc, outlined the abnormal conditions in which the City Committee must work: The main building was seized by foreign troops during the first hours of the occupation of Czechoslovakia; contacts with District Party Committees and other organs in the city are maintained only with difficulty; in the course of the six days, the Presidium has been forced to change its place of work four times, under a direct threat of tanks and machine guns.

In spite of these conditions, it was possible to summon the delegates of the Extraordinary Fourteenth Party Congress on very short notice. The task of safeguarding the Congress was taken over by the Prague working class and the People's Militia in Prague. In a most impressive manner, the Congress documented the unity of patriotic forces under the freely recognized leadership of the Communist Party.

As long as the main City Committee building remains under seizure, the City Committee will maintain its Secretariat on Mala Strana, on the square behind the St. Nicholas Church, in the Party-school dormitories. Secretary Stanislav Maxa is in charge of the Secretariat. (The telephone number is 0945.) All matters of the city Party organization may be addressed to this office, in person or by telephone. All workers of the City Committee are at work; none of them have lent themselves to collaboration, and they are fulfilling all tasks assigned to them by the City Committee Presidium with dedication in spite of all difficulties.

From Vecerni Praha, *August 27, 1968*

Comments from Some Members of the New Central Committee Elected at the Extraordinary Fourteenth Party Congress

We have sent, by a reliable route, a number of our newspapers and detailed reports to Comrade President Svoboda and to our delegation in Moscow. Subsequently we have received confirmation that he received the shipment.

We issued the slogan "February" for the militia [the militia had played a key role in the Communist take-over of February, 1948]. When we learned that the enemies had become aware of its significance, we announced that "February" was invalid. Our delegation in Moscow was thereupon faced with the accusation that we were renouncing the traditions of February, 1948.

We must constantly verify the reports from our delegation in Moscow addressed to our Government, as we cannot be certain that the reports are not falsified to distort the situation.

Concerning some well-known personalities, the following comments were made:

Svestka failed to come out for either side in any of the discussions and should be riding in armored cars too.

Kapek refused to accept any Party office and also declined an offer to travel to Moscow with our delegation.

Lenart was supposed to get one of the highest posts in the leadership of the state, according to the proposal of the traitors. When he learned about it, he announced that he stood behind the post-January policy.

Hajek—the Soviets want to recall him from his post and demand that he join Malik in the United Nations and in the Security Council. However, he shall remain loyal to our position.

Cisar—we have been able to free him, and we hope that you will see and hear him soon.

From Vecerni Praha, *August 27, 1968*

The Countryside Supplies Food to the Factories

The works committee of the Foundries received the following letter on Monday, August 26:

Dear Comrades:

The members of the Horka Poricany Agricultural Cooperative worked a Sunday shift on August 25, 1968, for the rebirth of our country and in support of comrades Ludvik Svoboda, Alexander Dubcek, and other patriots and in protest against the occupation of our country. The members of the cooperative decided to donate five tons of potatoes from this shift to the citizens of Prague and stipulated that the money obtained for these potatoes be turned over to the Fund of the Republic on behalf of our cooperative. In the next few days we shall deliver an additional three wagon-loads of potatoes to Prague.

The first shipment of potatoes was received by the foundry workers of Vysocany. The works committee immediately put the potatoes on sale and is donating the money to the stipulated purpose.

From the legal Kovak, *August 27, 1968*

4:10 P.M.

Czechoslovak Radio broadcast an announcement by Public Security that all main roads from Prague will be closed in both directions at 6 P.M. In case of violations, the occupation troops shall take harsh measures. Shooting cannot be excluded.

4:15 P.M.

Cestmir Cisar, member of the Presidium of the Central Committee and Chairman of the Czech National Council, has resumed his duties at the Secretariat of the new Central Committee.

From Rude Pravo, *August 27, 1968*

Letter of the Trade Unionists of the Elektrosignal Enterprise in Prague

We, the trade unionists of the Elektrosignal enterprise in Prague 7, support the appeal of the Government of the Czechoslovak Socialist Republic asking you to suspend your negotiations with the leading government officials of the Soviet Union and return with the entire delegation to our country to discuss the situation prevailing here with the constitutional organs—that is, with the Government of the Republic and the National Assembly.

We recommend that further negotiations with the Soviet representatives take place on the territory of our country.

5:10 P.M.

Czechoslovak Radio reported that the Presidium of the Czechoslovak Academy of Sciences issued a statement taking exception to the assertion that a number of international congresses have been organized by the imperialists.

5:25 P.M.

The continuing extraordinary eighty-fifth session of the Presidium of the National Assembly resumed (recessed at 6:05 P.M.). From the agenda: drafting of a letter of protest against the internment of Comrade Frantisek Kriegel; reports on the situation in the economy and on contacts with our delegation in Moscow.

5:30 P.M.

Czechoslovak Radio announced that the Czechoslovak State Bank denies the report that it has been occupied. The Czechoslovak Trade Bank has not been occupied either.

Resolution of the Leadership of the Czechoslovak Writers Union

The long uncertainty as to whether the Soviet Union is to play the role of an apostle or of a gendarme in the socialist camp has finally been overcome. The great socialist power is returning to the tried and tested traditions of Cossack diplomacy. By this retrograde and fascist-like action, the Soviet Union has deprived itself of any right to play a leading role in the international Communist movement. Armies of tanks cannot suppress the yearning of nations for freedom; ideas cannot be shot dead. There are not enough jails in Czechoslovakia to accommodate all those who are today raising and holding up the banner of freedom. We assume that all those who have dealt this deadly blow to the prestige of the Soviet Union and of socialism will be called to account for their actions: Leonid Brezhnev, Nikolai Podgorny, Aleksei Kosygin [East German Party leader], Walter Ulbricht, [Polish Party leader] Wladyslaw Gomulka, [Hungarian Party leader] Janos Kadar, [Bulgarian Party leader] Todor Zhivkov. On behalf of the Czechoslovak Writers Union, whose buildings in Prague have been seized by the occupiers and are being guarded by their tanks, we are turning to the intellectual community of the whole world. Raise your voice in defense of Czechoslovakia. Express loudly your opposition to this unjustified aggression. Boycott all activities of the occupiers anywhere in the world. Terminate all cultural agreements with this unclean alliance. Until the ocupation troops are withdrawn, cease all showing of their films, shows, and plays. Stop the circulation of their press. Freedom is indivisible; it is not only ourselves who are at stake but you as well. Demand that they immediately take their hands off socialist Czechoslovakia. They shall never break our determination to live in freedom and to bring up our children in freedom. We have spoken for the free leadership of the Czechoslovak Writers Union, which is working and acting.

From Rude Pravo, *August 27, 1968*

6:09 P.M.

The continuing extraordinary twenty-sixth session of the National Assembly resumed (recessed at 8 P.M.) with 191 deputies present. From the agenda: unanimous approval of a proclamation on the anniversary of the Slovak national uprising and of the proclamation of the National Assembly, the Government, and the Central Trade Union Council to all workers; reports on the health situation, particularly in Prague, and on the supply of food throughout the Republic; a criticism of the Government concerning the contacts with our delegation in Moscow.

From documents of the National Assembly

To the Czech and Slovak Nation, to the People of Czechoslovakia

On the eve of the anniversary of the Slovak national uprising [1] we recall with particular urgency that national freedom and independence can be achieved only by the struggle of a united people; you cannot beg for freedom on your knees. Freedom, independence, and sovereignty of the Czechoslovak Socialist Republic, as well as the hopes of a really human and dignified life of Czechs and Slovaks and of all the people of Czechoslovakia, were twice in this century born from a struggle against foreign domination, from a struggle for national and state independence.

[1] In which Alexander Dubcek, a Slovak, took part.

In January, 1968, we started out on the road of correcting the mistakes of our previous socialist development, the road of building socialism with a human face. At the moment when we were achieving our first successes in this effort, the hitherto peaceful work of the people of our country was disrupted. Our hearts were filled with concern and anxiety about the future of our state, concern about the road we alone freely entered after January. A brute force from the outside is attempting to bring us to our knees and to impose an alien will upon us.

Czechs and Slovaks, the anniversary of the Slovak national uprising reminds us that the freedom of our two nations is the main supporting pillar of the Czechoslovak statehood. Jan Kollar's verse comes to mind:

> He who is himself worthy of freedom
> Knows how to value freedom of others.

It arouses our emotions even more powerfully as we recall that the armies of socialist countries that, twenty-four years ago, were aiding the fighters for Czechoslovak freedom are today frustrating and destroying the heritage of the Slovak national uprising.

Czechs and Slovaks have lived in a common state for fifty years now. The results of the life of their state are—in spite of all the shadows of the past developments—highly positive. Our common republic, and particularly its socialist construction, has enabled our two nations to develop politically, economically, and culturally. Having drawn a lesson from the bad experiences of the pre-January period and from the years between the two world wars, we have decided to base the future state existence of our two nations on federative foundations. We have labored in order that, on the twenty-eighth of October, the National Assembly could adopt a constitutional law on the socialist federative arrangement of our state.[2] The work on this legislation was progressing in a highly promising way in the days immediately preceding the sad twenty-first of August. A solution of difficult problems, acceptable to both the Slovaks and the Czechs, was within reach.

[2] The law was adopted, despite the occupation, in October and went into effect on January 1, 1969.

Czechs and Slovaks, people of the Czechoslovak Socialist Republic: The National Assembly—the deputies whom you have elected—solemnly declare in this fateful time of testing to which we are being subjected by historical events that we are striving with utmost determination in order that foreign armies leave the territory of our Republic; the constitutional organs of the Czechoslovak Socialist Republic and their representatives elected by the will of the people and enjoying their full confidence may exercise their functions in freedom and sovereignty; all our people may live in a sovereign state, managing their own affairs according to their will; socialism in our country may grow out of a free labor of workers, peasants, and intellectuals, that it be a humanitarian socialism responding to the democratic and progressive traditions of the nations and nationalities of our country, that it be a socialism realizing the principles of the Action Program and of the Extraordinary Fourteenth Congress of the Communist Party; the constitutional law on the federative arrangement of the Czechoslovak Socialist Republic, which is in preparation, be discussed and approved, in close cooperation with the Czech National Council and the Slovak National Council and with all the components of the National Front, by the time of the fiftieth anniversary of the founding of the Czechoslovak Republic.

Czech and Slovaks, people of the Czechoslovak Socialist Republic, in these fateful days of trial, we ask you and we urge you: Persevere in your brotherly unity and solidarity, in your dignified and resolute attitude. Do not bow your head before the occupation. Remain loyal to the ideals of freedom, democracy, socialism, and a real proletarian internationalism. Remain loyal to the President of the Republic, Ludvik Svoboda, to the Cernik Government, to Smrkovsky's National Assembly, to Kriegel's National Front, to Dubcek's Central Committee elected by the Extraordinary Fourteenth Congress of the Communist Party of Czechoslovakia.

National Assembly of the Czechoslovak
Socialist Republic

From documents of the National Assembly

Proclamation of the National Assembly, the Government of the Czechoslovak Socialist Republic, and the Central Trade Union Council, to All Working People

Esteemed Friends, Men and Women Comrades:

One of the expressions of resistance against occupiers has always been a strike. However, the Presidium of the National Assembly and the Government of the Czechoslovak Socialist Republic wish to point out that, in the current period of the occupation of our country, strikes are sometimes used in a manner not in accord with our righteous struggle. We wish to point out that a short-term work stoppage of a few minutes is symbolic and tends to unify the resistance against the occupation of the Republic. Longer strikes, however, cause far-reaching losses to the national economy of the Republic without affecting the occupiers; in addition, long-term interruptions of work can only help the occupiers, by providing a pretext for the assertion that we are unable to govern ourselves and that the occupation measures were inevitable. Surely no honest working citizen of our Republic wants that.

We are therefore addressing an urgent appeal to you to work honestly, with dedication, discipline, and determination and at the present time to even increase your efforts at creating the values our country needs. Follow the work directives of your comrades from the enterprise management and do not let yourselves be confused by radicalist elements who, not realizing the harmfulness of their actions, urge you to restrict or to stop your work.

A disciplined, fruitful work is the national duty of every citizen of the Czechoslovak Socialist Republic at the present time. Fulfill this patriotic duty even in this period so painful for us all.

> Josef Valo,
> National Assembly
>
> Lubomir Strougal,
> Government of the Czechoslovak Socialist Republic
>
> Karel Polacek,
> Central Trade Union Council

From documents of the National Assembly and Czechoslovak Radio broadcast of 4:15 P.M.

Around 8 P.M.

Soviet troops left the building of the Presidium of the Government.

9:08 P.M.

The continuing extraordinary eighty-fifth session of the Presidium of the National Assembly resumed (recessed at 10:19 P.M.). From the agenda: reports on the activity of the Czech National Council and on the coordination of its work with the National Assembly; report on a conversation with Premier Oldrich Cernik, which took place at 8:30 P.M.; discussion on contacts with the Government and with our delegation in Moscow and on the attitude to the departure of the President of the Republic for Moscow.

From documents of the National Assembly

Commentary of the Day

It is impossible, in the long run, to call things by words other than those that really describe them. Terms cannot be confused or mixed up for long. This is also true about "liberation," which is the label they have tried to put on their aggression against our country, on the occupation of Czechoslovakia.

A country that does not need to be saved from anything or freed from anything, that is not asking for it and is actually rejecting it for weeks in advance as an absurdity—such a country cannot be "liberated." Such a country can only be occupied—unlawfully, brutally, recklessly. Not liberation but aggression, not rescue but occupation.

These are unpleasant truths, and one cannot be surprised that the occupiers do not want to read them on the asphalt of the roads, on the walls of houses, on the locomotives on the rails, on the sides of trucks, on millions of posters throughout the country or even—in not a few instances—on their own vehicles and other facilities. But they cannot do away with these truths, least of all by driving the "natives" into the streets under their automatics and forcing them to tear down the posters.

True, there is something peculiar in this case, something they cannot admit to themselves, something they have to mask and deny before each other. Are they not acting "in the interests of socialism," have they not come as "class brethren" performing their "noble internationalist duty?" It is totally inconceivable to them that they should be compared with those who subjugated this country in an equally brutal manner three decades ago. It is totally unacceptable for them to be compared, for instance, with the Americans in Vietnam.

They find it unacceptable, they protest violently. They spew out miles of magnetic tape of pitiful self-justifications and tons of paper printed over with high-sounding phrases, but they cannot change matters one bit. They did not come to liberate socialist Czechoslovakia on the twenty-first of August, but to trample it down; they did not come to save the Czechs and Slovaks, but to enslave them.

Let us recapitulate—bluntly and briefly: Stealthily, not like a government of a decent country, but like medieval conspirators, behind the backs of all the legal organs of this country, they joined in a compact with a handful of discredited political corpses and stool pigeons who feared punishment for their participation in the crimes of the 1950's and while still pretending to conduct a dialog in their formal contacts, they forcibly invaded the country. Like gangsters, they abducted the Premier of the legal government of a sovereign country, the Chairman of the legal parliament of that country, the First Secretary of the leading political party, and they restricted the freedom of movement and action of the head of state, the President of the Republic, a bearer of the highest medals of their own country.[3]

They trampled upon all agreements that had bound them with that country, and yet they had enough arrogance to claim that they were doing so precisely on the basis of those agreements.

They brutally surrounded the parliament of that country with their tanks and machine guns. They surrounded the residence of the head of the state and the seat of the government. They invaded the offices of leading cultural and other institutions. Within

---

[3] Svoboda is one of the very few foreigners to have received the Soviet Union's highest military decoration, Hero of the Soviet Union.

three days, they flooded that small country with twenty-six military divisions and a half-million soldiers, with thousands of tanks and even rocket weapons, which they aimed against our capital city. They drove the voices of this country, its press, radio, and television, underground, and they tried to replace them with their disgusting prattle disseminated out of [East] Berlin in an insulting distortion of our language. Although they are formally joined with us by ties of alliance, they placed their tanks around our military barracks and facilities of our armed forces, and they aimed their gun barrels against those who had until then been their allies.

They employed the methods of military and police terror. They were shooting at children and crushing people under the treads of their tanks, destroying roadways and homes, not sparing even the most precious cultural monuments, as witnessed by the disfigured front of the National Museum.

Encountering the calm of the people, a country that fails to offer a single proof in support of their nonsensical pretext for aggression, they started a futile barrage from all their weapons in the middle of the night—perhaps to be able to pretend to themselves that there is, after all, a need to fight.

They have brought in some selected cutthroats of their secret police in order to imprison the political and cultural elite of our nation and make it easier to install new collaborationists of the Moravec type.[4]

Can all this be called a rescue, can all this be called a liberation? How does it actually differ from the fifteenth of March, 1939? Is this not a replica of all that we already went through once? Of *Wehrmacht* and Gestapo, of blood and iron? Of injustice and arrogance, cruelty and recklessness?

Is anything changed by the fact that all this is being perpetrated not by enemies but by "friends," not by recognized aggressors but by allies, not by those of whom we might have expected it but by those whom we would never have thought capable of it?

Can they expect of us that, in condemning this crime, we, its

---

[4] A cabinet minister who urged cooperation with the "protectorate" set up by the Nazis in Bohemia and Moravia during World War II.

very victims, shall be less resolute, less eloquent than the whole civilized world, which is condemning them?

We want to honestly differentiate between those who bear the main responsibility for this criminal decision and those whose task it is to implement it, many of whom did not even know where they were, where they were going, what they were doing. But it is not easy to maintain such distinctions for long in situations such as ours after the twenty-first of August. More than twenty years ago, the International Court of Justice established the collective responsibility of the German people,[5] and it still remains true that "the most honorable duty of a soldier is to disobey a criminal order."

After five days of occupation, it is clear that the moral victory is ours. The short-sighted stage direction of the aggression has failed shamefully. The aggressors have encountered such a single-minded resistance by the two nations of our country that there is no precedent for it in history. Enraged, but to no avail, they are desperately seeking some authoritative collaborationists to provide a semblance of "legality" to the aggression after the fact. There simply are none. The occupation army is totally isolated, helpless, completely rejected. Throughout the country, orientation signs, street names, house numbers, name plates on doors have disappeared; the country is anonymous and mute. Arrest warrants and lists of victims have become worthless. The occupiers have seized our printing houses, but newspapers keep appearing several times a day with full freedom of expression. They have seized the radio, but the broadcasts go on in freedom. They have seized the television but failed to silence it, too. Already in these first days, the occupation has been politically defeated, defeated morally and psychologically, defeated and rendered ridiculous before the eyes of the whole world. The central expression of this defeat is the fact, above all, that, in spite of all the fabrications about a counterrevolution and a collapse of the socialist order in Czechoslovakia, it is precisely the Communist Party that has demonstrated its tremendous viability and, in accordance with the will of the people of the

[5] This is not true. Post–World War II tribunals have shunned the idea of collective responsibility.

entire country, has again assumed its position at the head of the national resistance in this fateful hour, at the head of the struggle for socialism and for state and national sovereignty.

We can hardly hope, given the treachery and brutality shown by this aggressor on the twenty-first of August, that there will soon arrive a favorable turn of events. But the adventurist,[6] anti-socialist, aggressive policy of the Brezhnev clique at the head of the Soviet Communist Party has no future. It is deeply contrary to the objective interests of the Soviet Union itself and of the Soviet people, and this contradiction is bound to engulf it sooner or later. Until then, we must persevere, we must overcome this grave crisis, we must defend our truth with minimum sacrifices and with maximum determination. A compromise is impossible: We cannot lose more than we have already lost or offer more than they have already stolen from us. The sympathies of the entire civilized world are on our side. Truth and justice are on our side. The future is on our side.

From Reporter, *No. 35, August 26, 1968*

How to Decimate an Enemy

On Friday, the fourth day of the forcible occupation of Czechoslovakia, the changing of the guards began. In the course of the last seventy-two hours, fresh units have been streaming in from all sides to replace the morally decimated and tired divisions of the Warsaw Pact. Only four days were enough for the occupation commanders to realize that although the two hundred thousand Soviet, East German, Polish, Bulgarian, and Hungarian soldiers were still remaining in their positions, their reactions, alertness, vigilance, and also their judgment had been impaired. No wonder. Falsely informed, they came to a country their fathers had liberated, and on every step they encountered the kind of resistance that could not be overcome with the most up-to-date, modern technology and planning that their generals were providing them with. They came into towns and villages

[6] A particularly interesting choice of words, for—as the author of the article undoubtedly knew—former Soviet Communist Party leader Nikita Khrushchev, who was ousted by his colleagues in 1964, had been accused of "adventurism."

where people kept explaining to them in their native language—learned in popular courses in Russian—that they were unwelcome, that nobody had called them in, that there was no counterrevolution here, that there were no West German revanchists. They could read dozens of slogans exhorting them to go back home. If they did not intimidate people with the power of their weapons, no one gave them food or water. People were turning their backs on them. This spontaneous expression of resistance on the part of the unarmed Czechoslovaks has morally disrupted the occupation force. No general staff in the whole world could have thought up such a plan. It was born in the heads of fourteen million Czechs and Slovaks, who are rebuffing their uninvited guests and showing by their psychological resistance that it is possible to face down even the mightiest army with calm and common sense. This is something the generals in the Kremlin never expected.

From Lidova Demokracie, *8th special edition, August 26, 1968*

What Conditions

There is a law, valid in all countries of the world, that a document signed under a threat of arms is invalid. If a burglar enters your house in the middle of the night, injures you, and with a pistol in his hand, forces you to sign a pledge that you will voluntarily turn your property over to him, that signature is good only as long as you are standing in front of the drawn weapon. Our representatives in Moscow are in exactly the same situation. Both our nations stand wounded before the barrels of tank guns. Svoboda, along with Dubcek and Cernik, has been in Moscow for several days now, lacking any information about the situation back home. While they are negotiating, shooting continues here.

Moscow's first condition, concerning the stationing of Soviet troops on our territory, is unacceptable because it would mean that a weapon would constantly be held against us. It could be accepted only if the Moscow military district would be exclusively occupied, for the same length of time, by Czechoslovak military units.

The second condition is to prevent any agitation against the Soviet Union. It is fully acceptable because the effects of the anti-Soviet agitation the Kremlin has mounted by having occupied Czechoslovakia are incomparably greater than any agitation by the most extreme right-wing organizations in the West. Moscow itself has carried out the most effective agitation against the Soviet Union. I would only have one supplement to this condition: Czechoslovak representatives pledge to see to it that the truth and nothing but the truth will always be written about the Soviet Union. They require the same of Leonid Brezhnev!

By their third, unacceptable condition, demanding the re-establishment of censorship, all the five countries admit that they do maintain censorship, and we all know what that means. A lie, when repeated a hundred times, becomes truth. *Tass* fabricates a news item, which is then circulated in all the five countries and repeated *ad nauseam* in their press, radio, and television until it sticks firmly in the memory of readers and listeners. No thanks, we cannot accept censorship, particularly not this kind.

The fourth condition asks us to relinquish any claims of neutrality and to remain in the Warsaw Pact. Calls for neutrality were heard in our country only at the moment when the Warsaw Pact was effectively torn to pieces by the aggression and when our people suddenly saw that the treaty guaranteed them not independence but occupation. It would be ideal if all countries of the world were neutral and released their soldiers to civilian life. Our army, one of the largest in the world in proportion to the size of the population, has never been used throughout the entire fifty years of the existence of the Republic. Our country is so small and in such an exposed position in Europe that we cannot harbor any illusions for the future as long as the present division of the world in power blocs lasts. It is therefore necessary to agree with this condition.

From Mlada Fronta, *August 26, 1968*

The Only Way

"On the first day, we were the only freely accessible hospital." Docent Korcak, M.D., has been at the Vinohrady Hospital for six days now. He looks fit and in fine fettle, and this is hard to understand because he says, "On Wednesday we received sixty-nine wounded. They were shot wounds, lacerations, and lesions, wounds caused by grenade fragments and shots from tank grenades—very grave and deep injuries. Shots in the abdomen, in the neck, in the chest, compound limb fractures."

Out of the sixty-nine, twenty-four are in the surgery ward today, five are in the department of plastic surgery. Out of the sixty-nine, four are no longer alive.

Most of the injured are young people. An elderly woman who lives on Wenceslas Square was walking with her husband to have a look at the radio building when the fighting there started. Her husband tried to protect her with his overcoat. The front part of his right foot was torn away. She has a crushed bone in her right hip and shell fragments in both eyes. "We are used to seeing all kinds of things; that's the kind of business we are in—but this was a shock even for us," says the doctor.

Next to the bed of each of the wounded patients are beautiful carnations, gladioli, asters—presents from the Prague gardeners. A young man with a crushed leg has a visitor, his father.

A railroad worker is telling about the train that carried the jamming equipment to mar the reception of our legal radio broadcasts: "I tell you frankly, that train should have been stopped at Cierna. But there was nothing peculiar about it— except that it was so short, eight cars only. At first we wanted to throw it off the track, but that could have had terrible consequences. Near Olomouc, it got ahead of a long freight train. Then it accidentally broke up into three sections, and it took four hours to fix. Exactly according to all regulations. Then I collapsed. Another maintenance man needed another four hours to fix it. Then it moved on to Trebova and, with repair work going on all the time, as far as Chocen. From there, we wanted to steer them on to Poland, but by that time they had maps.

"Suddenly they were in a great hurry because they had eaten up everything they had in their two parlor cars. Before Moravany, we threw the trolley wires down, and the train got all tangled up in them. That took two maintenance squads, and still they were unable to put it together. The Russians were quite nervous.

They wanted the machine to run on batteries, and they could not understand why it should not be possible when all the various pieces of equipment seemed to be functioning all right. In Pardubice, they wanted steam, but we told them that that was an electrified line. In Prelouc, a piece of the track was dismantled, then a trolley thrown off, and they decided that they would go on by way of Hradec. In Steblova, again a thrown-off trolley; it's a single-track stretch so there was nothing to be done. Not too quickly, anyway. Six Soviet helicopters picked up our dispatchers as hostages. We put fifteen freight trains in front of them, and there is no yard in Prague that could take all of that. Our own trains suffered because of it; everything was delayed. I myself got to Kolin with a completely empty passenger train. Now they are somewhere around Lysa on the Elbe. But such a Schweik-type operation cannot last indefinitely." [7]

A colleague from *Zemedelske Noviny* came to the Vinohrady Hospital with some sad news. There are seven wounded in the Frantisek Hospital: one skull fracture, one man with the arteries in his hands cut by flying glass, another shot through his arm and kidneys, the rest suffering shot wounds in the arms and legs. There was only one dead at Frantisek. His name was Semyonovich, and he was a Soviet soldier. His death was bizarre: His automatic, which was hanging over his shoulder, discharged accidentally and shot him through his back. His armed brothers responded instinctively: They shot him full of holes.

This is the sixth day of the occupation. Prague has 314 wounded, 110 of them in hospitals. Twenty-two dead. The doctors have a new experience—war surgery.

From Politika, *No. 3, August 27, 1968*

Statement of Employees of the Mir National Enterprise

Because of the betrayal on the part of the German Democratic Republic, which is participating in the occupation, we are suspending the treaty of friendship with Viktoria enterprise of Heidenau. We ask our friends in that enterprise, who during their recent visit at our plant showed great sympathies for our

[7] This was the first detailed account published of what happened to the train rushing Soviet radio jamming equipment to Prague.

political developments, to protest against the participation of the army of the German Democratic Republic in the occupation of Czechoslovakia.

From Zemedelske Noviny, August 27, 1968

Neutrality?

The military occupation of Czechoslovakia by socialist countries has trampled on the independence of Czechoslovakia and the basic principles of its foreign-policy orientation. Czechoslovakia never counted on an act of such brutal aggression on the part of its former friends and was not prepared for it. Even people who seriously studied the problems of relations among socialist countries never expected anything like this, not because they had any illusions about the foreign policy of the Soviet Union but because of the consequences of a military intervention in the Czechoslovak Socialist Republic for world developments, for the world Communist movement, and particularly for the future of world socialism. However, a fear of the consequences of the Czechoslovak road to socialism for the developments in some socialist countries outweighed the voice of reason and political realism.

The demand for neutrality expressed so frequently these days represents a turning point in the thinking of our public. However, no small country can assure its neutrality merely by declaring itself neutral. This demand is ill considered and can only be exploited by the occupiers. The needs of the present situation must be expressed, above all, by the resolute demand of the restoration of full independence and sovereignty of our country. As a basic demand, it implies, first of all, the departure of foreign troops. Although it is difficult at the moment to say in specific terms what the international political position of Czechoslovakia is going to be afterward and what the circumstances and possibilities of its foreign policy will be, one thing is already certain: Czechoslovakia is going to have a socialist foreign policy expressing the needs and interests of our nation in the newly created situation.

From Politika, No. 2, August 26, 1968

The Ten Commandments

1. don't know
2. don't care
3. don't tell
4. don't have
5. don't know how to
6. don't give
7. can't do
8. don't sell
9. don't show
10. do nothing

From Vecerni Praha, *August 26, 1968*

To All Readers of Rude Pravo [8]

To all who cherish socialist Czechoslovakia:

After a pause of several days caused by well-known occurrences, the readers of *Rude Pravo* are again receiving their daily paper, the organ of the Central Committee of the Communist Party of Czechoslovakia.

Rude Pravo remains loyal to its traditions as a revolutionary Communist newspaper; it remains loyal to the ideas of Marxism-Leninism; it remains loyal to the principles of proletarian internationalism and socialist patriotism.

We are an organ of the officially elected Central Committee headed by its First Secretary, Comrade Alexander Dubcek. Our organ has absolutely nothing to do with the Central Committee created at the so-called Extraordinary Fourteenth Party Congress, whose convocation and proceedings represent a chain of violations of the most elementary norms of intra-Party democracy.

Our political platform is a full realization of the policy line based on the decisions of the January plenum of the Central Committee and on the Action Program. We shall resolutely oppose all tendencies and attempts at a return to the pre-January period and its methods and practices, which have been rightly

---

[8] The following two articles from *Rude Pravo*, both labeled "illegal edition" by the Institute of History, were probably put out by conservatives under the orders of editor Oldrich Svestka.

condemned. We shall not permit the return to political life of people discredited before the Party and the people, who bear responsibility for the errors and deformations of the past.

We shall be implacable in our struggle against right-wing anti-socialist forces and counterrevolutionary elements, which misused the process of democratization in our society for attacks against the foundations of socialism in our country. We shall conduct the most resolute struggle against the bearers of revisionism, who are concentrating on an ideological and organizational break-up of the Party.

In these days, in a particularly complex situation and in a tense atmosphere, we wish to contribute our utmost toward a gradual general consolidation and calming down. We realize that it is an extremely complex task. Its full success depends primarily on a really truthful, objective informing of the citizens, which will make it possible for the overwhelming majority of people loyal to socialism to see through the false game and understand the real danger that is seriously threatening the basic interests of the working people. Its success depends on the responsibility of party, state, and economic organs in normalizing the conditions of life and work. We in *Rude Pravo* want to assist this process with all our energy. This is, in our opinion, the road to the creation of conditions that will make possible the departure of the troops of allied countries without risking a threat to socialism in our country.

Editorial Board of *Rude Pravo*

From Rude Pravo, *illegal edition, August 26, 1968*

"The Extraordinary Fourteenth Party Congress"—an Unheard-of Violation of Statutes

The so-called Central Committee elected by the so-called Extraordinary Fourteenth Party Congress has stated that it is "the only authorized leading organ of the Party in the period between congresses and requests all lower Party organs to be guided in their activities solely by the directives of this legal Central Committee and its Presidium." This unprecedented fraud, as outrageous as the whole convoking and organizing of the illegal farce around the Extraordinary Fourteenth Party Congress, is contained in the communiqué from the first session of this strange, illegal Party organ.

In this connection, it must be said clearly and uncompromisingly: To convoke a congress, to cancel the mandates of the current Central Committee of the Party and of the Central Control and Audit Commission, to elect a new Central Committee, to receive appeals, to approve letters and resolutions, and actually to usurp the right of "guiding the Party" is anti-Party, illegal activity, an activity utterly contrary to the Party statutes, which shall be judged and condemned as such.

What does this violation of the Party statutes, unprecedented and unheard-of in this history of our Party, consist of?

1. The regularly elected Central Committee, which has not yet been deprived of its mandate, decided to convoke the Congress on September 9, 1968. According to the valid statutes, only it was authorized to change that date. No one else was, or is, authorized to do that.

2. The convocation of the Extraordinary Fourteenth Party Congress was decided without authorization by the City Committee in Prague, which thus elevated itself to the Central Committee, although the Central Committee was fully capable to evaluate and decide the question of the date of the Congress. The Prague City Committee thus grossly violated the Party statutes, and its activity must be judged as anti-Party.

3. A third of the duly elected delegates of the Congress were unable to take part in the Congress because they were not aware of its convocation or of the place of its session. A number of delegates from more remote Czech regions and from Moravia were unable to attend the Congress, and delegates from Slovakia did not attend at all. The Congress therefore had no right to meet in session or even to decide on questions concerning the entire state, not to mention the fact that it had no right at all to elect a new Central Committee or a new Central Control and Audit Commission.

4. The documents that the so-called Extraordinary Fourteenth Party Congress was discussing had not been passed or approved

by the duly elected Central Committee, which has not yet been deprived of its mandate.

5. The Central Committee, legally elected at the Thirteenth Party Congress, had no opportunity to inform the Congress on the situation in the country that had brought about the necessity of the arrival of the Warsaw Pact forces in our country.

All this proves that the so-called Extraordinary Fourteenth Party Congress was not duly convoked in a manner corresponding with the statutes and that it absolutely could not have fulfilled its task in the present complicated circumstances. Its actions as well as its elections of new Party organs were anti-Party acts and cannot be considered valid.

Only the authorized Central Committee, elected at the Thirteenth Party Congress, can and must decide on the convocation of the Fourteenth Party Congress on a new date.

This organ cannot be replaced by anyone, much less by the extremist, ultra-rightest forces that undermined the Prague City Committee of the Party, elevated themselves to the function of the Central Committee, and proved again, as they had many times before, that precisely those who have their mouths full of humanism, revival, and democracy quickly put democracy aside when it ceases to suit them.

From Rude Pravo, *illegal edition, August 26, 1968*

8

TUESDAY, AUGUST 27

7:25 A.M.

Czechoslovak Radio announced that, according to a report from Moscow, the negotiations have ended. The delegation is on its way back to Prague.

7:30 A.M.

Czechoslovak Radio broadcast an appeal to have all bells and sirens sound for fifteen minutes at 9 A.M.

7:40 A.M.

Czechoslovak Radio reported that the leadership of the Central Labor Council requests all factory units of the organization and all strike committees to go into permanent session.

7:45 A.M.

Czechoslovak Radio broadcast a report of one of its newsmen who has walked around in Prague. A considerable portion of the heavy equipment of the occupiers is gone from the center of the city, from the Ministry of National Defense, from the Chotek Highway, and from the approaches to Klarov. Bridges have also been vacated.

8:05 A.M.

Czechoslovak Radio announced that early this morning our delegation returned from Moscow.

8:10 A.M.

Czechoslovak Radio reported that crowds of people awaiting our delegation have been gathering on and around Kladenska Avenue [the route from the airport] for the second day now.

8:15 A.M.

Czechoslovak Radio broadcast a tape-recorded interview with Smrkovsky obtained after the arrival of the delegation. "It's hard for me to speak. By means of the radio, I wish to pay my profound respect to this nation, which has accomplished so much. We have all come back, including Kriegel." [1] Smrkovsky said he doesn't know in what order but that reports will be given by Svoboda, Dubcek, Cernik, and himself.

8:22 A.M.

The continuing extraordinary eighty-fifth session of the Presidium of the National Assembly resumed. From the agenda: dissatisfaction with the Government's failure to communicate to the National Assembly information on the building of the Government Presidium being vacated and on the negotiations in Moscow being completed; report on the telephone conversation with Smrkovsky.

From documents of the National Assembly

10:37 A.M.

The continuing extraordinary twenty-sixth session of the National Assembly resumed (adjourned at 11:13 A.M.). The session

---

[1] When the Czechoslovak delegation arrived at Moscow Airport for the flight home, Frantisek Kriegel—a liberal Presidium member and a Jew, to whom the Soviets had the most violent objections—was missing. The Czechoslovaks refused to take off without him. In short order, the Soviets produced Kriegel, and he joined the delegation for the flight home.

was held under the chairmanship of Comrade Smrkovsky. From the agenda: welcoming Comrade Smrkovsky; report on the negotiations in Moscow by Comrade Smrkovsky.

From documents of the National Assembly

Preliminary Report of Chairman of the National Assembly Josef Smrkovsky

During the night, tanks made more noise around the building of the National Assembly than at any previous time. When we looked out of the window in the morning, they were all gone and only some churned-up soil showed where they had stood.

What happened was that our representatives had returned from Moscow at last. The arrival of the Chairman of the National Assembly, Comrade Smrkovsky, to attend the plenary meeting was being awaited all morning. Crowds of people, especially young people, have gathered in front of the parliament building. Czechoslovak as well as foreign newsmen and cameramen are quite busy.

As Comrade Smrkovsky stands before the members of the National Assembly, everyone is very quiet—in contrast to the tumultuous greetings that met him outside. He gives his detailed report on the negotiations in Moscow in a tired, somber voice. The session is adjourned without any discussion.

He does not comply with the wish of the people gathered outside to speak from the balcony. He is in a hurry to attend a meeting of the Central Committee.

From Mlady Svet, No. 35, 1968

11:50 A.M.

The continuing extraordinary eighty-fifth session of the Presidium of the National Assembly resumed (adjourned at 12:10 P.M.). From the agenda: steps to prevent disorder in Prague; reports from the Government; discussion on questions connected with the conclusions of the negotiations in Moscow; draft communiqué on the activities of the National Assembly.

From documents of the National Assembly

Commentaries and Statements Written Before Publication of the Communiqué on the Moscow Negotiations

I just returned from the center of Prague. I must have walked at least ten miles. I saw and heard quite a bit, and now I am to write a commentary.

I sit here, and I don't know how to avoid strong words and at the same time avoid sounding too uppity. Yesterday, we had a report about an ambulance that had been shot up, about the thievery of the occupiers and their brutality and vulgarity. Today, according to a Czechoslovak Radio broadcast based on an official news item released by the Government, the occupiers shot at two of our Ministers as they were leaving the Castle. The occupiers were seen stealing gasoline from cars and breaking store windows. Yesterday, our reporters recounted how they saw the occupiers at Harfa snatching transistor radios from people and destroying them on the spot. Yesterday, at 3 P.M., a Soviet armored vehicle knocked down a light post on a traffic island at Republic Square; on the same day, the occupiers broke into the White Swan Department Store. On the bridges across the Vltava River, the soldiers even made random searches of people's attaché cases. If anyone still retains any illusions, let him pay a visit to the morgues of Prague's hospitals—even though a corpse with a part of his head shot off is not a very appealing sight. Dr. L. is firmly convinced that a number of casualties (including fatal ones) were hit by dumdum bullets.

One can only grind his teeth and fight the tears brought to his eyes by futile anger. But we must keep our teeth clenched and remain cool to provide no excuse for the occupiers to launch mass repression.

The schools of higher learning have already been seized. The secret police of the occupiers is already arresting and deporting our citizens.[2] The occupiers shoot at people walking in the streets without warning or provocation—worse than at the time of the Nazis.

---

[2] This was apparently not true. Early reports of widespread arrests turned out to be rumors based on fear rather than fact.

The only thing we haven't got so far is a new Lidice.[3] Let us not provide any opportunity for a new Lidice to occur. It's quite possible that an incident of the right kind is just the thing being awaited by the collaborators and heirs of the *Chernosotnyenetsy* [Russian religious fanatics who persecuted others during Czarist times].

From the legal Kovak, August 27, 1968

Prague

The Communists as well as non-Party members on the staff of the Ministry of Economic Planning, meeting on August 27, 1968, declare that no agreement would be acceptable to us that would:

1. legalize in any way the presence of the occupation forces on the territory of the Czechoslovak Socialist Republic
2. restrict the freedom of expression and the personal freedoms of the citizens of the Czechoslovak Socialist Republic, including elections of constitutional officials and organs and Party functionaries (At the same time, we do not reject a constraint on the means of communication in questions touching on the Union of Soviet Socialist Republics, the German Democratic Republic, and the Hungarian, Polish, and Bulgarian People's Republics.)
3. in any manner interfere with the post-January course of the domestic and foreign policies of the Czechoslovak Socialist Republic
4. signify nonrecognition of the results, including elections, of the Extraordinary Fourteenth Congress of the Communist Party of Czechoslovakia.

We rely on you and trust your statement that no such agreement shall be signed.

We are of the opinion that the further development of socialism in this country and in the world would *be better served if we*

[3] Lidice was a Czech town near Prague, which the Nazis leveled to the ground after shooting all the men and deporting the women to concentration camps.

exposed ourselves to force while retaining our honor and the good will of the progressive public opinion than by accepting humiliating conditions of the occupiers.[4]

> Local Unit of the Communist Party of Czechoslovakia at the Ministry of Economic Planning

What Is at Stake Is the Character and Development of Our Nations

In the past thirty years, we have lived through many critical experiences that left their mark on our national character. This included the Hitlerian occupation, which humiliated our nations immeasurably and systematically deprived them of their spiritual leaders who could influence the national development. The effects of the occupation were hardly overcome, and a vision of socialism was hardly achieved—a vision of socialism in harmony with the character of our nations and their modern history—when Stalinism entered brutally into the activity of our Party and our whole life. Through the processes concerning the whole system of bureaucratic organization, Stalinism created an atmosphere of fear and insecurity particularly affecting certain strata of our nations. It imposed on us its truths—many of which proved to be false. In addition, it used its whole system of power to make people accept arguments that in many instances were false—as we see even today when we observe Soviet propaganda trying to justify before its own citizens the brutal occupation of our free socialist state just because we want creative socialism.

It took several years of concentrated effort by many Communists and citizens of this state to do away with a Party leadership that was subject to directives from abroad and was willing, in order to retain its position, to betray its own nations and assume attitudes in the area of domestic and foreign policy, economics, and so on that were alien to them. The only prerequisite was for us to begin creating conditions of life that would make it possible for our nations to develop soundly. This was accomplished after January—even though a number of concessions had to be made, including the retention of their posts by many dog-

[4] Italics in original.

matic politicians in whom the nation had expressed a lack of confidence. Nevertheless, we began to construct, step by step, that which we came to call democratic socialism, socialism with a human face, whose measure would be man and his happiness. A period of renaissance began for our nations. A revitalization was apparent in the respect for knowledge and truth, the feeling for fair play and justice, the democratization of the administrative organs of the society, the recognition of the human personality and its right to develop independently, the humanism connected with that, the devotion to freedom and independence, the equality of people. All this began to exert a benign influence on the life of our nations.

The forceful occupation of our country is a blow against this post-January development. It has become apparent, however, that the occupation has not destroyed the good qualities of our nations but, on the contrary, has awakened and mobilized them. The whole world watches our nations with admiration now. This obliges us not to accept anything that would hamper the awakening of our nations and deprive us of the confidence we feel in the moral and intellectual qualities of our people and their resolve to go on. Consequently, our nations cannot give up the life-giving sources from which they mold their history. The occupier is in a position to impose many things on our people temporarily, but none of them can be voluntarily accepted and recognized by any honest Czech or Slovak.

In this, our position is firm, and no concessions are possible. Our point of departure must remain the unemasculated Action Program of the Communist Party of Czechoslovakia and the program of the Government of our socialist Republic. This is our stand now, when the results and consequences of the Moscow negotiations are being speculated about. We believe that every honest politician in our country will realize this and act accordingly. Otherwise, he would seriously antagonize his own people.

I can state that the new leadership of the Party does realize it fully. It realizes that the Communist Party and the Communists are duty-bound to voice the opinion and defend the interests of the people and to fight for them purposefully. They are demonstrating it by very specific acts these days, and they will not retreat from it in the future, because only this can be the basis of the people's confidence in Communists.

From Zemedelske Noviny, *August 27, 1968*

The Blood of Children Was Shed

It happened on the Cyril and Methodius Square in the Karlin district of Prague. An armored car belonging to the Soviet occupation forces approached a house where a boy about fifteen years of age was painting on the wall in the Russian alphabet the most common sign of these days: "Go home!" The machine-gunner riding on the vehicle pointed his gun toward the boy. This was observed by a woman pushing a baby carriage. In the naive hope that the occupiers might be compassionate, she took her six-month-old child in her arms and stood by the boy. The occupier murdered all three with a single burst of his gun.

From Lidova Demokracie, *9th extra edition, August 27, 1968*

A Swell Borough

In times of peace, the sixth borough of Prague used to be called a swell borough. There were no factories with their pollutants, only parks, broad avenues, single-family houses surrounded by gardens, and modern buildings. A large number of public officials live here. There are many embassies in this area, the building of the Ministry of National Defense, of the General Staff, several research institutes, and other buildings of importance. But, in the last few days, the sixth borough has become the home of the largest number of occupation forces of any borough in the city. They impede traffic, the distribution of supplies, the whole life of the borough.

Summary of casualties in the sixth borough of Prague as of noon, Monday, the twenty-seventh of August, 1968: 1 dead; 1 seriously wounded; 2 lightly wounded. The funeral of Milan Kadlec took place at 2 P.M. on Tuesday and was attended by a large number of delegations from factories and various organizations.

The young people of the borough marked the first day of the occupation by collecting signatures for the statement of the District National Committee in Prague 6. This statement expresses support for our legal organs and demands an immediate withdrawal of the occupation forces. Sixteen thousand citizens signed on the first day alone.

The borough committee is working in full legality. A plenary meeting is held daily and is enlarged to include members of the District Supervisory Commission and chairmen of Party organizations at enterprises. All the Party organizations in the borough went on record as approving the results of the Extraordinary Fourteenth Party Congress and the resolution of the new Central Committee. During the six days, several dozen people applied for membership in the Party. The chairman of the Party organization was removed by the member Communists because he went on leave during the critical days and his conduct was unbecoming for a Party member. Fifteen new members who joined in the past few days include kindergarten teacher Jana Kotherova, an employee working in the foreign-trade sector, A. Tachezyova, and typesetter R. Cech.

Every day, citizens come to the District Committee and offer financial contributions and other assistance for damage repair and reconstruction in the city. The secretary of the borough committee declares: "We are acting lawfully. However, we are prepared to ensure the continued activities of the Party under all conditions.[5] We have only one complaint: poor distribution of the newspapers. They're being scattered around on the streets. We need them for enterprises and factories."

The occupiers confiscated the arms of the People's Militia at the airport and the Party's Higher Political School. Evidently, they thought that that, too, was a bed of counterrevolution.

Saturday and Sunday were regular working days for all enterprises in the Prague 6 borough. Normal work is impossible only at the airport, where, however, at least the maintenance of machinery is being continued. The airport is occupied, but despite that, at least one thousand employees voted for a resolution for freedom, Dubcek, and Svoboda. Research workers and other employees of the research institutes came to offer their assistance to

[5] A hint that this group, as well as many other organizations, was prepared to go underground if necessary.

the District National Committee and the District Committee. They assist in the distribution of food, and on Tuesday four hundred of them left to help harvest hops.

Drivers, maintenance workers, cleaning women, and others who used to work at the Soviet Embassy reported at the District Committee and requested transfers to other jobs because they did not want to work for the Embassy any longer. New jobs were secured for them.

Not a single member of Public Security turned traitor. Even off-duty members of State Security are offering their services to the legal organs. State Security in the borough has only two traitors: They now work as announcers for the occupiers' television. One of them is Milos Hladik, a former Secretary of the City Committee who was concerned with tasks in ideology.

The distribution of food is going along all right. All nursery schools where the children get their meals are in operation. The District National Committee secured care for the aged and the sick. They are being taken care of by members of citizens' committees, who shop and clean and cook for them.

Members of the Pioneer organization [the Communist Party's pre-teen and early-teen youth group] collected paper last Tuesday. In their announcement to the public, they said that the collection was being made to aid printing shops.

This is how life goes on these days in the borough that has a reputation for being swell.

From Politika, *No. 3, August 27, 1968*

What Sort of Information Did Brezhnev Have?

The occupation of our country must have been preceded by a lengthy period during which the Soviet leadership was collecting information. The reports could have been of several types, of which two were the most significant—information collected by the Soviet espionage service in Czechoslovakia, and information processed by the Soviet Embassy in Prague.

It seems that the espionage network in this country flopped, and the standard of the work of the Soviet diplomats in Prague is indicated by its results. When Brezhnev decided to intervene in

Czechoslovakia (and the decision must certainly have been approved by Messrs. Ulbricht, Gomulka, Kadar, and Zhivkov), he undoubtedly calculated on the basis of some information that people would be found immediately who would declare themselves to be the new Czechoslovak leadership, that at least part of the population would welcome the Soviet occupiers, and that units of Czechoslovak Security would quickly render the communication media harmless and intimidate the population by mass threats.

He miscalculated on each count. Perhaps this is now evident even to Brezhnev, as it is becoming evident to his soldiers whose units lost their way and groped around in our cities stripped of street markers and signposts.

Brezhnev and his colleagues in the Politburo should draw at least two conclusions from all this. They should disband their intelligence network in Czechoslovakia and read, instead of its reports, the free Czechoslovak press. They should replace their diplomats in Prague. Nobody will any longer shake the hands of those who are still here.

From Politika, *No. 3, August 27, 1968*

Broken Pieces Hard to Glue Together

The metaphor about a bull in a china shop has never fit any situation as closely as it does this one. All the commentators in the world who analyze the invasion of our country agree on that point. The progressive people in the world clench their fists over the asininity of the invasion, which can very well soil the concept of socialism in the eyes of so many millions.

Here are some of the innumerable acts of protest.

For the first time since 1956, both Houses of the British Parliament held sessions in London yesterday and sharply condemned the occupation of Czechoslovakia. The halls of Westminster resounded with the angry words of the leaders of all political parties.

President Saragat of Italy convened a meeting of the parliament for the day after tomorrow to discuss the invasion of Czechoslovakia. This will be the first time since World War II that the parliament will meet during summer vacations. In Rome, in the Communist-dominated districts, Emilia and Romagna, one protest demonstration follows on the heels of another.

In Austria, a general strike took place this morning to support our fight for freedom. Yesterday, work was stopped in the factories in France. People in Holland indicated their feelings by two minutes of national silence today at noon.

The Communist Party of France has already issued three appeals to the Soviet Union to withdraw its troops and has expressed admiration for the dignity of Czechs and Slovaks in these times of bitter betrayal.

From Vecerni Praha, August 27, 1968

Occupied Prague

Shot up. With its dead victims. With cannons pointing at people and at buildings. But this is only part of the picture. The occupation is now in its seventh day, and still the city is unbowed. The posters on the walls speak in one voice: "Go home, occupiers! Nobody asked you to come." Signposts show: "Moscow—1,800 miles."

Prague is still under occupation even though the occupiers withdrew from the center of the city today. People clench their fists as they walk past the National Museum and on Vinohradska Street [where most of the visible damage was done]. The citizens of Prague love their city. They swear to themselves: We shall never forget this! Our children, too, will be told about the morning in August when your tanks appeared in the streets, and they will hear from us about double-facedness and the betrayal of our friends.

No, don't worry, we are not forgetting the year 1945 when Soviet troops liberated us. But we evaluate deeds justly.

Prague under occupation: our city, which they did not succeed in bringing to its knees, as they did not succeed in bringing the people of our country to their knees. We are the masters in our house, in our city. And you have no business staying here!

GO AWAY!

From Prazske Noviny, published by Nova Praha

What Would Lenin Say About It?

It happened in the center of the city. First, the thunder of a helicopter; then, a shower of leaflets. No, these are not leaflets, they are something larger. Newspapers printed in the Russian alphabet—Moscow's *Pravda*. A newspaper people used to read with a pencil in their hand. A newspaper they used in their studies of the Russian language. Today it is a *Pravda* that is consistently printing lies about us. In the Sunday edition, it says again that "the counterrevolution in Czechoslovakia is growing increasingly bold. . . ."

It shocks you. Our little, honest, and proud people who love their Republic—railway employees, salesgirls, streetcar conductors, workers on their way to factories hurrying through streets where perfidious death is lurking, drivers distributing milk in the dangerous night and early morning hours, our intelligentsia—are they what *Pravda* calls counterrevolutionaries? Is this how far you have gone, writers and editors of *Pravda*, that, in spite of what your correspondents must have seen in Prague, you continue to insult our honest people? While misinforming over 200 million trusting Soviet people at the same time?

Copies of *Pravda* are floating down from above, but unfortunately they are full of lies about Czechoslovakia. No wonder, then, at what follows. People gather up some copies, make a pile, and put a match to it; others tear them up in disgust. This is what you have done to *Pravda*'s one-time marvelous popularity. *Pravda*, founded by Lenin. How deep you have allowed it to sink by misusing its pages to justify the occupation and the firing on innocent, defenseless people. Lenin must be turning in his grave, as the saying goes.

This, however, will not prevent you, writers and editors of *Pravda*, from printing another news item tomorrow: "The counterrevolutionaries in Prague burn copies of Lenin's *Pravda!*"

From Rude Pravo, *August 27, 1968*

Jiri Lukas in a New Post

Many people have mislaid their face in the past few days. Some are hiding it. One man is hiding behind the pictures from

Plicka's volume of Prague photographs. He is an announcer of the occupiers' television station, Jiri Lukas, editor-in-chief of the magazine *Prague-Moscow*, formerly on the staff of the Central Committee when Antonin Novotny was there, one-time assistant editor of *Kvety* and News Agency *Novosti*. He should now change his name, too, not only hide his face. Instead of Lukas, the name Judas would suit him.

Lukas is a typical careerist of the Novotny regime who always served spinelessly and tried to suppress everything progressive. Eventually, he was fired for serious moral transgressions after his position, even in Novotny's clique, became untenable. However, in order to be able to go on throwing around money in bars, he was given a nice job as assistant editor of *Kvety*. The progressive editor of this publication was crudely eased out of his job to make room for Lukas.

From Zemedelske Noviny, *August 27, 1968*

Not Even in the Darkest, Most Fantastic Dream

These days, as I listen at times to the programs of the Soviet radio and am struck by the fantastic, nonsensical, even simple-minded lies, I have to recall the period when I worked for Radio Moscow. I see the anteroom of the studio where I used to wait for the Austrian announcer to leave and for my turn to come. I see the microphones by which I used to sit down night after night to speak the first lines of the program: "This is Moscow Radio speaking." That was the beginning of my respect for the Soviet Union. It was there that I would relate news of the Soviet Union— demolished by occupiers but rising from the ashes—of the heroic and selfless work of the exhausted, impoverished, bleeding, pain- fully wounded Soviet people.

I got to know Leningrad when it still had the horrors of the blockade and of hunger fresh in its memory. I used to take walks along the beautiful embankments, and I could still read and touch with my palms the three- and four-year-old black signs that the rains could not wash off or the fogs and snows of north- ern winters dissolve: "Death to the German aggressors!" I used to read Mikhail Sholokhov and his school of hate—a searing, tenacious, rock-hard hate for the aggressors, the occupiers.

I was writing a book about Leningrad, and I wanted it to be a bible of brave, honorable, and desperate heroism and patriotism and of the best human qualities of the Soviet man.

For twenty years, I have worked for friendship with the Soviet Union. I worked with a clear and convinced heart, and the results of the work came out well because I was ardent and enthusiastic. I am sure the women of Chomutov [a city northwest of Prague] still remember our meeting, at which I gave my last talk on this subject, that they still remember the two women professors who took part, the zestfulness, the love, the fervent friendship that filled the decorated hall.

I recall how I was present at the founding of the School of the Czech Language at Moscow's University, how I worked with Professor Bogatyrov on his first Czech-Russian dictionary. I wonder how Professor Bogatyrov, our devoted friend for forty years, felt now when he left for home from the International Congress of Slavists in Prague. He could testify that there has been no chaos and no counterrevolution in this country.

A few days ago, I was in Treptov, near Berlin, and stood in front of the grandiose statue of a Red Army soldier holding a huge sword in one hand and a child in his other arm. A monumental and overwhelming symbol of strength and kindness, of the victor and the protector. How many people were there on that warm summer day! How many fell silent under the overpowering impression—remembrance and gratitude. All sorts of nationalities were represented there, where we stood in silence and wept, looking at the hero and the child, feeling ready to offer any sacrifice, any testimony, any act of duty.

The thought never crossed our minds that in a few days the soldier with the sword would come to our country and that the feelings we would be looking at him with would-be humiliation and incredulous surprise.

These days, I often meet a Russian lady in the woods, a warmhearted and good mother whose married daughter lives in this country. "Such a beautiful country, so kind, so many gardens and flowers are here. And such care taken of the graves of our sons." I recall the graves of six thousand Soviet dead at the Opava

cemetery. The army of the occupiers has already passed through
Northern Moravia. Perhaps they noticed the loving care. They
are not aware of the fact that our children have been taught to
take care of that cemetery, that every year on Christmas Eve a
whole forest of Christmas trees is lit up there. Could anyone
believe that in one day, in one fatal hour, we shall turn our backs
on those very uniforms, that our hearts might bleed, but that we
would not hand them a drink of water? And the Soviet soldier
would look at our sorrow and anger and not understand it because he, too, has been deceived? Propaganda is obviously so
all-powerful that one cannot escape it under these regimes, and
it creates chasms so wide that they cannot be bridged in a
few days.

And could I, myself, believe that I, personally, am writing these
lines so full of lament and disappointment and incurable sorrow?
When the first issue of *Rude Pravo* was published in May, 1945,
a buff-colored sheet printed in haste, it carried articles by two
women writers, Marie Pujmanova and myself.

Could anyone in the darkest, most fantastic dream foresee that
twenty-three years later I would be writing for publication in
Rude Pravo a confession of my grief and disillusionment, which
hurts so unbearably at the threshold of my old age?

Jarmila Glazarova

From Rude Pravo, *August 27, 1968*

Do Not Harm a Hair of Their Heads, But Do Not Give Them a Drop of Water!

The pen is shaking in my hand, my voice falters. For twenty-
five years I have been teaching my children to love the Soviet
Union, to see Moscow as the guarantor of our national and state
independence. All this is in ruins now. The very same faces, the
very same uniforms my children know from the pictures of the
unforgettable days of May, 1945, which I have taught them to
respect as the faces of our liberators, are being seen by them, by
their very own eyes, in an awful context. They see them spilling
Czech blood, firing at our national monuments; they witness their
unprecedented, cynical kidnapping of Alexander Dubcek and

Oldrich Cernik, representatives of our sovereignty. The number of crimes committed these days in the streets of Prague cries to high heaven.

They tell lies to the world, claiming that we called on them to help, but they are unable to give the name of one single person who did. They lie, claiming that they protect Prague, while in fact they ruin it by the treads and cannons of their tanks. They lie, claiming that they have come to give us fraternal assistance, while in fact they shamelessly and incomprehensibly terrorize the Czech nation. They claim to be fighting for Communism—against Czech and Slovak Communists who try to redeem the Party. They induced the birth in our hearts of something terrible: hate of this deceitfulness, a burning feeling of being insulted, an inextinguishable flame of anger. But also the birth of something beautiful: pride of one's own people, country-wide unshakable unity, resolve to resist until the end, not to retreat, not to give up, not to fall on our knees before the occupiers, not to accept any compromise. The whole world sees our moral superiority, and perhaps even many of the simple Ivans and Sergeis see it, judging by how they look away as they meet us in Prague's streets. It's of no avail, fellows: You may be personally very good-hearted, but you came here as occupiers, you came as bandits of the night, you befouled our native land. Our children are learning and will learn to hate you even though we taught them to love your fathers. And we, the fathers here, look on, humbled and impotent but with unbroken character. We shall survive this blow, we shall overcome the humiliation of betrayal and infamy. But if we should tear the words "love" and "peace" from our hearts and throw them up, blame it on your "government" and on yourselves. You are dishonorable occupiers, and he hit it right on the mark, whoever it was who wrote on a wall in Prague: "Do not harm a hair of their heads, but do not give them a drop of water!"

Jan Drda

From Rude Pravo, *August 27, 1968*

Fear

I saw fear in the eyes of the occupation troops. They were standing guard over an old doorman in a passage leading to a large garage. They were undoubtedly decent young men who never imagined a week ago that they might shoot and kill anyone. But not far from where they stood was our first dead.

The fear that the soldiers had in their eyes was a peculiar kind. Each type of fear is really a state in which a man feels helpless. But the fear of a man who is holding a submachine gun in his hand and who is backed by almost a million of his fellow soldiers, tanks, amphibious trucks, and aircraft, who is a member of the largest force in the world, armed to the teeth—this type of fear is really shattering. These soldiers are actually helpless. There is nothing in their own personal and cultural make-up that would enable them to understand why our citizens turn their backs on them. These soldiers have found themselves in the position of teamster Vanya in one of Chekhov's works. Vanya happens to get a translation of *The Three Musketeers*, reads it, shakes his head, says: "I don't follow at all, some foreigners," and then gets dead drunk.

The rulers of Russia who ordered these young boys to invade a small country in the center of Europe have thrown their soldiers back into an old trauma of Russian history. Russian history is marked to a considerable degree by a convergence and merging of things "Caesar's and God's," the state and the church, the Party and the Government—simply by all that is called caesaropapism. Of course, Russian history is also a history of resistance against this caesaropapist tradition, since the best minds of Russia were always aware of the fact that the caesaropapist model of life deprives man of his most essential faculty—the faculty to create— and submerges him in a horrifying passivity that results in man's disrespect for himself and in his slavishness. The spiritual as well as external world of a man subjected to this slavishness is narrowed into an airtight compartment, and one can live in it only if the airtightness is holy in the literal sense of the word. When the Czar decrees that the dress of all saints shall be painted in gold on all icons, to resist means not only to demand a different painting technique but also to assail the Czar's position of power. To declare that grass is green (if some authority has designated it blue) requires the courage of a Copernicus, for it means to become a free man face to face with the machinery of a threatening world power. Does a simple soldier who stands guard by the gate of a garage have courage like that? Probably not. But the rulers of Russia, who have put him into this trauma, have become entrapped in their own guile. For, in a country governed by contempt for one's own people, Vanya will eventually throw *The Three Musketeers* into a corner and get drunk in order to drown his fear.

No, don't think that I am likely to underestimate that fear. What we are now living through, what they have perpetrated on us, that, too, is a crime of fear. They were afraid of us. They are afraid of us. Because, even under the guns of their million-strong army, we are free men.

From Sesity, extra edition, August 27, 1968

The Ideology of Superior Force

One wouldn't believe one's own ears as one listens to the arguments of Soviet propaganda in these tragic days. We had been astounded by the writings of the Soviet press since the spring of this year, and we always questioned whether the Soviet leadership was well informed. Now we know that the questions were relevant. Today, we are simply embittered and shocked by the cynicism with which Soviet propaganda mutilates objective truth to make it fit into the prescribed and primitive precept.

There is evidence of this in the attacks of the last few days on the Extraordinary Fourteenth Party Congress. There is no need to take up the outspoken lies and distortions. It is sufficiently well known that the delegates to that Congress were democratically nominated in the basic organizations of the Party and then elected at regular meetings of district and regional conferences. It is well known that the elected delegates are men who had renounced the errors committed by the Communist Party in the past twenty years under strict tutelage of Moscow, errors whose existence cannot be denied even by today's Soviet propaganda.

It is also well known that the delegates to the Extraordinary Fourteenth Party Congress have elected into the leadership of the new Central Committee Alexander Dubcek and those of his closest collaborators who have at last succeeded in elevating the prestige of the Communist Party from the dust in which it had shamefully lain to a point higher than that it had ever before achieved in Czechoslovakia. The confidence put in the leadership of the Communist Party, in Comrade Dubcek, and the others and the unity of all the sections of the population made it possible to accomplish something that could not have been achieved otherwise: to convene the Congress half a month ahead of time and, moreover, under very difficult conditions. The occupation forces tried to prevent the Congress from being held. They interned Comrade Dubcek and many others. If it were not for the workers in the factories, for the People's Militia, and for the concentrated assistance of plain citizens—both members and nonmembers of the Party—the occupiers would have accomplished what they had actually come to this country to do: prevent the consolidated Party from beginning to build socialism with a human face, to which man of the second half of the twentieth century, no matter what country he is a citizen of, could look with hope and expectation.

The transparent argument of the Soviet sermonizers to the effect that the Extraordinary Fourteenth Party Congress was held in irregular circumstances—that is, secretly—will not hold water. One needs merely leaf through the history of the All-Union Communist Party of the Bolsheviks (even in its officially distorted version) to find voluminous evidence of the fact that the Party must, in the interest of its ability to act, adjust to objective conditions. The Soviet Party used to do that, and many of the congresses in the history of the workers' movement in Russia could be called irregular with much more justification than the legal, democratically arranged Extraordinary Fourteenth Party Congress.

Why, then, did the Extraordinary Fourteenth Party Congress become the target of the propagandistic cannonade of the Soviet ideologists? The Communist Party of the Soviet Union combined the ideology of the Party with the great-power politics of the state organs. For it, there is no equality between a great power and its satellites. The Soviet Communist Party refused to recognize at its Twentieth and Twenty-second Party Congresses that small Communist parties have just as much right to sovereignty as big ones. The ideologists of neo-Stalinism still consider it their right to make final decisions concerning the development of all Communist and workers' parties. The ideas and feelings of people, which constitute the source of socialism's creative development, are for the ideologists merely objects to be manipulated. The result of this anachronism in the thinking of the official Soviet ideologists and leaders is the tragic failure to understand what caused the Communist parties not only in Czechoslovakia but in the whole world to unite in condemning the occupation of Czechoslovakia.

From Svet Prace, *extra edition, August 27, 1968*

Josef Schweik Tells It as It Is

"Technology, Mrs. Müller, is a great blessing for mankind," sighed Josef Schweik as he massaged his legs. "Take radio, for instance. I walked all through Prague, and then I switched on Radio *Vltava*, and I saw that my walking was all in vain because I had missed the most important things happening in Prague. It was only from Radio *Vltava* that I learned, on the basis of reliable reports from Moscow, and here I quote their very words, Mrs. Müller, that one can see all over Prague how soldiers and officers of the allied forces are fraternizing with the population, how they are answering innumerable questions, how they are assisting the people in evaluating the political situation, and how they are clarifying the noble aims the troops have come to fulfill. That's what they said, Mrs. Müller, and I'll tell you, if I didn't have that rubbing stuff on my hands, I would wipe the tears off on my cheeks, that's how touched I am to know how well I'm able to understand their language."

"And did they also report, Sir," asked Mrs. Müller, "that a secret cache of arms was found in the Ministry of Mr. Boruvka?"

"That's right, Mrs. Müller, and that also proves what I'm trying to tell you. Prophetic information, that's a feather in anybody's hat. The news that a cache of arms had been discovered at the Ministry of Agriculture appeared in Moscow's newspapers on

Saturday, and, true enough, the cache was discovered on Sunday by the brave occupation troops. They just confirmed, so to say, that Moscow's *Pravda* had the story right."

"And Mr. Hajek from the Ministry of Foreign Affairs is on the run, Sir," Mrs. Müller whispered.

"That's right, Mrs. Müller," said Josef Schweik, lifting his sad eyes for a moment to look at his landlady. "That Mr. Hajek also has a talent for prophecy, which is hard to find. Just imagine, Mrs. Müller, he was on the run at a beach in Yugoslavia several days before the allied armies suddenly decided to crush the counterrevolution in our country, even if they had to plow it up from the ground first. And to top it all, Mr. Hajek is now running across the sea to the United Nations, which, for a Minister of Foreign Affairs, is something unheard of."

Mrs. Müller, leaning on her broomstick, was following the explanation of Josef Schweik gratefully.

"And to think, Sir, how the inflamed anti-Party elements in the editorial offices of *Rude Pravo* seized Mr. Svestka so that he had to be liberated from captivity by Soviet troops!"

By now Josef Schweik was already tying the string of his underpants and rolling down the trouser-legs. Mrs. Müller helped him into his coat, and he reached for his pipe.

"I'll go now and have a glass or two at the U Kalicha [At the Chalice], Mrs. Müller. I hope old Bretschneider won't be there any longer, that someone has come to 'liberate' him, too." [6]

2:35 P.M.

Czechoslovak Radio reported on the morning meeting of the Government in Prague Castle under the chairmanship of Oldrich Cernik. During the course of the meeting, President Svoboda arrived. The Government discussed a report on the negotiations of the Czechoslovak Government and Party representatives in Moscow. The meeting will be resumed in the afternoon.

---

[6] U Kalicha is the beer hall in Prague that Schweik's creator Jaroslav Hasek frequented. Bretschneider was Schweik's nemesis. See Book I, Chapter 1, of Jaroslav Hasek's *The Good Soldier Schweik* (New York: New American Library, Signet Books, 1963).

2:40 P.M.

Czechoslovak Radio broadcast the text of the communiqué on the Czechoslovak-Soviet negotiations held in Moscow from August 23 to August 26, 1968.

Czechoslovak-Soviet negotiations took place in Moscow from August 23 to 26, 1968, with the participation of, from the Czechoslovak side, Comrade Ludvik Svoboda, President of the Czechoslovak Socialist Republic; Comrade Alexander Dubcek, First Secretary of the Central Committee; Comrade Josef Smrkovsky, Chairman of the National Assembly, member of the Presidium of the Central Committee; Comrade Oldrich Cernik, Chairman of the Government, member of the Presidium of the Central Committee; Comrade Vasil Bilak, member of the Central Committee, First Secretary of the Central Committee of the Communist Party of Slovakia; Comrade Frantisek Barbirek, member of the Presidium of the Central Committee, Deputy Chairman of the Slovak National Council; Comrade Jan Piller, member of the Presidium of the Central Committee; Comrade Emil Rigo, member of the Presidium of the Central Committee; Comrade Oldrich Svestka, member of the Presidium of the Central Committee; Comrade Milos Jakes, Chairman of the Central Control and Audit Commission; Comrade Josef Lenart, alternate member of the Presidium of the Central Committee, Secretary of the Central Committee; Comrade Bohumil Simon, alternate member of the Central Committee; Comrade Dr. Gustav Husak, Deputy Chairman of the Government; Comrade Alois Indra, Secretary of the Central Committee; Comrade Dr. Zdenek Mlynar, Secretary of the Central Committee; Comrade Colonel-General Martin Dzur, Minister of National Defense; Comrade Dr. Bohuslav Kucera, Minister of Justice; Comrade Vladimir Koucky, Ambassador of the Czechoslovak Socialist Republic to the Soviet Union.

From the Soviet side: Comrade Brezhnev, Secretary General of the Central Committee of the Communist Party of the Soviet Union; Comrade Kosygin, Chairman of the Council of Ministers of the Soviet Union, member of the Politburo; Comrade Podgorny, Chairman of the Presidium of the Supreme Soviet of the

Soviet Union, member of the Politburo; Comrade Voronov, member of the Politburo, Chairman of the Council of Ministers of the Russian Federation; Comrade Kirilenko, member of the Politburo, Secretary of the Central Committee; Comrade Polyansky, member of the Politburo, First Deputy Chairman of the Council of Ministers of the Soviet Union; Comrade Suslov, member of the Politburo, Secretary of the Central Committee; Comrade Shelepin, member of the Politburo, Chairman of the All-Union Central Council of Soviet Trade Unions; Comrade Shelest, member of the Politburo, First Secretary of the Central Committee of the Communist Party of the Ukraine; Comrade Katushev, Secretary of the Central Committee; Comrade Ponomarev, Secretary of the Central Committee; Comrade Grechko, Minister of Defense of the Soviet Union; Comrade Gromyko, Minister of Foreign Affairs of the Soviet Union.

During the talks, in a free comradely discussion, the two sides considered questions relating to the present development of the international situation, the activization of imperialism's machinations against the socialist countries, the situation in Czechoslovakia in the recent period, and the temporary entry of troops of the five socialist countries into the territory of the Czechoslovak Socialist Republic.

The participants expressed their mutual, firm belief that the main thing in the present situation is to carry out the joint decisions adopted in Cierna nad Tisou and the provisions and principles formulated by the Bratislava conference, as well as to implement gradually the practical steps following from the agreement reached during the talks. The Soviet side stated its understanding of and support for the position of the leadership of the Czechoslovak Communist Party and the Czechoslovak Socialist Republic, which is determined to proceed from the decisions adopted at the January and May plenary meetings of the Central Committee of the Czechoslovak Communist Party, in the interest of improving the methods of management of the society, developing socialist democracy, and strengthening the socialist system on the basis of Marxism-Leninism.

Agreement was reached on measures aimed at the speediest normalization of the situation in the Czechoslovak Socialist Republic. The Czechoslovak representatives gave information on the planned immediate measures aimed at meeting these goals. The Czechoslovak representatives stated that all the work of the Party and state organs in all the sectors of their activity will be directed at ensuring effective measures in the interest of the socialist system, the leading role of the working class, and the Communist Party and developing and strengthening friendly relations with the peoples of the Soviet Union and the entire socialist community. Expressing the unanimous striving of the peoples of the Soviet Union for friendship and brotherhood with the peoples of socialist Czechoslovakia, the Soviet representatives confirmed their readiness for the broadest sincere cooperation on the basis of mutual respect, equality, territorial integrity, independence, and socialist solidarity.

The troops of the allied countries that temporarily entered the territory of Czechoslovakia will not interfere in the internal affairs of the Czechoslovak Socialist Republic. Agreement was reached on the terms of the withdrawal of these troops from the territory of Czechoslovakia, depending on the normalization of the situation in the Republic. The Czechoslovak side gave information that the supreme commander of the Czechoslovak armed forces had issued appropriate orders aimed at preventing incidents and conflicts capable of disturbing peace and public order. He also instructed the military command of the Czechoslovak Socialist Republic to be in contact with the command of the allied troops.

In connection with the discussion in the United Nations Security Council of the so-called question of the situation in the Czechoslovak Socialist Republic, the representatives of the Republic stated that the Czechoslovak side had not requested the submission of this question for consideration by the Security Council and has demanded its removal from the agenda. The leading representatives of the Czechoslovak Communist Party and the Soviet Communist Party confirmed their determination to resolutely carry out in the international arena a policy meeting the interests of strengthening the solidarity of the socialist community and the cause of peace and international security.

As heretofore, Czechoslovakia and the Soviet Union will resist with determination the militaristic, revanchist, and neo-Nazi forces that strive to reverse the results of World War II and to encroach on the inviolability of the existing borders in Europe. Both sides also confirmed again their determination to fulfill unswervingly all commitments under multilateral and bilateral agreements concluded between socialist states, to strengthen the defensive power of the socialist community, and to increase the effectiveness of the defensive Warsaw Pact. The talks were held in an atmosphere of frankness, comradeship, and friendship.

From documents of the Ministry of Foreign Affairs

2:50 P.M.

Czechoslovak Radio broadcast a statement by the President of the Republic Ludvik Svoboda.

Dear fellow citizens!

After four days of negotiations in Moscow, we are back among you, in our fatherland. We have returned together with comrades Dubcek, Cernik, Smrkovsky, and other comrades. Neither you nor we felt at ease. We were with you all the time in thought, wondering how you were living through these difficult days. We are truly glad that we are home again among you. We received with deep sadness news, in particular, of the loss of life, the most valuable thing there is, mainly among the young. We feel deep sympathy for those whose dear ones have died.

We have been drawing strength during the negotiations from the innumerable demonstrations of confidence. I thank you for it sincerely. I am sure we have not disappointed you. We have been helped by the prudence and high discipline of you all, Czechs and Slovaks, workers and our armed units.

The developments in our country in recent days threatened every hour to produce the most tragic consequences. As a soldier, I know what bloodshed can result in a conflict between civilians and an army with modern equipment. Consequently, as your President, I considered it my duty to do all I could to ensure that this does not happen, that the blood of peoples that have always been friends is not spilled senselessly, but that at the same time the fundamental interests of our fatherland and its people are safeguarded. In saying this, I do not want to deny the fact that painful wounds caused by the events of these days will long remain. Yet we are truly interested in the renewal of confidence and sincere cooperation between countries linked by destiny to a common road. The place of our country in today's world is and cannot be anywhere but in the socialist community. As I stressed in my previous pronouncements, I left for the negotiations in Moscow in agreement with the Government, feeling that the solution of a complicated situation must be based on accelerated normalization of the activities of the constitutional and other legitimate organs of our socialist state, our society, and its leading representatives. As I already told you from Moscow—and as you can see for yourselves—I have returned with all these comrades, who are forthwith resuming the offices to which they have been democratically appointed and in which you have supported them with your full confidence.

This is the first and for us important step toward the normalization of life in our country. Naturally, the departure of the armies of the Soviet Union and the other socialist countries from our territory bears on this. We have, above all, achieved agreement in principle on a gradual implementation of the complete departure of the armies. Pending this, their presence is a political reality. The prudence and discipline you have been manifesting until now are the necessary pre-condition for the final solution of this problem. I am telling you this with full responsibility as your President, as a patriot, and as a soldier.

Dear friends, in the last few days you have showered us, the constitutional representatives of the state and of the Communist Party of Czechoslovakia, with expressions of confidence and loyalty. This is a great asset, a great force on which we count in our efforts to ensure the further, consistently socialist, development of our country. In the spirit of the January, April, and May plenary meetings of the Central Committee of the Communist Party of Czechoslovakia, we want to continue to develop the socialist social system and strengthen its humanist, democratic character, as expressed in the Action Program and the Government's policy declaration. Together with the whole National Front, we want to carry on building our country as the real homeland of the working people. We shall not retreat a single step from these aims. We shall naturally not allow them to be misused by those to whom the interests of socialism are alien. To that end, all of us must now purposefully and with determination direct our efforts.

We appeal to you all, my dear fellow citizens, workers, farmers, members of the intelligentsia, to you, my dear young friends. In these difficult days, I call on you to unite and ask you to continue to manifest wisdom and circumspection.

Let us unite all socialist, patriotic, and creative forces and work for the well-being of the peoples of our Czechoslovak Socialist Republic!

3:05 P.M.

Czechoslovak Radio broadcast a round-table discussion with commentaries on the Moscow communiqué.

4:55 P.M.

The continuing extraordinary twenty-sixth session of the National Assembly resumed (adjourned at 6:29 P.M.). Present were 216 members.

From the agenda: reading of the communiqué on the Moscow negotiations; discussion of the present situation; unanimous approval of a communiqué on the activities of the National Assembly.

From documents of the National Assembly

Approximately 5:30 P.M.

Czechoslovak Radio broadcast a statement by the First Secretary of the Party, Comrade Alexander Dubcek.

Dear fellow citizens, comrades,

It is difficult for me to find words to express gratitude for the enormous show of confidence with which you have overwhelmed me and the other comrades for whom you have been waiting. Your high morale, your circumspect course and attitude, and the firmly expressed conviction that all properly elected officials of the Party and the central organs would return to their functions was not a vain hope. We are again among you in our work. We thank you. We can again renew the activities of the central organs of our Republic, of the National Assembly, of the Government, and the activity of the National Front.

This activity, like the life of our people, will take place in a situation whose reality does not depend on our will alone. We were fully aware of this fact during the entire time, just as you feel it—and all of you are certainly aware of it. It is the great merit of our circumspection, the circumspection of the people of our Republic, that you abided by the appeal of the Presidium of the Central Committee, of the President of the Republic, Comrade Ludvik Svoboda, and of the Government of the Republic, that no greater open clashes and no additional bloodshed occurred. It is necessary to prevent further suffering and further losses at all costs, because they would not alter the real conditions, and the abnormal situation in our homeland would be prolonged. The fact that we are determined to prevent bloodshed does not mean that we want passively to submit to the situation that has been created. On the contrary, we are doing everything in order that we may find—and we are convinced that we shall find—ways and means of devising and, together with you, implementing the policy that will in the end lead to a normalization of conditions. In this conviction we are being strengthened by the results the representatives of the Soviet Union have achieved in the negotiations we concluded yesterday in Moscow. The Soviet representatives, too, want to contribute to the normalization of our relations.

In today's reality, we are faced with the task of finding a way out of the present situation in Czechoslovakia. First, we have an agreement on the phased departure of troops of the five states from the territory of our Republic. Consequently, any distrust aroused about this matter is groundless and harmful. That agreement, that standpoint, is the fundamental prerequisite for our future activities. We have agreed that troops will be moved immediately from villages and towns to areas reserved for them. This is naturally connected with the ability of our own Czechoslovak organs to ensure order and normal life in individual areas. In this respect, the Government of the Republic has already proceeded today to take appropriate measures in order that our organs may implement steps to regulate our civil life. It would therefore be very imprudent and dangerous to take any actions that would hold up the movements and eventually the departure of the troops of the five states from our country. The final aim of our entire endeavor is to effect the complete withdrawal of these troops as soon as possible. On the basis of the Moscow negotiations, the Government is already taking specific steps in this direction.

Work is going on concerning other measures. We ask you, dear fellow citizens, to help us prevent any provocations by those who are interested in increasing the tension of the situation, which is already very tense indeed, and whose forces are directed against socialism. What we need, above all, in this period is order. We need the conscientious discipline of all our citizens, all inhabitants of our Czechoslovak socialist fatherland, just as we have had up to now. Moreover, in the next period we shall need this conscientiousness even more, for a lot will be at stake, and much will depend on our course, on our work, on how all of you help to perform this work. I want to point out most seriously that the normalization of conditions includes the requirement that each individual should not act on the basis of passions and mass psychosis without knowledge of the facts. In this complicated period, we must not succumb to passions and psychoses. If this happened, we would hardly be able to regulate life in our country, and believe me, we are determined to do everything in this respect that is in our power.

The normalization of conditions is the basic prerequisite for our being able again to concentrate our efforts on proceeding without major mistakes or extended delays along the path in which you have put your trust, along with us, and in which you still believe, in my opinion, even though we now live and work under complicated conditions and in a complicated period. We have interpreted your support in these days as support for the idea of a more successful development of socialism in our country along the path formulated since the January plenary meeting of the Central Committee and during the preparations for the Party's Extraordinary Fourteenth Congress. This support will strengthen us all the more and will be an obligation for us not to abandon, in this complicated time, our striving for the expression of humanist and socialist principles.

It might seem a paradox that I speak about this just now. But we must have faith in our strength and faith in our people, because only in unity, in the unity of our course, in the unity of our deeds, can we assure the success of our future policy. We are returning to work with the determination to create conditions for continuing this policy with as few mistakes as possible. It will not be easy, and it will therefore be necessary to exert much effort. Such is the reality, and from this we must embark on our work. To ignore the real situation could lead in some places only to adventure and to anarchy. That would not be good, and it would not be good for the implementation of the important tasks we now face. You know that the new situation in our country confronts us with new questions and that there are new points of view. The first thing we need is the quickest possible consolidation and normalization of the situation in the country. I know that it will be very complicated, but we must see it as the fundamental condition for further steps. For this very reason, we trust that you will assist us today in the same way you have supported us before—on the basis of a realistic assessment of the situation —with your continued confidence and active participation. We trust you will do this if we must carry out some temporary, exceptional measures restricting the degree of democracy and freedom of expression that we have achieved. I ask you to understand the kind of time we live in. The sooner we are able to achieve a normalization of conditions in the country and the greater the support you give us, the sooner we will be able to take further steps on our post-January course. We do not want to seek the road to the solution of our problems by ourselves. We rely not only on our own strength, but primarily on your strength, on your moral strength, on your character, on your independent thinking based on prudence, circumspection, and proceeding from reality in our country.

This reality must not be ignored. But the broadcasts of some radio transmitters, after the speech of the President of the Republic, Comrade Svoboda, have been spreading mistrust and doubts about the Moscow negotiations and about the measures being prepared for the withdrawal of troops. We warn very emphatically against such a course. Inflammatory words are easily broadcast into the atmosphere. It is necessary to see the link between such speech and responsibility for additional loss of life, and material damage, which even now is far from small.

Your support, calmness, prudence, and the activity of the Party and other mass and social organizations in these days have confirmed again the experience we had already gained since January of this year—that it is necessary to be in close touch with the people, to consult with them systematically, to lean on their good sense and experience, to pay attention to their views and express them in our policy. We wish to continue this way. I know the ideals you fight for. I know that you will never retreat from the idea of socialism, humanism, national independence, and our Czechoslovak sovereignty. I believe, and I say this to you all, that in my life I cannot and will not do anything other than work for the realization of these ideals of my people. With this in mind, I and the other comrades negotiated in the past few days, and with this in mind, I want to work and serve my fatherland in the days to come. There are a great many questions for which we must seek and find answers. You yourselves know best how many fateful questions have appeared during the last week—from renewing order, to the withdrawal of troops and the solution of many problems in the life of each one of us. All this requires a well-considered answer as soon as possible. I assure you that I intend to consider, along with you, our future steps in the new situation that has arisen and to begin solving the most urgent problems as soon as possible.

Allow me now to address a few words to all Communists, rank-and-file members, as well as functionaries of our Party. Comrades, we all—whether we work in the basic organizations or in the highest organs of the Party—are strong only if we have the confidence of the people. This increases the degree of the responsibility we bear for doing everything in the area of practical politics in the interest of the people and doing it even under today's extraordinary and incredibly difficult conditions. It would be the greatest disaster for the Party if its soundest substance, if all its forces that fought to clear the path to the post-January policy of the Communist Party of Czechoslovakia, were now to disintegrate, if a lack of confidence were to arise within the sound forces of the Party. This would inevitably mean the disintegration of the only force capable of extricating our nation from the present complicated situation.

I want you, members and officials of the Party who have worked at home during these days, to understand those of us who have negotiated away from home. We will jointly and as soon as possible deal with all the questions that have arisen in these truly extraordinary and exceptional circumstances. I ask all functionaries of Regional and District Committees and basic organizations of the Party, all delegates to the Extraordinary Fourteenth Party Congress, that during the next few days they fully respect in their Party work the instructions I shall issue in my capacity as the First Secretary of the Central Committee. I mention this because I and the comrades who have worked in the regions and districts and here at the center shall have to discuss the additional steps needed to unify the work of all Communists on all levels, to unify the steps of the Communists who have worked here at home, for further implementation of the policy of our Party.

I assume, at the same time, the exercise of my function of Commander of the People's Militia, which is part of the title and function entrusted to me. In the very near future, we shall solve all necessary questions at a plenary meeting of the Central Committee attended by representatives of the delegates to the Extraordinary Fourteenth Party Congress. We must consult with those Communists, with those leading officials of our Party, who worked while I and other comrades were unable to take part in the work of our Party. I want to state quite frankly that we paid dearly for the experience we now have, that we must conduct our policy with determination and consistency. We must also take care to see to it that the present complicated situation is not taken advantage of by elements and tendencies to which socialism is alien. We shall guard decisively and consistently our socialist policy in Czechoslovakia for the future.[7]

[7] Here Dubcek, obviously exhausted, paused—according to some accounts he almost fainted—and reportedly received an injection that allowed him to go on with his speech.

Dear listeners, I ask you to forgive me if every now and then there is a pause in this largely improvised speech and impromptu appearance. I think you know why it is. All of us who negotiated in Moscow during the past few days are profoundly grateful to you for your prudent and genuinely Communistic work. Without it, it would not have been possible to prevent an aggravation of the situation and to maintain circumspection and the true moral and political unity of our people. I would also like to thank the members of the army, the National Security corps, and the People's Militia for showing such high morale, which helped to avoid great conflicts. That has been right, that is the way to proceed according to the order of the President of the Republic. I thank you all, all our people, from the bottom of my heart. Believe me, your confidence constitutes for us all an obligation, and we will never in our lives forget this obligation and will always feel responsible to you for our actions. We understand our work only as service to our people, a service to our Czechoslovak socialist homeland. We all know today that the future course will not be easy, that it will be complicated—that it will be more complicated and also take longer than we thought, especially with regard to the fulfillment of the Action Program. But whichever way life goes today, we must keep in mind that we must think over carefully how to fulfill in this new situation and these new conditions the program of our Communist Party of Czechoslovakia, the program we espoused in January and April and in subsequent measures of the Central Committee of the Communist Party of Czechoslovakia. It would not have been possible to do otherwise. Subsequently, too, we stood on this position and stand on it now, and this position of ours will be the point of departure for the next period.

The nation and our people belong to the community of the socialist nations in other countries. We believe that, in spite of everything that has happened and that we are going through today, the relations between our nations and the nations of other socialist countries will be resolved in such a way as to be in harmony with this reality. I cannot put it any other way. For the very reason that our nations, the Czechs and the Slovaks, are people of a profoundly human nature with internationalist feelings, their relations with the nations of other socialist countries—as well as with the nations, the people, the working people of the Soviet Union, and of other countries, too—are relations of international feelings. We must not abandon these relations because we will be working things out not only today but tomorrow, too, and the relations in this respect will certainly be aimed at drawing closer with these nations, resolving the relations in such a way as to be in harmony with, and corresponding to, the reality that our nations and other nations are socialist nations. I beg you not to allow any provocations, not to let panic enter our ranks. In this difficult situation, we cannot do otherwise than to exert all our strength, all our reason, in order to be truly able to pass muster in our future work. A nation in which everyone will be guided by reason and conscience shall not perish. I ask you all, my dear fellow citizens, Czechs and Slovaks, Communists and members of the other political parties of the National Front, I ask all the workers, farmers, I ask our intelligentsia, all our people, let us remain united, calm, and, above all, prudent. Let us realize that only in that and in our loyalty to socialism, in our honor, in our endeavors, in our character, is a guarantee of the road forward.

Statements About the Moscow Communiqué

Communiqué on the Session of the Central Committee and Central Control and Audit Commission

Members of the Central Committee of the Communist Party of Czechoslovakia and Central Control and Audit Commission, elected at the urgent session of the Extraordinary Fourteenth Party Congress, resolved at their meeting of August 28, 1968, to support in full discipline the leadership of the Party headed by Comrade Alexander Dubcek and to contribute to the unified effort of the whole Party to solve the complicated tasks of the present serious situation in our country. The political steps unanimously agreed on will now be carried out by the members in the area of their activity. In this they can lean on the expressions of confidence addressed to the Central Committee from a great number of provinces, districts, and enterprises.

Comrades, citizens of the Czechoslovak Socialist Republic!

At this moment of history, we consider it our duty to thank you for your unprecedented bravery, discipline, and faithfulness to the ideas of democratic, humanistic socialism, for your unity, and your sincere patriotism. The high moral qualities of our people have gained for us the sympathies of working people all over the world and are helping us to overcome the results of the tragic events in our country.

We particularly appreciate the selflessness and sacrifices of workers in industry and agriculture, in the health services and transport, in food distribution and power supply, the unbeatable will of all the people to secure the continued functioning of our economy and fulfillment of the basic needs of the people. A special word of thanks should go to the workers in Vysocany [the industrial section of Prague], without whose cooperation the political work of the leading organs of the Communist Party in the critical days would not have been possible.

We thank members of the People's Militia for their high conscientiousness, alertness, and selflessness, for taking their stand alongside our people. The members of our People's Army and a decisive majority of our Security corps have won the respect and gratitude of all their fellow citizens by their conduct.

We also thank all those who work in the mass media of communication, who, being unable to go to their usual places of work, have succeeded in establishing, with the assistance of specialized enterprises and of many citizens, new posts where they are able to work and who have communicated the will as well as the feelings of the people in the fateful hours of trial.

Comrades, citizens, we value your patriotic, socialist performance highly.

We are with you; be with us!

From Rude Pravo, *August 28, 1968*

To All the People of Czechoslovakia!

Dear fellow citizens!

Our thoughts are with you all the time. We share your feelings, and we understand you. We are aware of our responsibility in return for the confidence you have given us. We beg you in the name of everything that is dear to our nations: Do not allow your emotions to carry you away into actions that would result in a national catastrophe. Everything depends on you, on your decisions. Make your decisions in a statesmanlike and wise manner. We know that you can.

The main question of today is: Can we find a way out of the actual situation and can we govern ourselves at this grave time? Or shall we allow acts by irresponsible or imprudent people or by forces alien to socialism to provoke measures by the troops that are on our territory? Does anyone who loves our socialist homeland want the troops to return to the streets of our towns from which most of them have already departed and will continue to depart? Does anyone think that we don't know how to govern ourselves? We trust we can under any circumstances.

You have demanded that the representatives you elected should resume their functions. They are grateful to you and will feel obliged to you for it for the rest of their lives. We ask you at this time for only one thing: Support that for which we have returned to our functions, that which is the prerequisite for your and our efforts to be meaningful. Support the efforts for consolidation so that the troops can begin gradually to leave our territory and eventually to depart altogether. Oppose with us everything that stands in the way of these efforts. Help us prevent provocations; prevent any gamble with the fate of our nations. In this lies the whole meaning of our actions. This is the pre-condition for us to continue with the policy in which you have expressed your confidence.

Your confidence is an obligation to us. However, it is our duty, with which you have entrusted and charged us, to govern. Make that possible for us if you ask us to serve you.

> Ludvik Svoboda,
> President of the Czechoslovak Socialist
> Republic
>
> Josef Smrkovsky,
> National Assembly of the Czechoslovak
> Socialist Republic
>
> Oldrich Cernik,
> Government of the Czechoslovak Socialist
> Republic

Alexander Dubcek,
Central Committee of the Communist Party
From Rude Pravo, *extra edition, August 28, 1968*

To All the People of Czechoslovakia!

The National Assembly, proceeding from the unanimous will of the people expressed in hundreds of resolutions that are arriving at the address of the National Assembly, regards it necessary to make the following statement:

1. The National Assembly continues to regard the occupation of the Czechoslovak Socialist Republic by forces of the five states of the Warsaw Pact as illegal and in violation of international treaties, the Charter of the United Nations, and the Warsaw Pact.

2. The National Assembly expresses thanks to the President of the Republic, to the representatives of the National Assembly, of the Government, of the Communist Party of Czechoslovakia, and of the National Front for their efforts during the Moscow negotiations and appreciates their efforts aimed at doing away with today's abnormal state of affairs in our country.

3. The National Assembly is convinced that the only place for this country is in the community of socialist nations and states.

4. The National Assembly is convinced that our army is capable of securing our western frontiers and calls on the Government systematically and resolutely to insist on the establishment and consistent fulfillment of specific time limits for the speediest possible withdrawal of foreign troops from our country.

5. The National Assembly demands that the undisturbed, free activity of all constitutional, Government, and state organs and institutions, and of all legal mass media of communication, should be made possible and secured without delay. At the same time, we insist that all our citizens who have been illegally detained and imprisoned by Czechoslovak or foreign organs since August 21 be released.

6. The National Assembly emphasizes that it unswervingly adheres to the principles and policies contained in the Action Program and in the policy declaration of the Czechoslovak Government. The members of the National Assembly pledge they

will exert maximum effort to ensure that our process of democratization continues without onerous features.

7. The National Assembly will debate in the near future the Government report on the results of the negotiations in Moscow and a Government statement. The National Assembly continues to base its actions on the documents it has adopted since August 21, 1968.

8. The National Assembly calls on all the people to maintain firm unity and to prevent provocations that could provide a pretext for new interventions against the interests of the people and our Government. Only by calm reason and circumspection can we extricate ourselves from a situation that has come about through no fault of our own, return to normal life even under difficult conditions, and continue in the construction of the Czechoslovak Socialist Republic according to the desires and ideas of its people.

National Assembly of the Czechoslovak
Socialist Republic

From documents of the National Assembly, August 28, 1968

Defense Minister Dzur on the Situation

In answer to our reporter's question, what is demanded by the present situation, especially with respect to its military aspects, the Minister of National Defense replied:

The orders issued previously are still in force. Their aim was to prevent an armed confrontation and mass shedding of blood and to firmly secure the western border of our Republic. I have issued no further orders, especially after the assurance given by the forces of the five countries that no attempts will be made to disarm any units of our army. I am of the opinion that the first requirement today is to prevent conflicts and possible bloodshed at any cost.

In the present tense situation, even a small provocation could result in a great conflagration, with catastrophic consequences. Yes, the situation is still extraordinarily serious, but after our negotiations in Moscow, I am sure that there exists a way out—naturally attainable only if peace is maintained. I have just sent a letter to the delegates to the Congress of the Communist Party of Slovakia. I say in this letter: As you meet, please bear in mind the political reality of the serious situation in which our Republic has found itself and apply the necessary prudence and realism. I am certain that, through the joint effort of both nations, the Czech and the Slovak, and under the leadership of the Central Committee of the Czechoslovak Communist Party, we shall find a way out of even this difficult situation.

From Rude Pravo, *extra edition, August 28, 1968*

Premier Cernik on the Situation

Czechoslovak Radio broadcast a statement by the Premier Oldrich Cernik.

Dear friends, comrades!

I come before you with great emotion to thank you for the greetings and for the trust that you expressed in the past days in the Government and in me personally. I am returning to work in an exceptionally difficult situation in our country, which has affected our feelings and the life of our families.

As you have been already informed, I participated in the negotiations of the President of the Republic in Moscow. On this occasion, dear fellow citizens, I would like to note with deep appreciation the statesmanlike wisdom, the patience, prudence, and political perspicacity of our President Ludvik Svoboda. Permit me to make use of this opportunity to express to him, on behalf of the Government, our sincere thanks and deep respect.

The first result of the Moscow talks will be the restoration of the functioning of the legitimate constitutional organs of the state and their legally elected leading representatives. We agreed on the principle of the foreign troops' departure and on the settlement of the consequences of their stay in our country. We are interested, just as you are, in their complete and speedy withdrawal. But we must be patient and continue to be prudent. The withdrawal will be carried out gradually and in several phases.

In the interest of normalization of our life, all the forces will first leave the cities and withdraw to new areas. The individual phases of the complete departure of troops from our territory remain to be specified and will be taken up by the appropriate Government officials. We received assurances that foreign troops will not interfere in the internal affairs of the Republic. The direction of all the spheres of the state administration remains fully subordinated to the Government and the other state organs. Concrete steps for the strengthening of the socialist system, the realization of which we have prepared, or will now prepare, for implementation, are exclusively an internal matter. But it must be understood that this is now influenced by the extraordinary situation in our country, and as a result, the steps will often be extraordinary in nature and of temporary validity. I beg you to understand, however, that these are matters that will take time, patience, and further negotiations. Still, we must work with resolve, with the necessary prudence, and also with greater consistency, against those who would threaten our socialist way.

I share fully the unity of the people, which has been shown lately and particularly in the past few days. It has been a source of strength and hope not only for yourselves but also for me. I would like to stress especially the stand taken these days by our youth, inasmuch as it is possible to single it out. Its great selflessness and devotion to the fatherland fills us with certainty that it will be good hands into which our generation will hand over the results of its efforts.

At every step, we were thinking of you and only of you, dear fellow citizens, of your children, of your future. In such moments, everyone understands what it means to love one's people, to love one's country, its history, its present, its culture and work. We were also aware of your confidence in us and support for us. In this support, the great strength of the people of our state again manifested itself, the firmness of spirit and will that grows from ancient historical roots.

We were constantly concerned not only for the cultural, spiritual, and material values created over centuries by the work of the people of this country; we also felt full responsibility for the preservation of these values for future generations.

The past days have produced a great manifestation of unity of both our nations and all nationalities. The firmness of the relation between Czechs and Slovaks has become very clear, and it has been also confirmed that this trial has strengthened it further. I should like with all my heart to thank especially the entire Slovak people for the warm and sincere words with which they expressed themselves in favor of the preservation of a united and firm republic. I greatly value the resolute stand taken by the Slovak National Council. As Chairman of the Government, I want to stand at the head of a government that will remain the government of all our people of both our nations and all nationalities, a government that enjoys the full confidence of the working class, the farmers, the intelligentsia, and all sections of society, and a government that wants to repay its constitutional mandate of confidence—so repeatedly confirmed by the people in the recent dramatic days—through devoted service to the cause of socialism and to the interests of the sovereign Czechoslovak socialist state.

Permit me, in particular, to say a few words to the members of the army, Security, and People's Militia. In the night of August 20–21 and also in the days that followed, you fulfilled the order of the army command, which was confirmed by the Presidium of the Central Committee, by the President of the Republic, and by the Government, thus preventing bloodshed not only of soldiers but also of the civilians of our country, as well as great material losses. If this had not been possible, the way out of the present situation would be incomparably more difficult; the prudence, organization, and discipline of the armed forces is one of the important conditions for the normalization of affairs in the Republic.

We are of the opinion that thanks are due to the Government of the Republic, which, in a grave moment and without the participation of some of its members, did not allow its activity to become paralyzed and firmly stood with the people of this country and with the President of the Republic. I promise to all of you that I am ready to act in the future in such a way as would enable us to extricate our Republic from the complicated and difficult situation and fulfill the aims of the Government's program. In this, we shall always be guided by the principle: What the people cannot do, no other force can do.

Dear friends, people now ask us with tears in their eyes: Have your decisions and attitudes been right? I am determined to continue with the policy, the foundations of which were laid by the January meeting at the Central Committee. I want to continue to fulfill the program started by the Government, for it was on its basis alone that the Government obtained the confidence of the people in the area of domestic as well as foreign policy, where it is necessary to fulfill all the obligations that devolve on us from bilateral and multilateral agreements and negotiations, including agreements in foreign trade, where we can insist on the fulfillment of obligations by the other side only if we also fulfill them.

Everybody will certainly understand that the fulfillment of the long-term tasks of socialist construction, which I consider basic, has not been an easy matter so far and is even less so today. I am convinced that the Government, which has been enjoying the full confidence of the people from the very outset of its activities, will use all its powers in these difficult days, too, to secure the needs of the people and the normalization of public and economic life. I trust that we will be able to rely on your intelligence, supported by the feelings of our nations, and on the high statesmanlike feeling of responsibility of the people of this country.

I intend to guide the activities of the Government toward the solution of the consequences of the events of recent days. The Government is already preparing certain measures in this respect. Within a few days, it will work out a document in which it will address the governments of the Soviet Union, the German Democratic Republic, the Polish People's Republic, the Hungarian People's Republic and the Bulgarian People's Republic to begin negotiations as soon as possible on the gradual withdrawal of foreign troops from Czechoslovak territory. Within two weeks, materials for economic negotiations with Moscow will be prepared; they will include proposals for correcting the consequences of the events of the past days.[8]

It is urgently necessary to normalize conditions for the functioning of the basic organs of the state, including the Government.

[8] Following the end of negotiations in Moscow, reports circulated that the Czechoslovak Government planned to hand the Soviets a bill for $500 million for damage inflicted on the country by the occupation. As the Soviets tightened their grip on Czechoslovakia, nothing more was heard about this claim for indemnification.

In particular, it is necessary quickly to restore communications and transport, to strengthen the organs for the maintenance of public order, especially in the large cities. Citizens would surely welcome it if the National Committees were organizing, in co-operation with Public Security, services for the maintenance of order, calm, and the security of you all. Special attention must be paid to the normalization of the situation in Prague, and for that reason the Government intends to discuss within two days the applicable proposals made by the City National Committee in Prague.

The Government approved today some extraordinary measures concerning the press, radio, and television required by the abnormal situation, in which it is necessary fully to assert the Government's influence on the radio, television, and the Czechoslovak News Agency.[9]

At the same time, it is necessary to ensure that the events of the past few days will not have worsened the people's basic living conditions. For that reason, it is necessary by all means to secure the harvest and the agricultural products because the damage caused by delays here would be irreparable. It is necessary to secure the smooth flow of supplies and fuel for the winter to the population and also to secure supplies for industry in order to hasten its normalization. The proper and smooth running of schools, health services, and financial institutions, the payment of wages, pensions, and other financial benefits must be made possible. The return home of citizens of the Republic who are abroad on holiday or on official business must be facilitated.[10]

To avoid any worsening of the living conditions of the people, effort to maintain calm and order must be made. It is therefore necessary to organize more determined steps against the force that would try to undermine civil discipline, to create provocations, and so on. In connection with the solving of these questions, we have begun negotiations today for the settlement of the con-

[9] Censorship, which had been formally lifted by the National Assembly in June, was legally reimposed by the National Assembly in September. Initially, the new restraints involved self-censorship, but by the end of the year stricter measures seemed imminent.

[10] According to reliable estimates, about seventy thousand Czechoslovaks were out of the country at the time of the invasion.

sequences for the national economy of the activity of foreign troops.

In addition to these talks, the Government will strive, even under today's extraordinary, difficult conditions, to maintain legality according to our laws and regulations. Extraordinary measures arising from the extraordinary situation can be of only temporary duration. It is not always going to be easy, and a lot is going to depend on your understanding and on the ability of all organs of the state, especially the National Committees at all levels, to find the right decisions.

Yesterday's negotiations of the Government with the chairmen of the Regional National Committee convinced me that the National Committees in recent days played an important role in solving the abnormal conditions of the lives of the citizens. I thank them for their work, and I am certain that they are going to continue working enthusiastically and selflessly in the future.

The Government has decided that, as soon as possible, following an evaluation of the situation that has arisen, it will submit to the National Assembly of the Republic a program for the normalization of our national life, a program for the active removal of obstacles and abnormalities brought about by the presence of foreign troops in our country. All of us at every level of management must now come forth with clear, practical ideas and thus establish a national and moral unity founded on concrete acts at every step.

In such acts, the attitude of our people toward realistic conditions will manifest itself. I understand your feelings, dear fellow citizens. But, believe me, we can extricate the Republic from a difficult situation only with a cool head. Only a responsible, sensible approach will make it possible for us to fulfill, albeit at a slower pace, the tasks we have set for ourselves.

I would like to ask you in this connection to avoid hasty judgments. Contradictory and very distorted information can easily arise in an unclear situation. Let us avoid unconsidered radicalism, which could frustrate our progress and our solutions for the present situation. I am convinced that the way out of the situation that has arisen requires cool heads and prudence.

I appeal to all workers in the factories and in agriculture, in the cultural and the scientific sphere, to the workers in all state and economic organs, to help the Government in this serious situation with their dedication to work. I am sure that at this time, too, you yourselves know best how to direct your efforts so that our country does not suffer additional losses. The road to the fulfillment of our aims—aims we have not compromised and do not intend to compromise—will be hard, requiring patient, prudent, and dedicated work by us all. However, I believe firmly that, no matter how difficult it may seem today, the idea and the works of socialism and its human face will emerge victorious in the Czechoslovak Socialist Republic from these difficult days. However, that will be possible only if we continue to be united.

I believe firmly in the people of this country. I ask you to give your confidence to me and to the Government in the difficult and complicated work that awaits us in creating the conditions for the realization of the program of further construction of socialism as set forth in the post-January development of our country.

From Prace, *August 29, 1968*

Statement by Josef Smrkovsky

Czechoslovak Radio broadcast, on August 29, a statement by Chairman of the National Assembly Comrade Josef Smrkovsky.

Dear fellow citizens of the Czechoslovak fatherland, dear friends:

In the past I spoke to you many times, perhaps too many times. Sometimes I spoke of things that were on your mind at that time, and whenever I did, I always knew it because it was easier for me to speak. Today I would like to tell you that never before has it been so difficult for me to speak as it is now.

The only thing that has been giving me strength in recent days are you, our people, the Czechs and Slovaks and all others, who in this most difficult trial have been behaving so well that I am at a loss to find words to express my gratitude and my respect to you all. I bow to you. I bow to our people, to the sacrifice they have made, and I bow to their courage and prudence.

I do not wish to repeat what has already been said in the statements of the President, Comrade Svoboda, of the First Secretary of the Central Committee, Comrade Dubcek, and of the Premier, Comrade Cernik. Allow me to speak for myself and say what I feel. I am almost sixty years old, and I have been through quite a few things in my life.[11] You know my biography, and you know that my life has not been easy. However, I never thought that something even more difficult, even more difficult decisions, were in store for me. Now I know. The past few days have been the most difficult experience I have ever lived through in my life. And I also know that the days to come will not be easier.

I know very well what is chiefly on your minds now; it has also been on our minds, not only today but throughout our stay in Moscow: the question of how it will all turn out for us and for our Republic.

This is neither the time nor the place to look back, to draw a balance sheet of our post-January development. The events of the past few days have shown that we have underrated several factors in our previous efforts—namely, those that have substantially affected our development, primarily external and international factors, which have come to produce the greatest and most difficult complications in our efforts. You know that our Party policy gradually became the subject of criticism and pressure from the neighboring socialist countries, pressure that on August 21 reached formidable proportions. Our country was suddenly occupied by an enormous military power against which it was absolutely hopeless and impossible to resist.

Unfortunately, and such is the sad reality, the situation is not novel or unusual in the history of our nations. This has happened more than once in Czech and Slovak history, and as a matter of fact it has happened already for the second time in the twentieth century. Therein lies the tragedy of small nations whose fatherland is located in a particularly sensitive place on this continent. Therein lies the tragedy of the efforts for new socialist advance, the tragedy of those who try to march in front, the tragedy of the attempts of people who set great and noble aims for themselves. Such an effort is never easy, and it is twice as difficult for small

[11] Smrkovsky, a Communist leader in Prague even before the Communist take-over in 1948, was jailed by the Stalinist regime in 1951 for four years, an experience that is said to have been a key factor in his emergence as a liberal reformer.

nations, involving twice as much risk of failure, frustration, and misunderstanding. I think we were aware of this risk. I think we had a feeling that we would have to pay for all this, but—and I should like to stress this—we did not expect to have to pay such a price as we were confronted with on the night of August 20–21.

Since that moment, a mortal danger has existed not only for all our post-January efforts but literally for the most fundamental, truly existential values of us all—for the state and its sovereignty, for freedom, for the management of our domestic affairs, in fact, even for the existence and security of every citizen.

Our negotiations in Moscow were of an unusual nature. You know that we did not arrive there all at one time, and you also know the circumstance under which some of us got there and negotiated. I don't think I should go into detail: The topic is still too difficult and painful for me just as it is for Comrade Dubcek and the others.

As everyone can figure out for himself, to make decisions in this situation was extremely problematic. The occupation of our country by Warsaw Pact troops was a stern reality. Our communication with home was limited; we received extremely little or no information, and sometimes we had to depend more on our faith in the firm attitude of our people than on any factual knowledge of the situation. However, the attitude of our partners was made known to us rather accurately, and we also guessed that there might be certain difficulties in which the external military intervention found itself politically. We knew that the world sympathized with us but that the great powers would accept a compromise solution rather than anything else. Under these circumstances, we were confronted with a dilemma from which there was no escape.

We could have rejected any type of compromise and prodded the development of things to the point where the foreign troops would stay on our territory permanently, with all the consequences this would have for the sovereignty of the state, the political rights, the economy, and for possible new human sacrifices such a contentious development would likely have caused. I emphasize that we did bear in mind that there is a certain point at which nothing is left but to reject any submissive settlement, at which it is better to expose one's breast to the bayonets in the interest of the honor and the character of the nation.

At the same time, however, we were of the opinion that such an extreme moment had not yet come and that, in spite of all that happened, alternatives existed that we, as politicians responsible for the destiny of the state, must not leave unexplored. Accordingly, we tried once more to find a way out based on an acceptable compromise. In this, too, we were aware of the consequences, particularly moral and historical consequences, that such a settlement could have.

I ask you to believe us that at that moment our personal fate —even though as normal people we were not indifferent to it— was of secondary consideration to us. The crucial question was whether there was any possibility of extricating the Czechoslovak state and socialism from a crisis into which it had fallen through no fault of its own.

Such a possibility began to emerge when the clear and united attitude of the Czech and Slovak people toward the entry of foreign troops on our territory fully manifested itself and influenced the attitude of our partners as well as our personal situation. In these circumstances, we then decided to embark on the second road, the road of compromise, which offered hope for a continuation of the path begun in January. This was recognized by the other negotiating side as the basis of a possible settlement.

But our deliberations were not easy even then. They went on virtually for a day and a night, and we realized that the outcome could be regarded by the people of our country and by history either as acceptable or as a betrayal; we were also aware of the problematic and limited nature of our mandate. I ask you to believe that we did not keep silent, that we did clash sharply and repeatedly—both with our partners and among ourselves—and that we used every argument available to us.

All this finally crystallized into a solution whose outlines you know, mainly from the speeches of the President, the First Secretary of the Central Committee, and the Chairman of the Government, who—in contrast to the official communiqué—spoke in a language that is closer to us and that we understand better.

As most of you already know, the main points of the agreement are roughly as follows:

1. Our internal life, the transformation of Czechoslovak socialism in the spirit expressed by the Central Committee after January, will continue.

2. All this political life will be directed not by a government that has been imposed but by the existing and duly elected organs of the state. In this sense, too, the National Assembly of which I am the Chairman will exercise the functions with which it is charged by the constitution and other laws.

3. Czechoslovak foreign policy will continue on its present course.

4. The troops of the Warsaw Pact powers are in occupation of Czechoslovak territory temporarily, as the communiqué declares. These troops and other organs of these countries will not interfere with our country's internal affairs and will leave our country after the situation in the Czechoslovak Socialist Republic has been normalized.

5. The Czechoslovak Communist Party will continue to exercise its political function in our national community in the spirit of the Action Program. Every reasonable person will agree that precisely in the crisis of the past few days this Party of ours has proven its abilities, that it has been the only force capable of leading our nations. We are all convinced that it will continue to give proof of this capability in the future as well, and that, united around Dubcek's leadership, with a cool head and reason, it will also solve all its internal problems for the good of the January line.

These are the fundamental points of agreement brought forth by the Moscow negotiations. Now the question is bound to be asked by all: What guarantees are there for the agreed points?

I tell you frankly that, despite all the help we have had from our friends, of whom we now have many and whom I thank from the bottom of my heart, in the situation that now exists in the world, our country has no other real guarantee and hope than its own good sense and, above all, its unity. Let us make the best of these qualities of ours, which so often before helped to put us back on our feet. Let us gather our will power, clench our teeth, and continue marching along our road toward the ideals we inscribed on our escutcheon after January.

I beg you, after the first wave of pain and bitterness has passed, to view the results of the negotiations with a cool head and, so to say, to use your well-proven good sense.

The point is this!

The troops of the Warsaw Pact are to remain here for some time, as the Premier has said, even though the Government is entering into negotiations for their phased withdrawal.

We shall be forced now to take exceptional measures in the area of the press, radio, and television, in order to prevent anything being written or said in these media that might run counter to the foreign political needs and interests of the Republic. In the sphere of the right of association and assembly, the measures required of us will result in the dissolution of the political clubs and will prevent the formation of any new political parties. The Government will have to be granted, temporarily, certain special, full powers. All these measures will be taken on the basis of laws that will be debated by the National Assembly in the next few days.

We all realize that these are measures that slow down and render more difficult the creation of democratic socialism. We believe that you will understand why this has to be and that you will not impute evil motives to the leadership and to the state. We believe that you will understand that all this is indispensable to the normalization of the situation, the departure of the foreign troops, and a renewed acceleration of the rate of our socialist democratization.

I am speaking to you about the results of the Moscow negotiations in the full knowledge of the immense responsibility that today burdens the shoulders of the supreme authority of our Republic, the National Assembly, at whose head, by your will, I stand.

The National Assembly has acquitted itself honorably of the task that confronted it during the recent eventful days. The overwhelming majority of the members of the National Assembly have shown themselves to be courageous, sovereign, free representatives of their people, have shown themselves to be capable, even in the presence of foreign troops on our territory, of protecting the legitimate character and sovereign exercise of the prerogatives and rights of our constitutional authorities. With the same sense of responsibility, this National Assembly intends to approach its tasks in the situation as it exists following our return from Moscow.

The National Assembly has already issued its statement on the situation, a statement with which you are familiar, and it has requested the Government of the Republic to submit to the National Assembly within the next few days a report on the Moscow negotiations, together with an account of its position on their results and its suggestions regarding the measures to be taken for the comprehensible normalization of life in our country.

It goes without saying that the National Assembly will debate this statement of the Government in full awareness of its, the Assembly's, rights and prerogatives, its responsibility and co-responsibility as the organ that, according to the constitution of the Czechoslovak Socialist Republic, must approve any and all agreements touching on the sovereignty and territorial integrity of the Republic and its internal political structure.

I have already indicated the way our thoughts went during the talks in Moscow. We also knew that we would have to come before the people and the constitutional organs of the Republic with an account of the position we have taken and that we will also be brought before the merciless tribunal of time and history. For, during these past few days, we really stood at a true crossroads of history, where one's thoughts must turn to the fundamental values that have to be protected unconditionally if our nations are to get their breath again and resume their forward march along their true road, which is in harmony with their sense of their own history and existence.

Your attitude, dear fellow citizens, during the recent eventful days, demonstrated your loyalty to the underlying sense of our history in a manner that has found a favorable reception, recognition, and admiration throughout the world. This was our greatest source of strength in the immensely difficult task that we had to cope with there, beyond the borders of our country.

I thank you with all my heart, comrade workers, members of

the People's Militia, who have transformed our factories into bastions of strength and resolution and who have proven once again how great a historic responsibility rests on your shoulders in this country. I also thank you, farmers, who have had to harvest the fruits of your year's work and secure for us "our daily bread" in the shadow of tanks and aircraft.

Thanks also to you, representatives of science and culture, and above all to the representatives of the press, radio, and television, and to all members of the intelligentsia, for your conduct, which was true to the finest traditions of Czechoslovak science and culture. And special thanks to you, our dear youth, the future of this country, thanks to you, boys and girls, for your enthusiasm and energy, courage and prudence. Thanks to you, too, comrades in the army and in Security who have remained on the side of the people. Thanks and respect are also due to our women, our mothers, who have had to live through days of anxiety, suffering, and grief, but who remained a firm support for us.

Today, on the anniversary of the Slovak national uprising, I would especially like to thank the Slovak nation for its stand on the unity of our socialist Republic and to assure it that we shall do everything to ensure that the legal steps concerning the federalization of the state are adopted within the proposed time limit—that is, by next October 28. I believe that we shall put our mutual relations, both on the state and on the Party level, fully in order and that there is sufficient good will on both sides for this to be achieved. I ask that we do not allow ourselves to be upset in this regard by any temporary or secondary elements and that we concentrate calmly and with confidence on the attainment of a favorable solution to our fundamental problems.

And finally—just like Comrade Cernik—I should like, on behalf of the National Assembly as well as on my own behalf, to give thanks to the President of the Republic, Army General Ludvik Svoboda, for his intervention at the moment that was the worst one for our state and for ourselves personally.

At the same time, dear fellow citizens, I ask you to have understanding also for us, on whose shoulders has rested the heavy burden of negotiating and making decisions. We, too, had to act and decide in the shadow of tanks and aircraft on our territory.

I assure you that we acted and made our decisions as patriots and soldiers, as men who were thinking not of themselves or their own lives but of the life and future of our nations. For the sake of that life and future of the Czechs and Slovaks and all the people of our country, I now turn to you with the appeal and request that lent us so much strength during the recent days: We are with you; be with us! Let us bear in mind Svatopluk's three legendary rods.[12] Let us not allow our ranks to be divided, for that would be a real disaster and a real defeat for our cause, a defeat for socialism, for our free Czechoslovak Socialist Republic. And that must not happen!

From Prace, August 30, 1968

[12] Svatopluk, a legendary nobleman, urged his three sons to remain together and demonstrated the wisdom of his advice by showing that three rods can be broken one at a time but not together.

9

EPILOGUE

Attitude of the Czechoslovak People to the Moscow Communiqué

We Have Not Been Defeated

A resolution of the all-enterprise assembly of CKD, Prague, adopted unanimously in the presence of some two thousand workers.

We are addressing this proclamation to all employees, regardless of their political affiliation or of their attitude in the period before the occupation of our country. It is necessary to say to you quite openly that the Soviet Union is an imperialist state with all its characteristic attributes. Therefore, it is neither the homeland of socialism nor a shield of socialism. It merely uses the cloak of socialism until Soviet power interests are threatened any respect. When the interests of the Soviet empire are threatened, it uses the means of occupation and of physical, cultural, and political repression with all the consequences resulting therefrom.

We warn against the false illusion that this is a matter of misunderstanding or even of error. We warn against the illusion that everything will be set straight and that normal conditions will be restored. We warn against the false illusion that our leading Party and state representatives, democratically elected, could have achieved any success in principle or perhaps even "neutrality and sovereignty" during the talks in Moscow, to which they had been dragged as slaves and where they were treated as slaves.

We warn each other against the idea that we should oppose the Soviet armed forces with our bare hands. We so warn because, sitting behind their armor plates, they are people of Asiatic manners and low culture. They are people who are ignorant of the history of this nation and who are here only to defend the aims of their emperors. If order is not restored in our country and if it becomes necessary, this country will be occupied by an unlimited number of troops. For them, the empire is everything, and nations are nothing.

We warn each other against overestimating the world's solidarity with our struggle. We are, of course, glad to know that we were on the right road, and we want to continue on this road. It is true that the overwhelming majority of people in the world are on our side, but their possibilities are limited.

In spite of all these warnings, we wish to stress that our people, our Czechoslovak socialist state, has not been defeated, because it was unable to fight. It has been knocked down to its knees and it shall have to try, as it has so many times in its history, to rise from its kneeling position, under its heavy burden, and to lift its eyes upwards. What, then, is to be done? Most of us are people accustomed to heavy labor and to difficult life. There are intelligent and highly capable people among us. There are brave and honorable people, true democrats in their hearts. We are turning to you with an urgent appeal.

Let us go on living in comradeship and honor, as we have lived in these recent days. Let us not be swayed in our views on socialism, democracy, and patriotism. Let us stay firmly together, and let us not permit anybody to be wrested away from our midst.

Let us not allow the liquidation of the democratic institutions we have built, be it Party, political, or Government institutions, including trade union organs, our works committee, and Party organs. These institutions must become our rallying point, because the twentieth-century emperors sometimes need democratic institutions in order to surpass another emperor in economic matters.

Those of you who still have some strength left and who are able to contribute to the cause of democratic socialism, do not leave the Communist Party. We shall have to go on working, legally as well as with other means. You who are able, stay in the ranks of the People's Militia as long as you can.

But let all of us do one thing. Let us maintain a total passivity to everything that is Soviet. If the Soviet Union is displeased by what we are writing and saying about them, let us not write or say anything about them at all. Let us therefore, for the time being, ignore even their culture.

Technicians and workers in the economy, continue to devote maximum attention to the economics of our country and of our enterprises. Let us use every day to make ready for democratic socialism. Above all, do not forget that our value lies primarily in maintaining and further developing our cadres.

Trade unionists and youth workers, go on with your untiring work. Use every opportunity. If it becomes possible, travel as much as you can in order to gather fresh strength.

This, then, is all that we as members of All-Enterprise organs (Party and trade union) are able to tell you in this fateful hour. We are proud that we have not, as of now, found a single collaborationist in our ranks. We thank you for your dedication and understanding in these historic days. We are still with you; be with us.

Long live democratic socialism, the aim of our human endeavor in this world.

> All-Enterprise Committee of ROH
> [Revolutionary Trade Union Movement],
> CKD Prague, National Enterprise
> The Foundries

From Avantgarda, *No. 1, August 29, 1968*

Tell the People the Whole Truth: The Position of the Communist Party University Committee in Prague

Citizens:

We reject any conditions that would mean a capitulation or a violation of our state sovereignty. Such "conditions" are unacceptable for our people. It is a capitulation that actually means hidden occupation. We are asked to give it a semblance of legality. Better an outright occupation than capitulation.

We ask that our legal state and Party organs defend the following demands: an immediate, unconditional, and total withdrawal of all occupation troops and a full transfer of the administration of the country into the hands of our state organs; the respecting of all the consequences and principles of our democratization process; recognition that the Extraordinary Fourteenth Party Congress and the legal Party organs elected by it are the only authorized spokesmen of the Communist Party; full compensation of all damages caused by the occupation.

Citizens! We can defend ourselves only by a proud and calm resistance such as we have demonstrated in recent days. Let us not be provoked. The occupiers are waiting for that. Prevent the collaborationists from taking over any positions. Remember them. Support the sovereignty of our state and of our organs with every means.

We, the Communists of Prague universities, are turning to the workers of Prague enterprises with an appeal to form joint committees for the protection of socialism, freedom, and sovereignty.

From Avantgarda, *No. 1, August 29, 1968*

Telegram from the Leadership of the Central Committee of the Czechoslovak Youth League, August 27, 1968

To the President of the Republic, Ludvik Svoboda, Prague Castle
To the Government of the Czechoslovak Socialist Republic
To the National Assembly of the Czechoslovak Socialist Republic

While we fully understand your incredibly difficult position and while we fully respect you personally and all your efforts for the rescue of the nation and of our state sovereignty, we cannot accept the Moscow communiqué.

It is our opinion that neither the President alone, nor the Government alone, nor the National Assembly alone can today decide on the future fate of the country.

We demand that you immediately hold a plebiscite on the results of the Moscow negotiations.

From a mimeographed leaflet

To the Central Committee of the Communist Party

The extraordinary plenary session of the Prague 1 District Committee of the Communist Party, held on August 27, 1968, having acquainted itself with the communiqué of the Moscow negotiations, considers it necessary to stress the following:

1. We cannot accept the published communiqué as an expression of the free will of Czechoslovak representatives, because the negotiations were conducted while the Czechoslovak Socialist Republic was occupied and also because some of the participants had lost any right to speak on behalf of our nations.

2. We insist on a complete withdrawal of the occupation troops and on the restoration of full sovereignty of the Czechoslovak Socialist Republic.

3. We continue to recognize the conclusions adopted by the Extraordinary Fourteenth Congress of the Communist Party of Czechoslovakia, and we demand that the Fourteenth Congress immediately resume its interrupted session under the leadership of Comrade Dubcek, in order to solve the new situation now that it has been fully informed of the whole, though cruel, truth.

4. In these grave hours, we stand behind comrades Dubcek and Svoboda and behind the measures of the legal Party and state organs of our country.

We ask and beg all citizens that, in view of the given reality, they remain calm, because that is our only weapon today, supported by the power of truth and reason.

Communist Party District Committee,
Prague 1

From a mimeographed leaflet

Position of the Workers of the Czechoslovak Air Lines

The all-enterprise committee of the Communist Party of Czechoslovakia in the Czechoslovak Air Lines, meeting in an extraordinary session today, has discussed and adopted the following unanimous position:

1. We disagree with the contents of the communiqué and with the results of the Moscow negotiations. We are convinced that

the negotiations took place in abnormal conditions, under duress, and without any possibility of contact with duly elected legal Party and Government organs. There were individuals in the Czechoslovak delegation who do not enjoy the confidence of our people.

2. We adhere to the statements and decisions of the Extraordinary Fourteenth Party Congress and to the new Central Committee elected by it.

3. We demand a nationwide referendum on these matters of principle affecting our entire country.

This statement has been endorsed by the ROH works committee [Revolutionary Trade Union Movement] and the all-enterprise committee of the Czechoslovak Youth League.

From a mimeographed leaflet

Position of the Workers of the Naradi National Enterprise

We, the workers of Naradi [Tools] national enterprise in Prague 10, representing 7,061 employees, have adopted the following stand regarding the communiqué on the Moscow talks, as broadcast at 3 P.M. today:

1. We consider the conditions stipulated by the communiqué as absolutely unacceptable for our two nations, and we feel bitterly disappointed and betrayed.

2. Among the signers of the agreement were individuals who no longer had any mandate to sign such a document and who therefore represented nobody.

3. At the same time, we express our conviction that the conditions for the negotiations for our delegation, in a country that had sent its troops into our territory, were outside the framework of international law and that they were dictated from a position of strength.

4. We reaffirm that we consider the Extraordinary Fourteenth Party Congress and the Central Committee elected by it as the only and supreme representative of the Party. We stand behind the decisions adopted by it without reservation.

5. Being aware of the tremendous difficulties and irregularities of the Moscow negotiations, we continue to maintain full confi-

dence in comrades Svoboda, Dubcek, Cernik, Smrkovsky, and we request them to remain in their functions under any circumstances.

From a mimeographed leaflet

Position of Workers of the Elektrocas National Enterprise

The Communist Party works organization, the ROH works organization, and all employees of the Elektrocas national enterprise, having gathered today at their places of work, have decided to adopt the following position on the current political situation:

1. We disagree with the formulation of the communiqué issued in conclusion of the negotiations of representatives of the Czechoslovak Socialist Republic and the Soviet Union, and we demand an immediate withdrawal of all occupation army units from our territory, so that the political and economic life in the state can be normalized in freedom.

2. We fully endorse the Action Program of the Party and of the National Front. We believe that the results of the Moscow negotiations are the maximum expression of what could have been achieved under given circumstances and pressures.

3. We fully support the new Central Committee and its Presidium headed by Comrade Dubcek. We reaffirm that the Central Committee, elected by the legal and valid Extraordinary Fourteenth Congress of the Party, enjoys the support of an overwhelming majority of the people. We express our love to Comrade Dubcek and Comrade Svoboda, and we promise to follow their earnest words spoken to us after their return from Moscow.

Position of the Editors of Student

To the National Assembly of the Czechoslovak Socialist Republic
To the Central Committee of the Communist Party
To the Government of the Czechoslovak Socialist Republic

Comrades,

The representatives of the Czechoslovak Socialist Republic at the negotiations in Moscow have completely capitulated before the brutal force of the occupiers. Regardless of the pressures they were exposed to, their action is tantamount to a betrayal of this Republic, betrayal of its people.

In ratifying the results of the Moscow negotiations, we shall lose everything: our freedom, our honor, our conscience. We shall become, as so many times before in our history, a nation of slaves. We shall not only betray ourselves but we shall also betray the historic task that has been assigned to our country: to shake the inhuman structure of Stalinism and to find the human form of the socialist system.

Therefore, if you wish to continue to call yourselves representatives of the Czech and Slovak people, if you wish your names not to be forever stained by the shame of betrayal and humiliation, if you wish this day not to enter the history of our nation as a new Munich, do the following:

The National Assembly, as the supreme legislative organ of this country, should immediately reject the results of the Moscow negotiations.

The Government of the Republic should immediately reject the results of the Moscow negotiations.

Comrades, let us be Czechs and Slovaks, let us be Communists, let us be citizens of this country. Rather than endorsing treason, let the occupiers disband your organs.

From Student, *5th special edition, August 27, 1968*

The editorial staff of *Student* has asked us to publish the text of its letter addressed to the President of the Republic, Ludvik Svoboda, to the First Secretary of the Communist Party, Alexander Dubcek, to the Chairman of the National Assembly, Josef Smrkovsky, and to Premier Oldrich Cernik.

Esteemed Comrades,

Allow us to express our considered opinion of our attitude to the results of the Moscow organizations, as published in the latest, 5th special edition, of *Student*.

We consider the published attitude as unfortunate, both in content and in style. It was drafted after the speech of the President of the Republic and after the broadcast of the communiqué by Czechoslovak Radio, at a moment when it seemed to us that everything had collapsed—that even more had collapsed than what had been lost when the occupying forces invaded our country. We are still convinced today that, in that situation, we were sharing the feelings of a majority of this country's population (mainly the part of it that is close to us in age and mental make-up)—a country that apparently is destined to have its history filled with terrible tragedies.

Some of us still think that the ideals of democratic socialism— the best thing that the people of this earth can bestow on themselves and for which we tried to fight in our magazine with all our resources—shall not be realized during the life of our generation. But, on this point, each of us should be speaking for himself, and we are writing to you collectively.

Perhaps it took us too long to realize that your attitude in the course of the Moscow negotiations cannot be called treason. Our position was adopted much too early, before we were able to think rationally and before we became aware of the awesome particulars.

Perhaps our letter will be understood. Perhaps we were understood when we were publishing our magazine under the most humane conditions, which not only this Republic but any other state ever knew, largely thanks to you.

Perhaps you will understand, too, that this editorial staff shall no longer publish the magazine, not even if the current conditions permitted it. We cannot, no matter how terribly much we would want to. Perhaps you shall understand that, too.

Editors of *Student*

From Mlada Fronta, *August 31, 1968*

Position of the Institute of History

The Institute of History of the Czechoslovak Academy of Sciences in Prague adopted the following resolution at an All-Institute meeting on the morning of August 28, 1968.

Our attitude to the aggression of the five countries against Czechoslovakia has been continually expressed in our statements and appeals since the first day of the occupation. Yesterday, after the publication of the communiqué on the Moscow negotiations and after the speeches of the President of the Republic and the First Secretary of the Communist Party, we also expressed our attitude toward the situation in a statement handed over to the legal Czechoslovak Radio; it is an integral part of this resolution.

We continue to reject the conditions of the *diktat*, accepted under unheard-of pressure, and in particular, the cynical phrases of the Moscow communiqué. We stand, without reservation, behind the policy line adopted in January, 1968, and especially behind all the decisions of the Extraordinary Fourteenth Party Congress and the resolutions and statements of the Central Committee elected at that Congress. Just as in the past seven days, when, along with all the people, we were making decisions concerning our attitudes and activities independently and in line with the conditions in which we were living, we intend to maintain our own independent thinking and initiative in the future as well.[1]

There is no reconciliation with the occupiers. A free people cannot live on its knees.

Sent to: the office of the President of the Republic, the office of the Premier, the Chairman of the National Assembly, the Secretariat of the Central Committee, and the Czechoslovak News Agency.

Dear Fellow Citizens:

Having heard the communiqué on the Moscow negotiations and the speeches by the President of the Republic and the First Secretary of the Communist Party, the entire personnel of the Institute of History of the Czechoslovak Academy of Sciences, which has been speaking to you during the past seven days on behalf of Prague historians, states the following: [2]

For us, for our nation, for the entire Czechoslovak people, there is no way back. We promised each other in that unforgettable message that we would never leave the road upon which we had started. These seven days, which can never be erased

---

[1] The Institute was true to its word. Witness this book.
[2] Telephoned to Czechoslovak Radio at 7:30 P.M., August 27, 1968, but not broadcast.

from our minds, have only strengthened our determination and irrevocable decision to follow our own path.

The most precious result of the united struggle of the entire nation against the occupation is the fact that the people of this country have taken their fate into their own hands. This sovereign people, determined to defend its freedom and independence, must be able to express its position on any agreement that may be deciding its fate, possibly for a whole generation, and it must be respected by anyone who wants to have its confidence.

We stand without reservation behind all decisions of the Extraordinary Fourteenth Party Congress and behind the Central Committee elected at that Congress. Without a recognition of the results of the Extraordinary Fourteenth Party Congress, there can be no Party unity. This is the feeling of those of us who live among the people as rank-and-file members of the nation, and it must be clear as well to the politicians who speak on the nation's behalf and ask for its confidence.

We are in favor of calm and prudence. We are not adventurists; we do not want nonsensical sacrifices. But both the old and the recent historical experiences tell us: Any concession in matters of principle in dealing with force is a step along a steep incline, a step on a road whose end cannot be seen. What may today appear merely as an inevitable act of realistic policy will tomorrow turn out to be the beginning of capitulation.

We continue to stand behind the workers of the legal Czechoslovak Radio stations. We express our confidence in them.

There is no reconciliation with the occupiers. A free people cannot live on its knees.

From the archives of the Institute of History of the Czechoslovak Academy of Sciences

Position of Mlada Fronta

To the President of the Czechoslovak Socialist Republic, Comrade Ludvik Svoboda

To the First Secretary of the Communist Party, Comrade Alexander Dubcek

To the National Assembly of the Czechoslovak Socialist Republic

To the Extraordinary Fourteenth Congress of the Communist
Party

To the Lord Mayor of the capital city of Prague

Driven out of our building, having to work in makeshift conditions, we have been united throughout in our resistance as well
as in our sympathies and feelings. We wish to maintain this unity
in the future. It is difficult, but we shall try. We feel that maintaining our unity is politically the most important thing that we
must strive for in these days.

Therefore, we can say nothing else at this time other than what
we have been saying ever since the first day of the forcible
occupation of our country.

1. We fully trust the First Secretary of the Communist Party,
Comrade Alexander Dubcek. We have understood his speech,
and we wish to be guided by his advice because we see in Alexander Dubcek a statesman of an extremely high character, purity,
and humanity.

2. However, we intend to continue to call things by their
proper names—say "honor" when we mean honor, say "lie" when
we mean lie, say "occupation" when we mean occupation. We can
never forget what the leadership and the armies of the five
Warsaw Pact countries have done to us. It cannot be undone
politically or morally. Too much has been betrayed and sullied
here for us to be able to forget.

3. Therefore, we understand the results of the Moscow nego-
tions as being imposed under pressure, and we do not identify
ourselves with them.

4. We fully support the results of the Extraordinary Fourteenth Party Congress and above all its political evaluation of
the situation. We recognize the Fourteenth Congress as the only
valid one, and we recognize only those Party representatives who
were duly elected to the Central Committee by the Fourteenth
Congress. We recognize no one else, particularly none of those
who betrayed us in the difficult hours. We not only do not recognize them but we condemn them resolutely. We demand an
immediate departure of the occupation troops and of the foreign

security units, and we insist equally resolutely on a full indemnification for damages caused by the occupation.

5. We declare that we shall never leave the road our nations, our Party, and all our people voluntarily, freely, and with full responsibility entered in January of this year. We continue to insist on political freedoms, without which democratic socialism cannot be maintained or developed.

6. We demand that the results of the Moscow negotiations be discussed by the National Assembly, by the Central Committee of the National Front, by the Central Committee, by the permanent Fourteenth Party Congress, as well as by an Extraordinary Congress of the Slovak Communist Party.

7. We demand that the unlawful occupation of the Czechoslovak Socialist Republic be discussed and condemned by the United Nations.

8. We demand that an international conference of Communist and workers parties be convoked in Prague without delay. The conference should discuss the situation in the international Communist movement and the relations among Communist parties.

9. We demand that the safety and freedom of movement of all citizens of the Czechoslovak Socialist Republic who have not transgressed against the laws of our Republic be guaranteed.

10. In the interest of a speedy normalization of internal conditions in our country, we request the Lord Mayor of the capital city of Prague to discuss with the competent commander of the occupation armies a prompt relinquishing by the occupation troops of the *Mlada Fronta* publishing house in Prague 1, Panska Street No. 8, which they have forcibly seized, in order that we may be able to contribute with our work toward an early consolidation of the situation created by the forcible occupation of the Czechoslovak Socialist Republic by the armies of the five Warsaw Pact states.

Unanimously adopted at a meeting of employees of the *Mlada Fronta* editorial and publishing house.

From a mimeographed leaflet, August 28, 1968

Position of the Teachers and Students of the Faculty of Journalism and Information of Charles University

We, the teachers and students of the Journalism and Information Faculty of Charles University, gathered at a public party meeting on August 28, 1968, declare unanimously:

In the grave situation of the recent and present days, the high moral qualities of the people of this country became apparent and will enter not only our history but the history of the human struggle for freedom and justice. In awareness of this, we stand fully behind comrades Dubcek, Svoboda, and Cernik and firmly behind the decisions of the Extraordinary Fourteenth Party Congress and the newly elected Central Committee.

However, as citizens of a free country and as Communists, we demand that the fact be made clear before us and before the whole world that the temporary retreat from some of the principles we were fighting for has been imposed on us by a *diktat*. Moreover, the Moscow communiqué has been signed by some individuals with whom we as honorable citizens do not want to have anything in common.

We, the teachers and students of the Faculty of Journalism and Information, are particularly affected by the possibility of limitations of the freedom of speech and expression. We declare that we insist on maintaining basic civil liberties codified by all the revolutions of the past but above all by the Great October Socialist Revolution. We also insist on preserving the high moral standards of publicist activity of our radio, press, and television.

We understand that the representatives of our Party and Government shall, even in the present difficult situation, strive for the realization of our just demands, and we assure them of our full support. We want to refrain from any expressions of shallow radicalism or despondency, but we shall not accept capitulation in any form.

We demand that the Central Committee do away with the traitors who have dishonored themselves forever by their collaboration. We do not want them to dishonor us too by their continuing presence in the Party.

We thank all students and graduates of our school who in

these grave hours were in their places as dedicated and enthusiastic publicists. We trust that not one of them will lend himself in the future to the propagation of anything that is contrary to our conscience and truth. Our greatest strength lies in high moral qualities.

From a mimeographed leaflet

Position of the Editors and Co-workers of Literarni Listy

Dear Friends of *Literarni Listy*,

This editorial staff, having gained your confidence in recent years, would like to tell all of you how we see the present situation, what we think about the future possibilities for us all.

We declare:

All agreements counting on any form of occupation of the Czechoslovak Socialist Republic are unacceptable to the nations of Czechoslovakia. We reject the Moscow communiqué, which is contrary to the decisions of the Extraordinary Fourteenth Party Congress. The representatives of our Party and state were acting in an irregular situation, deprived of contact with their nations, and under brutal pressure. Enforced agreements are not binding for us.

The sovereignty of our nations depends on the sovereign position of its state and political organs, which must be able to exercise their functions in freedom. We therefore reject the conditions, which are a *de facto* denial of this sovereignty.

One cannot continue a consistent development toward socialist democracy while at the same introducing censorship. The staff of *Literarni Listy* has decided to publish a magazine only if it is able to continue working in accord with its convictions and with its conscience. We shall never again accept the "realistic" policy of filtered truths.

The unity of our nations has proved itself in conditions of violence. It manifested itself in active resistance characteristic of decent people.

Let us not allow ourselves to act otherwise now, when force and violence strive for legitimization. We would hardly achieve anything with guns and pistols, except a senseless shedding of blood. Momentary heroism is romantically beautiful but ineffective and unnecessary. Let us seek the heroism of permanent resistance. Be implacable. Do not yield, but do not succumb to hysteria.

Even in the present grim situation, we are not without weapons. The seven days of the occupation have shown that our nations are capable of inventing, in the most difficult circumstances, new ways of resistance, dissent, and protest.

Today we call on our public, and on our young people in particular, to continue these forms of resistance. A silent demonstration during a march or a sit-in, a living newspaper of slogans and placards in the streets, in shop windows, and on walls, a boycott of the occupationist propaganda, and expressions of solidarity by all honest people of our country—such things have a greater power than you might think.

Do not adopt the eye-for-eye, tooth-for-tooth morality. The world has seen that the invincible strength of a socialist and democratic Czechoslovakia lies in its ethical and moral position worthy of a mature European state.

To strengthen this moral superiority under any circumstances today and at any time in the future—that is our lasting program.

We were with you. We are with you; be with us!

From Literarni Listy, *special edition, August 28, 1968*

Proclamation of the Presidium of the Central Trade Union Council and of the Chairmen of the Trade Unions, August 28, 1968

Men and Women Comrades, Trade Unionists, Working People of the Czechoslovak Socialist Republic:

The speeches of the delegation members after their return from Moscow have convinced us that they did all they could in the given circumstances, that they exerted every effort for the maximum defense of the rights and desires of our people. But the justified demand of the Czechoslovak people for an immediate withdrawal of the occupation forces has not been fulfilled. In the speeches by comrades Svoboda and Dubcek, you heard the cruel news, so unfavorable for us. We recognize that this is an oppressive reality that does not depend on our will and on our possibilities alone. In spite of that, we continue to insist on the withdrawal of foreign troops, and we cannot agree that their departure should be delayed. We trust that you, comrades, shall do your utmost to see that, in further negotiations, guarantees are gained of a full withdrawal of foreign occupation forces from our territory. We shall support you in this.

Let us continue in the process of the revival of our social and political life. Let us continue in realizing the Action Program of the Communist Party of Czechoslovakia. Let us create all the prerequisites for the realization of the program of the Revolutionary Trade Union Movement.

The entire progressive world was on our side in these exciting days. Trade unionists, regardless of their political affiliation, were daily showing their solidarity with the Czechoslovak Socialist Republic. They, too, should have our thanks at this time. To them we are sending our comradely and fraternal greetings.

Through the unity of the ROH—for socialism, for the freedom and sovereignty of the Czechoslovak Socialist Republic.

Position of the Workers of the Semi-Conductor Enterprise

To the Deputies of the National Assembly of the Czechoslovak Socialist Republic in Prague, August 28, 1968

Esteemed Comrade Deputies:

The workers of the Semi-Conductor enterprise of the CKD in Nusle thank you for your intrepid attitude and for your courage in this difficult time caused by the invasion of our territory.

Do not permit the personalities in whom we have trusted since January to disappear from our public life. We could not reconcile ourselves with any changes the occupiers might want to enforce in the positions of the members of the Government, the National Assembly, and in all other functions to which comrades have been duly elected and appointed in accordance with our constitution.

We know that it is not possible at the present time to immediately relieve of their functions all collaborationists and traitors to the Czechoslovak people, but you should find a way of making it known that you are dissociating yourselves from them.

You have our full confidence!

Should the work of our state or public organs be interfered with or rendered impossible in any way, we are determined to call a general strike.

We are convinced of the deep truth of a quotation that should be an encouragement to all people of good will in the whole world: "When humanity begins to think, a new epoch of history begins; and humanity has begun to think over the fate of Czechoslovakia."

Position of the Workers of the Lokomotiva-Sokolovo Plant, August 28, 1968

The workers of the CKD Lokomotiva-Sokolovo plant, having heard the report on the course of the Moscow negotiations, express their fundamental disagreement with the conclusions adopted.

We demand that the following points be considered and adopted:

1. Guaranteeing of the normal functioning of the duly elected organs—that is, the President of the Republic, Ludvik Svoboda, the Government of the Republic headed by Comrade Oldrich Cernik, the National Assembly headed by Comrade Josef Smrkovsky, the Central Committee of the National Front headed by Comrade Frantisek Kriegel, and the Central Committee headed by First Secretary Comrade Alexander Dubcek.

2. Recognition of the new Central Committee elected at the Extraordinary Fourteenth Party Congress.

3. Complete withdrawal of the occupation troops from the territory of the Czechoslovak Socialist Republic, including their political and security units, and indemnification for damages caused by the occupation.

4. An immediate dismissal from their posts of all collaborators and traitors, who no longer represent anybody.

5. Guaranteeing of all civil rights and democratic freedoms of the citizens of our Republic and granting of protection to all those who have been publicly and socially active in the post-January development and particularly in the course of the last week.

6. Recognition of our sovereignty and of our own specific road to socialism in the spirit of the Action Program and of the policy statement of the Government of the Republic.

At the same time, we assure you, esteemed comrades, that we stand firmly behind you, that we expect further expressions of your attitude, and promise not to do anything for the time being that would further complicate the present difficult situation in our country.

Resolution from a Convocation of Functionaries, August 28, 1968

We have heard with emotion the speeches by comrades Svoboda and Dubcek, and we indignantly condemn the dictated Moscow communiqué. After the treacherous occupation, after the abduction of our representatives, and after the acts of violence perpetrated by the occupation troops, the act of inhuman pressure exerted on our representatives is another evidence of the power policy of the ruling circles of the Soviet Union, which did not hesitate to sacrifice human lives as well as our traditionally friendly relations.

Our people, having experienced the disappointment of the Munich betrayal of 1938, are today united and determined not to acquiesce with the humiliating occupation by a former friend.

We express thanks to our representatives, Svoboda, Dubcek, Cernik, and Smrkovsky, for their courage in the course of the unequal negotiatioins in Moscow, and we assure them of our full support in our common struggle for the restoration of pre-occupation life in our country. Although we still have full confidence in these representatives of ours, we cannot accept the contents or the form of the Moscow communiqué.

In the interest of preserving the unity of our people, we demand the publication of all agreements, even partial, arrived at in the course of the negotiations with the representatives of the occupation countries.

We therefore declare:

1. We shall never acquiesce in the occupation of our territory, and we insist on an immediate and unconditional departure of the occupation troops. Removal of the occupation troops is the first prerequisite of a normalization of life in our homeland.

2. We want to hear the whole and full truth, immediately, on all agreements, including the partial ones.

3. We fully endorse the actions of the Extraordinary Fourteenth Party Congress and the Central Committee elected at that Congress, and we identify ourselves with the Congress documents.

4. We shall bring to life in this country the full scope of the Action Program of the Communist Party adopted at the April session of the Central Committee. We want to realize socialism with a human face.

> Functionaries of the Communist Party, ROH, and other National Front organizations of the Tesla enterprise, Strasnice

Position of the Workers of Tesla Holesovice, Enterprise No. 7, Vrsovice

We have heard the radio speech by Comrade Alexander Dubcek with immeasurable pain and bitterness. We fully understand what he said and also what he was unable to say at this time. We are convinced, however, that, under given conditions and in the given imbalance of power, he achieved the maximum by his fearless, courageous, and honorable attitude.

However, we disagree with the formulation of the communiqué on the negotiations of our and the Soviet delegation in Moscow. It obscures the real state of affairs by well-worn phrases. In addition, it was co-signed by people who at that time no longer had a proper mandate for signing such an important and fateful document and who thus represented no one.

We reaffirm that we consider the Extraordinary Fourteenth Party Congress and the Central Committee elected by it as the sole and supreme representative of our Party in the present situation. We endorse the decisions adopted by it without reservation.

We shall of course normalize the working conditions in our enterprise so that the damages caused by the abnormal situation are removed as soon as possible. That of course presupposes the immediate departure of the occupation armies from the territory of the Czechoslovak Socialist Republic.

Position of the Workers of the Kablo Enterprise, August 28, 1968

To the Presidium of the Central Committee
To the National Assembly of the Czechoslovak Socialist Republic
To the Government of the Czechoslovak Socialist Republic

Esteemed Comrades,

We have heard the speeches by our President, Ludvik Svoboda, and by the First Secretary, Comrade Alexander Dubcek, with deep concentration. Proceeding from the present reality, which made it impossible for our representatives negotiating in Moscow to decide freely, and from the words of all the speeches, we declare that we fully support our First Secretary, Comrade Dubcek, all decisions of the legal Extraordinary Fourteenth Party Congress, the President of the Republic, Comrade Svoboda, our Government headed by Comrade Cernik, the National Assembly headed by Comrade Smrkovsky, the National Front headed by Comrade Kriegel, and all legal, democratically elected representatives of our Czechoslovak state, which is so dear to us.

We ask you, comrades, particularly in these hours so grave for our future, to remain in your functions and so lead our people on a legal road to our goal of democratic socialism.

We insist on the immediate departure of the occupation troops, which have brutally trampled upon our freedoms and influenced the thinking and the feelings of all our people. We demand a speedy repayment of all losses caused in our territory by the occupiers, even though the lives of our innocently murdered children and citizens can never in any manner be reimbursed and replaced.

We express our fundamental disagreement with the communiqué signed at the conclusion of the Moscow negotiations. We shall never accept the Moscow *diktat!*

Trust us, we trust you!

In the name of 902 workers of the Kablo enterprise in Hostivar.

This resolution has been signed by 540 employees of our enterprise who work the morning shift. The signatures of the afternoon- and night-shift workers will be supplied tomorrow.

Resolution

The employees of the Metallurgical enterprise in Prague 10, Strasnice, submit the following resolution to the Central Committee, to the Central Trade Union Council, and to the National Assembly:

1. We consider the conditions stipulated in the communiqué on the Moscow negotiations unacceptable for our Party and for our two nations.

2. The agreement was co-signed by people who at that time no longer had the proper mandate to sign such a document and therefore represented no one.

3. We reaffirm that we consider the Extraordinary Fourteenth Party Congress and the Central Committee elected by it the only and supreme representatives of our Party in the present situation. We endorse its decisions, adopted thus far, without reservation.

4. We continue to consider the realization of the Action Program as the basic line of the work of the Party and fully stand behind the results achieved in its fulfillment since the January plenum of the Central Committee.

5. We demand that the Extraordinary Fourteenth Party Congress continue its session and adopt a stand on the situation created in our country. We assume that it shall proceed, as it has proceeded thus far, from the basic interests of both of our nations.

6. We are aware of the complexity and difficulty of the Moscow negotiations, and therefore we express our full confidence in comrades Svoboda, Dubcek, Cernik, and Smrkovsky, and we ask them to remain in their Party and state functions under any circumstances.

7. We demand an immediate departure of the foreign troops from our territory (or the setting of a date for their departure as soon as possible and the announcement of that date to our people).

8. We demand full indemnification for all the damages caused by the occupation armies.

Approved by all employees on August 28, 1968.

Position of the Workers of the TOS National Enterprise

To the Central Committee of the Communist Party
To the National Assembly of the Czechoslovak Socialist Republic
To the Government of the Czechoslovak Socialist Republic

With bitterness and feelings of injustice, we have heard the communiqué on the negotiations between representatives of the Czechoslovak Socialist Republic and the Soviet Union, the speech of the President of our Republic, Comrade Ludvik Svoboda, and the speech of our First Secretary of the Communist Party, Comrade Alexander Dubcek.

From the all-enterprise assembly called on August 28, 1968, we are sending you the following unanimous resolution:

1. We unreservedly trust comrades Svoboda, Dubcek, Cernik, Smrkovsky, and the other comrades who were negotiating in Moscow on behalf of our nations and with the authorization of our nations.

2. We promise to support their further negotiations, and we declare that whatever they decide will also be a decision of our will and in our name.

APPENDIX 1

LEADERS OF THE COMMUNIST PARTY OF CZECH-OSLOVAKIA AT THE TIME OF THE INVASION

Presidium
    Full members
        Frantisek Barbirek
        Vasil Bilak
        Oldrich Cernik
        Alexander Dubcek
        Drahomir Kolder
        Frantisek Kriegel
        Jan Piller
        Emil Rigo
        Josef Smrkovsky
        Josef Spacek
        Oldrich Svestka
    Candidate members
        Antonin Kapek
        Josef Lenart
        Bohumil Simon
Secretariat of the Central Committee
    First Secretary, Alexander Dubcek
    Secretaries and members
        Cestmir Cisar
        Evzen Erban
        Alois Indra
        Drahomir Kolder

Josef Lenart
Zdenek Mylnar
Stefan Sadovsky
Vaclav Slavik
Oldrich Volenik
Control and Audit Commission
Chairman, Milos Jakes

APPENDIX 2

MEMBERS OF THE GOVERNMENT OF CZECHOSLO-VAKIA AT THE TIME OF THE INVASION

President of the Republic, Ludvik Svoboda
Chairman of the National Assembly, Josef Smrkovsky
Government
    Premier, Oldrich Cernik
    Deputy Premiers
        Peter Colotka
        Frantisek Hamouz
        Gustav Husak
        Ota Sik
        Lubomir Strougal
    Minister of Agriculture and Nutrition, Josef Boruvka
    Minister of the Chemical Industry, Stanislav Razl
    Minister of Consumer Industry, Bozena Machacova
    Minister of Construction, Josef Trokan
    Minister of Culture and Information, Miroslav Galuska
    Minister of Economic Planning, Frantisek Vlasek
    Minister of Education, Vladimir Kadlec
    Minister of Finance, Bohumil Sucharda
    Minister of Foreign Affairs, Jiri Hajek
    Minister of Foreign Trade, Vaclav Vales
    Minister of Forestry and Water Conservation, Julius Hanus
    Minister of Health, Vladislav Vlcek
    Minister of Heavy Industry, Josef Krejci
    Minister of Internal Trade, Oldrich Pavlovsky

Minister of Interior, Josef Pavel
Minister of Justice, Bohuslav Kucera
Minister of Labor and Social Welfare, Michal Stancel
Minister of Mining, Frantisek Penc
Minister of National Defense, Martin Dzur
Minister of Technology, Miloslav Hruskovic
Minister of Transport, Frantisek Rehak
Minister-Chairman of the Central Board for Power, Josef Korcak
Minister-Chairman of the State Price Board, Vaclav Hula
Chairman of the Central Board for Communications, Karel Hoffman
Chairman of the Central Commission of People's Control, Stefan Gasparik
Chairman of the Economic Council, Lubomir Strougal
Chairman of the State Statistical Council, Jan Kazimour
Chairman of the Supreme Court, Otomar Bocek
Prosecutor General, Milos Cerovsky

APPENDIX 3

LEADERS OF THE SLOVAK COMMUNIST PARTY AT THE TIME OF THE INVASION

Presidium
  Full members
    Frantisek Barbirek
    Vasil Bilak
    Vojtech Daubner
    Herbert Durkovic
    Miloslav Hruskovic
    Jan Janik
    Ondrej Klokoc
    Julius Loerincz
    Viktor Pavlenda
    Anton Tazky
    Josef Zrak
  Candidate members
    Koloman Boda
    Robert Harencar
    Michal Pecho
Secretariat of the Central Committee
  First Secretary, Vasil Bilak
  Secretaries and members
    Samuel Faltan
    Miloslav Hruskovic
    Jan Janik
    Michal Pecho
    Maria Sedlakova
    Josef Zrak